The Economic Psychology of Everyday Life

From childhood through to adulthood, retirement and finally death, *The Economic Psychology of Everyday Life* uniquely explores the economic problems all individuals have to solve across the course of their lives.

Webley, Burgoyne, Lea and Young begin by introducing the concept of economic behaviour and its study. They then examine the main economic issues faced at each life stage, including:

- the impact of advertising on children,
- buying a house and setting up home,
- changing family roles and gender-linked inequality,
- redundancy and unemployment,
- coping on a pension, and
- obituaries, wills and inheritance.

Finally, they draw together the commonalities of economic problems across the life-span, discuss the generational and cultural changes in economic behaviour and examine how the economy constrains non-economic aspects of individual psychology.

The Economic Psychology of Everyday Life provides a much-needed comprehensive and accessible guide to economic psychology which will be of great interest to researchers and students.

Paul Webley, **Carole B. Burgoyne**, **Stephen E. G. Lea** and **Brian M. Young** are all members of the Economic Psychology Research Group at the School of Psychology, University of Exeter.

International Series in Social Psychology
Edited by W. Peter Robinson
University of Bristol, UK

This series provides a showcase of original contributions of the highest quality, as well as thorough reviews of existing theories suitable for advanced students and researchers. Many will be useful as course texts for higher level study; applied topics are well represented and social psychology is defined broadly to include other psychological areas like social development, or the social psychology of abnormal behaviour. A reflection of contemporary social psychology, the series is a rich source of information for dissertations, new research projects and seminars.

Recent books in the series:

Adjustment of Adolescents
Cross-cultural similarities and differences
Ruth Scott and W. A. Scott

Adolescence From Crisis to Coping
A thirteen nation study
Janice Gibson-Cline

Personal Relationships across the Lifespan
Patricia Noller, Judith A. Feeney and Candida Peterson

Children as Consumers
A psychological analysis of the young people's market
Barrie Gunter and Adrian Furnham

Understanding the Older Consumer
The grey market
Barrie Gunter

Changing European Identities
Social psychological analyses of social change
Glynis M. Breakwell and Evanthia Lyons

Making Sense of Television
The psychology of audience interpretation (2nd edition)
Sonia Livingstone

Social Groups and Identities
Developing the legacy of Henri Tajfel
Edited by W. Peter Robinson

Stereotypes during the Decline and Fall of Communism
György Hunyady

Also available in the Routledge Research International Series in Social Psychology

1. Cooperation in Modern Society
Promoting the welfare of communities, states and organizations
Edited by Mark van Vught, Mark Snyder, Tom R. Tyler and Anders Biel

2. Youth and Coping in Twelve Nations
Surveys of 18–20-year-old young people
Edited by Janice Gibson-Cline

3. Responsibility
The many faces of a social phenomenon
Hans-Werner Bierhoff and Ann Elisabeth Auhagen

The Economic Psychology of Everyday Life

Paul Webley, Carole B. Burgoyne,
Stephen E. G. Lea and Brian M. Young

First published 2001
by Psychology Press Ltd
27 Church Road, Hove, East Sussex, BN3 2FA

http://www.psypress.co.uk

Simultaneously published in the USA and Canada
by Taylor & Francis Inc.
325 Chestnut Street, Suite 800, Philadelphia, PA 19106

Psychology Press is part of the Taylor & Francis Group

© 2001 Paul Webley, Carole B. Burgoyne, Stephen E. G. Lea and Brian M. Young

Typeset in Times by Keystroke, Jacaranda Lodge, Wolverhampton
Printed and bound in Great Britain by Biddles Ltd, Guildford and King's Lynn

British Library Cataloguing in Publication Data
A catalogue record for this book is available from the British Library

Library of Congress Cataloging in Publication Data
The economic psychology of everyday life / Paul Webley . . . [et al.]
    p. cm. — (International series in social psychology)
  Includes bibliographical references and index.
  ISBN 0–415–18860–1 — ISBN 0–415–18861–X (pbk)
  1. Economics—Psychological aspects. 2. Consumers. I. Webley, Paul.
  II. Series.

HB74.P8 E324 2000
330′.01′9—dc21   00–040285

ISBN 0–415–18860–1 (hbk)
ISBN 0–415–18861–X (pbk)

[14410]

Contents

Preface

This book has been over four years in the writing. This might seem rather excessive for what is, after all, quite a slim volume. Our hope is that the passing of the years has enabled our ideas and our writing to mature, and that the book is robust, full-bodied and a pleasure to consume.

Our aim has been to provide an accessible and reasonably thorough (though not exhaustive) coverage of the most important issues in the rapidly developing area of economic psychology. The majority of economic psychologists are social psychologists by training and inclination, and so this book fits well in a series on applied social psychology. But it is important to be clear at the outset that economic psychology is a genuinely interdisciplinary enterprise: it draws on, and feeds back to, its main parent disciplines (economics and psychology) as well as the social sciences as a whole. So readers with backgrounds only in social psychology will encounter theories (such as buffer-stock models of saving) and techniques (such as those of experimental economics) that are unfamiliar to them. They should not be anxious on this score: we have made very little use of formal economic models and there are hardly any equations in the text.

The book does have a distinctive 'Exeter' flavour, as all four of us are members of the Economic Psychology Research Group at Exeter University. This flavour is reflected in two distinctive features – a concentration on the economic problems that people have to solve on a day-to-day basis and a life-span developmental approach. This means that we have concentrated more on what people actually *do* in their economic lives and less on how they think about economic matters. So, although there is substantial research on lay explanations and social representations of economic phenomena (and indeed we have done some work in this area ourselves), it is not discussed here. A life-span approach to economic psychology is genuinely novel. We have not used an explicit life-span theory, but have dealt with areas (e.g. paths to economic independence in late adolescence, the economic psychology of the elderly) that have previously been neglected.

Above all, we hope that we have managed to convey our enthusiasm for economic psychology and that some of the readers of the book will decide that this is the area for them. Economic psychology deals with real problems that matter to people, and with issues that pervade all of our lives. It needs new ideas, new techniques and new people. So join us!

Acknowledgements

We have been teaching economic psychology now for over twenty years, and the students we have taught over that period have all contributed, in one way or another, to this book. We are grateful to them, and particularly to those who have taken our seminar courses in the last four years, who have read and commented on early drafts of chapters. We also owe a great deal to our collaborators from other universities (particularly David Routh, Alan Lewis, Ellen Nyhus and Roberto Burlando) and to the members of IAREP (International Association for Research in Economic Psychology), who over the years have provided us with many helpful comments on our work.

The book would probably never have appeared without the support of four people. Peter Robinson, the series editor, never lost faith in us (despite severe provocation) and Alison Dixon, the editorial assistant at Psychology Press, was unfailingly polite in nudging the project along. Christine de Wilde acted as a very effective progress chaser when we had rather lost momentum, and Elizabeth Webley did a fine job in identifying lacunae in the manuscript and getting it into the form required by the publishers.

Part of the book was written whilst Paul Webley and Stephen Lea were on sabbatical leave. It is a pleasure for Paul to be able to thank the CentER for Economic Research, University of Tilburg and the International Centre for Economic Research, Turin for their hospitality and financial support. Both Paul and Stephen are grateful to the University of Exeter for allowing us to take full-year sabbatical leave.

1

An Introduction to Economic Psychology

What is Economic Behaviour?

We all think we know what economic behaviour is – it is about buying a computer, thinking about investment options, looking at a saving advert and wondering whether we ought to put some money by, choosing a holiday, and evading one's taxes. But do we really? The behaviours in the opening sentence all seem economic but how about this list: deciding to have children, stealing a car, making a Christmas present, washing one's clothes. Or walking to work (as opposed to going by car), visiting a friend who lives nearby (as opposed to one who lives further away), giving a friend a lift. By some formal definitions all of these behaviours (and indeed virtually all behaviour) can be seen as economic (Webley and Lea, 1993b). The central concept usually deployed here is scarcity: as Robbins (1932, p. 16) wrote 'Economics is the science which studies human behaviour as a relationship between ends and scarce means which have alternative uses'. Economists do not need to confine themselves to those domains we traditionally think of as 'economic' (markets, pricing, labour supply) and the intellectual imperialists such as Becker (1976, 1991) have striven hard to extend the scope of economics to explain, among other things, criminal and family behaviour. An alternative view sees economic behaviour simply as those areas that are generally seen as economic (buying, work, saving, etc.), usually as these are activities that go through the market (see Webley and Lea, 1993). But none of these definitions (nor others) take us very far: the pragmatic approach used here is to focus on those problems facing individuals at different points in their life that are best understood (or at least illuminated) from an economic psychology perspective. Thus we do deal with saving but don't deal with mate choice (although one could).

Approaches to Economic Behaviour

It is possible to regard the study of economic behaviour as just another branch of applied social psychology, where at worst one simply applies standard social-psychological theories to economic phenomena (e.g. applying attribution theory to understand people's explanations for poverty) and at best one develops theories that have more general application (Langer's, 1975, 1983, ideas of illusion of control and mindlessness might be an example of this). We do not take this view. Our belief is that economic behaviour is best understood by a truly interdisciplinary approach that draws on both economics and psychology (and related disciplines). This is not an easy option: economics and psychology have, in the past, had an uneasy relationship, as the conventions of inference and theory construction are very different. Economists have often shown 'aggressive uncuriosity' (Rabin, 1998) towards psychological research and psychologists have often been dismissive of a science based on what seem to them to be absurdly unrealistic assumptions. Nonetheless we believe that a truly interdisciplinary approach will bear fruit in the long term and benefit both parent disciplines. Here we outline some of the alternative perspectives that have been brought to bear in the two disciplines.

Optimality – the economist's approach

To simplify greatly, economists (or strictly speaking neo-classical economists) begin with the assumption that people are self-interested utility-maximisers – they are selfish and rational. So, faced with an interesting question, say the effect of the introduction of fees on applications for university places, the first step would be to construct a model of the behaviour in question. This would consider the quantifiable benefits of university education (the lifetime increase in earnings as a result of having a degree), the risks (the probability of ending up without a degree), and the costs (for example, of renting student accommodation, of forgone earnings). The model would make a number of simplifying assumptions, for example that universities come in only two types (high- or low-status) or that the choice is between a university in one's home town or in a distant city. The model would be of the behaviour of units in the system: in our example this could be individuals or households, in other cases it could be firms, regulators or the government. The model is then developed, but always on the assumption that the economic units (of whatever kind) are behaving in their own interests and in the most optimal way. It is important to bear in mind that such models do not usually predict the behaviour of individuals (a particular individual may be altruistic, badly informed or make poor judgements): what they do is to predict average behaviour, or what will happen, all other things being equal. So our model might predict that fees would reduce the number of mature applicants for university places (as the impact on their lifetime earnings of having a degree is less and the cost of taking up a place is higher) or might predict that fees would not reduce the overall number of applications but that students would become more likely to be home-based.

Social psychologists often dispute the claim that people are rational and make optimal decisions (they also argue against the assumption of self-interest, but less forcefully). They point to the extensive experimental evidence on decision-making (see, for example, Gilovich, 1991; Plous, 1993), which clearly shows that people often act contrary to rationality assumptions. Psychologists are frequently dismissive of economics as a consequence. We believe that this is misguided on two grounds. First, as we pointed out above, economics does not usually try to predict the behaviour of individuals (any more than a physicist tries to predict the flight pattern of a particular falling autumn leaf). It tries to produce predictions that work well on the average. So the fact that individuals can be shown to act irrationally does not matter as long as aggregate predictions do work well (this is the pragmatic defence of the rationality assumption advanced by Friedman, 1953). We are not so sure this condition is met (indeed, unlike models of weather systems, there is little evidence that models of the economy are getting any better, Wren-Lewis, 1996) but the argument itself is a reasonable one. Second, and much more importantly, it has been convincingly argued by Rachlin (1980) that any behaviour that is consistent can be described as rational. This may require some redefinitions and extensions to the basic theory (for instance, taking into account the costs and benefits of searching for information or the costs of remembering previous decisions) but does not alter the fact that it is fairly pointless trying to 'disprove' rationality (for an extended discussion of this issue see Lea, 1994).

Extension of the optimality approach to the whole lifetime

As we said above, economists try to model behaviours on the assumption that people are trying to maximise utility. This means that when dealing with behaviours such as saving, house-buying and career choice, costs and benefits need to be considered over the very long term. Life-cycle models in economics basically assert that people maximise their utility over their lifetime. A typical model of labour supply, for example, would involve an individual maximising utility (which would be a function of hours worked and leisure); a typical model of saving would involve an individual smoothing consumption and integrating income and consumption streams in order to maximise utility. The following quotation is a very clear example of this approach: 'An individual maximizes a lifetime utility function whose arguments are an aggregate consumption good, annual hours of leisure during work weeks and annual hours of leisure during nonwork weeks subject to a lifetime wealth constraint' (Reilly, 1994, p. 463). This may seem very unrealistic as it seems to imply that people have very long time horizons. Put in concrete terms it suggests that one of the factors entering into the decision to take a particular job at age 21 will be the quality of the pension deal on offer. But, again, psychologists' criticisms of these life-cycle approaches are often misplaced. First of all, these are models of what people do and not how they think: it is possible to behave rationally (to act in the optimum way) without having worked out the likely consequences of different choices (that is, to have engaged in rational thought). Second, life-cycle models in economics are now very complex and sophisticated and take into account different time horizons and time preferences; we shall make some use of those in Chapter 5.

The household life-cycle

The idea of the household life-cycle (at first called the 'family life-cycle') was introduced into the study of consumer behaviour by Wells and Gubar in 1966. This approach basically relates spending and other economic behaviour to transitions in the family situation. These might be, for example, the birth of the family's first child, the departure of the last child from the household or the death of a spouse. The original model excluded non-traditional households (e.g. people who stayed single or parents who never married) and so a number of researchers have suggested modifications to the original scheme. Here we present the Murphy and Staples (1979) version and its associated diagram (Figure 1.1), which is probably the most widely used. This maintains the idea of progression through stages but recognises that there are alternative routes through the life path.

The traditional family (with seven stages of adulthood) is represented by the middle row, from young single through to older unmarried (widow or widower). There are routes off this representing the major departures from the traditional family: those who do not have children and those whose marriages end in divorce (though Murphy and Staples exclude those who remain single all their lives). This model is more descriptive than theoretical though there is an implicit claim that life stage will be a strong predictor of economic behaviour over and above age and income. The model may give us some handle on changes in economic behaviour during adulthood.

For example, Wilkes (1995) investigated household spending patterns using a very large sample (over 7,000) of respondents to the US Consumer Expenditure survey. Even with this sample some categories had to be collapsed (a serious problem in much earlier research): it was not possible, for instance, to distinguish middle-aged divorced families who had never had children from those who currently do not have dependent children. Wilkes shows that including stage of household life-cycle improves the ability to predict expenditure on different product classes over and above what can be achieved using income, age, education and family size:

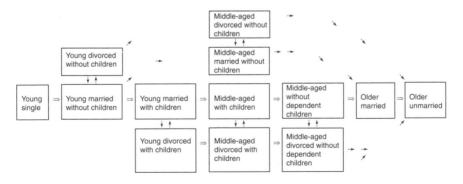

FIGURE 1.1 The modernised household life-cycle model
(after Murphy and Staples, 1979)

in other words the concept of the household life-cycle does add something. His results reveal three distinct spending patterns. The first is for spending to rise with the shift to married status, then drop with the arrival of children, rise again as families mature and then drop off during the last stages of the life-cycle (the pattern is a sine wave with two maxima). This pattern is found for, among other products and services, eating out, and buying of cars, furniture and clothing. A second, but less frequent, pattern is found for home improvement products, insurance and medical services, which is one of generally increasing expenditure across the life-cycle. And finally, spending on two products (alcohol and stereo equipment) shows a general decline across the life-cycle, which is interpreted by Wilkes as a shift from a self-indulgent perspective to a more sober family-oriented approach to expenditure.

Although Wilkes is generally positive about the usefulness of the household life-cycle approach, Nyhus (1998) is rather more critical. She points out that twenty years ago Arndt (1979) described the family life-cycle model as 'one of the most over-quoted and under-researched concepts' and that this remains a fair description of the current state of affairs. There have been few empirical tests of the model and it seems to add little (in terms of predictive power) to a more straightforward economic life-cycle approach (see for example, Nyhus, 1998; Wagner and Hanna, 1983). Since it is more complex than the latter and has less theoretical grounding, this should give us pause for thought. Nonetheless, from our perspective, it at least provides a framework for thinking about economic choices across the life-cycle.

Developmental psychology

Economists have until fairly recently ignored children (with some honourable exceptions – for example, Harbaugh and Krause, 1999) and have disregarded the value of a developmental approach to understanding behaviour. Broadly speaking, there are two main kinds of theory – one that looks for the origins of economic behaviour in childhood (e.g. Freud, 1908), the other that plots the development of children's understanding of the economic world (generally through the use of Piagetian stage models, e.g. Berti and Bombi, 1988). Each presents only a partial picture: 'origin' theories underestimate the importance of adult experiences and, in particular, the impact of economic constraints and opportunities, whilst Piagetian stage theories overemphasise the significance of adjusting to the adult economic world and minimise the importance of the child's own behaviour. Both have tended to regard particular ways of thinking and behaving as natural and inevitable, as opposed to being the result of historical and cultural processes.

We can see this if we look at the way each approach deals with money. Freud (and some later psycho-analysts such as Ferenczi, 1926) essentially saw both adults' approach to money (what one could call styles of economic behaviour, such as stinginess or being a spendthrift) and money stuff itself as a consequence of anal eroticism. The assumption is that all children experience pleasure in eliminating faeces and enjoy playing with these first products. Children then move on to play with mud, and stones, and eventually coins and paper money. Depending on the nature of the toilet training a child experiences, he or she may become miserly (an 'anal retentive'), if training is early and rigid, or a spendthrift ('anal expulsive'). Now, money itself has, historically, come in a wide variety of forms. Some of these may be interpretable in psycho-analytical terms (the huge stone millstones on Yap thus imply a monumental anality) but others (cattle, woodpecker scalps) are rather harder to fit into this framework. And whilst it is true that being miserly may be partly a matter of character and disposition it can also be a reaction to particular economic circumstances. This has led more recent psycho-analytic writers (e.g. Bornemann, 1976) to doubt that the nature of money is derived from the anal character. We actually know very little about how consistent people are in their styles of economic behaviour (an issue to which we will return in Chapter 5).

The neo-Piagetian approach to money gives us rather different insights. It tells us nothing about money *per se* but reveals how children come to understand its use. The literature suggests that children pass through a series of stages in attaining an adult understanding of money, though the number of stages described ranges from a low of three to a high of nine. For instance, Strauss (1952) described nine categories through which children progress in their understanding of monetary meaning. These ranged from stage one (where children realised that money can somehow buy certain things) through stage four (a recognition that the shopkeeper must be paid by the customers for goods bought in order for him or her to earn money) to stage nine (where children fully understood the notion of profit). Berti and Bombi (1988), by contrast, describe four stages in children's developing understanding of payment for work. At the first stage (4–5 years) children had no idea of the origin of money, whilst at the second, children saw the origin of money as independent from work. At stage three, children think that change given by shopkeepers is the origin of money and finally at stage four (7–8 years) children associate money with work. What is striking about this study is that it treats money as something clearly defined that children have to come to understand to function as effective economic agents. Money is seen as unproblematic (which it is not) and children's informal behaviour is ignored. We will discuss these issues in more detail in Chapter 3.

We will conclude this section by briefly describing a different kind of developmental theory, the Eriksonian psycho-social approach. Although, to our knowledge, this has not been applied to economic issues other than the issue of treasured possessions, it does resonate with the approach we will take of focusing on the main economic problems facing people at different stages of their lives. Erikson (1963, 1982) proposed that there were eight stages of psycho-social development each of which has a prototypical developmental task and distinctive psycho-social crises that can ensue. For example, in the first stage (oral–sensory), the child has to solve the problem of establishing basic trust; in the fifth (puberty), the adolescent must resolve the problem of identity versus role-confusion; and in the sixth (young adulthood), the adult must deal with the conflict between intimacy and isolation.

Erikson (1982) also identifies the core pathologies of each stage. These pathologies are not passive limitations of individuals but are active (misguided) strategies that protect them from unwanted associations. Thus the core pathology of early adolescence is isolation, whilst of early adulthood it is exclusivity. Erikson's model is like a staircase: at each stage the achievements of the previous stage provide the resources with which to deal with the problems and challenges of the next.

Newman and Newman (1991) make extensive use of Erikson's approach and believe that a relatively small number of tasks (quite a few of which are economic in character) dominate a person's efforts. For instance, one of the main ways in which identity is expressed in Western society is one's occupation, so it is not surprising that career choice is crucial in helping resolve the central question of adolescence, 'who am I?' Economic decisions are also important at later stages: work and lifestyle (in early adulthood) and the management of a career or household in middle adulthood.

Erikson's approach suffers from all the normal problems of stage theories and its concepts are sometimes abstruse and difficult to operationalise. But it is valuable in identifying the main problems that people have to resolve as they progress through life, and insightful in characterising some of the stages and their associated pathologies.

Expressive/communicative

Social scientists who have focused on the social context of economic behaviour have given us a rather different perspective. Perhaps the first to do so was Veblen (1899), who introduced the idea of conspicuous consumption, the notion that rich people buy expensive goods just because they are expensive in order to signal their wealth and class. This suggests that we should try to understand the goods people buy and exchange as a system of communication, which is the approach taken by Douglas and Isherwood (1996). As they say, 'The most general objective of the consumer can only be to construct an intelligent universe with the goods he chooses' (Douglas and Isherwood, 1996, p. 43). This means that not only in the obvious domains (buying a car, a picture, a tie, a blouse) but also in the less obvious ones (a meal, a lawnmower, a spanner) one is communicating with other members of society. In developing this idea, Douglas and Isherwood make use of the notion of consumption periodicities. This refers to the frequency with which different goods are consumed: thus, in our households at least, milk is a high-frequency good and champagne a low-frequency one. Periodicity acts as a signal, though not the only one, of rank and status. Champagne, for us, marks an occasion (such as celebrating the completion of this long-overdue book) as special, whereas milk would mark an occasion as routine. This applies not only to consumption but also to production. There is a tendency, the world over, for tasks to cluster, so that there is a category of people who carry out high-frequency tasks such as fetching the water, making meals, etc. (and who are of low status) and a category of people who carry out low-frequency tasks, and who are of high status: for example, the traditional and now less common household division of labour in the UK involved the wife cleaning the house, cooking and performing child care (high frequency, low status) whilst the husband cleaned the car, wired plugs and decorated (lower frequency, higher status).

That economic behaviour can usefully be considered as a form of communication is perhaps best seen in studies of gift-giving. Gifts can indicate social distance and relative intimacy; they can communicate how we see the recipient and how we would like to be perceived; they can even be insulting (sometimes deliberately). The 'language' of gift-giving is an imperfect one, however; so choosing the right present can be very difficult and it is not always easy to interpret the gifts one receives (Burgoyne, 1999). A good example was related to one of us by a relative, who reported that her husband had given her a blank cheque as a wedding anniversary present. Since they have a joint bank account, she felt initially rather hurt (a blank cheque involved no thought and somehow implied that she needed his permission to spend money from the account) but she subsequently decided to interpret the gift as an example of generosity. The communicative function of gifts is also evident in academic studies. Webley, Lea and Portalska (1983), for instance, showed that money was unacceptable as a gift for the respondent's mother, and Webley and Wilson (1989) that money was more acceptable as a gift when it passes down a status hierarchy. Burgoyne and Routh (1991), in a more ecologically valid study (a diary study of Christmas giving), confirmed this and provide the explanation that it is partly because money may communicate inappropriate messages relating to status and the nature of the relationship that it is unacceptable as a gift to someone of higher rank. Money is also felt to be unacceptable as a way of repaying neighbourly help, except in the case of a 'loan' of some food (Webley and Lea, 1993b): here too, it sends the wrong messages (that the neighbour is being paid for a service).

The communicative approach has been developed and extended in recent years by a number of researchers (Belk, 1988; McCracken, 1990; Lunt and Livingstone, 1992; Dittmar, 1992), who have all in different ways tried to tie together the communicative and identity aspects of economic behaviour and produce a fusion of traditional consumer research with other social-scientific disciplines. Belk (1988), for example, introduced the notion of the extended self as a way of highlighting how people incorporate possessions into their definitions of themselves. It is not only that possessions can reflect identities (our extensive collections of books reflect, for example, our identities as scholars) but they can be used to construct an identity. So Paul's acquisition of a Lambretta scooter, when he was a 16-year-old, was part of a doomed attempt to construct an identity as a young lad about town. According to Belk, anything that a person sees as theirs is included in the extended self: this can include bits of the countryside or even sports teams as well as the more obvious personal possessions. These possessions are used to provide stability, to give our lives permanence and also supply a record of it (exemplified best by souvenirs and special gifts). Dittmar (1992) provides more detail on the importance of identities in economic behaviour. She shows, for example, how men and women not only prefer different things but relate to their possessions in different ways. So a man's motorbike is not only likely to be larger and more powerful, but possession of it will be seen as differentiating him from others (he is a 'biker') whereas a women's motorbike is more likely to be given a name and is more likely to be important to her if it was given to her by someone and therefore symbolises a relationship. McCracken (1990) also stresses the importance of products as ways of constructing and communicating the self. McCracken's studies on how people decode clothing show that the latter is a rather coarse form of communication but that it is good at communicating social category membership. Lunt and Livingstone (1992), by contrast, link individual identity construction with the prevailing discourses in society. In their view, people, in constructing and reconstructing their identities, must do so within the discourse that sees the consumer society as progressive and facilitating or within the discourse that sees the consumer society as a materialist dead-end.

All of these authors reject what they see as the old-fashioned idea of the self as something outside of the process of consuming. For them the self is constructed by and through economic acts. They are also highly critical of the individualistic approach to economic behaviour, as this is seen as ignoring the crucial role played by culture (for more examples of this kind of approach see Edgell, Hetherington and Worde, 1996). The value of the expressive/communicative approach is that it forces us to take the emotional and social aspects of economic behaviour seriously: one problem is that it is extremely difficult to make use of its insights, for example predictively, or in terms of the economic modelling of behaviour.

Economic psychology

There is no single economic-psychological approach to economic behaviour. Economic psychology is very eclectic, and so at any economic psychology conference one would see a very wide range of theories from micro-economics and from social psychology being used. It is also not unique (see Webley and Lea 1992): it has no distinct theories, no distinct methods and its focus on interdisciplinary economic issues is shared by behavioural economics and socio-economics. What is special about economic psychology is that it recognises the importance of the wider context (especially the economy) and the value of drawing on economic theories and evidence as well as on psychology. A number of people have attempted to define the economic-psychological approach – perhaps the best of these is Wärneryd (1988), who has argued that at the micro level economic psychology is already well established.

Though there are no distinctive theories, economic psychologists are most likely to make use of the following approaches: (i) the notion of satisficing (Simon, 1956, 1982), (ii) the notions of framing and prospect theory (Kahneman and

Tversky, 1979; Tversky and Kahneman 1981), (iii) mental accounts (Thaler, 1980, 1985, 1993), (iv) the approach of Etzioni (1988, 1992), (v) notions derived from behavioural psychology, such as melioration (Herrnstein and Prelec, 1992) and myopia (Ainslie, 1991, 1992), (vi) attitudes, particularly the theory of planned behaviour (Azjen, 1985). The first three (satisficing, framing, mental accounts) are all concerned with the way decisions are actually made and the impact of decision-making processes on the outcome. They are bounded rationality approaches and accept selfishness. Etzioni, by contrast, questions selfishness but accepts rationality. The last two (behavioural psychology, attitude theory) are non-rational positive theories of economic choice. But all of these approaches have something in common – they are all trying to predict economic behaviour from the mechanism of economic choice instead of (or as well as) its objectives.

Simon (1956) introduced the term 'satisficing' (originally a Northumbrian synonym for satisfy) to refer to the behaviour of a decision maker who chooses an alternative that is 'good enough': that is, one that meets or exceeds particular criteria but is not necessarily the best alternative. This recognises that the real world is so complex that to optimise (to select the best alternative) requires far too much computational effort. Now it is possible to treat satisficing as a form of optimising where an individual takes into account the cost of searching for alternatives, though, as Simon points out, this adds to the computational burden. Satisficing may be particularly useful (and especially prevalent) when people are taking decisions where the dimensions involved seem to them to be incommensurable. For example, an applicant choosing between possible universities may find it hard to compare one with great sports facilities with one with a fine academic reputation with one in a stunningly beautiful location. To choose between the University of Playing Fields, Nobel Prize University and Bellavista University is very difficult, as it involves trading off between things that seem completely different. (Students opting for the University of Exeter are, of course, spared the necessity of such trading off.) The usual response to such situations is to refuse to make the choice and search for a new alternative that is at least acceptable on all of the relevant dimensions. Similarly, where a choice involves one person's gain but another's loss, there will be a search for an alternative where both have satisfactory outcomes.

A similar concern with the cognitive limitations of decision makers is found in the work of Kahnemann and Tversky (e.g. Kahnemann and Tversky, 1979; Tversky and Kahnemann, 1981, 1991) who have produced a stream of publications which describe (and account for) robust oddities in people's decision-making. Social psychologists have made extensive use of, for example, prospect theory but probably do not realise that its impact on economics has been just as great. An example should suffice to give a flavour of their approach. It is (almost) a psychological truism that people tend to be much more concerned with how an outcome differs from some reference point than with its absolute value. So a particular temperature is experienced differently depending on what temperature an individual has adapted to. If the reference point is the current financial position, Kahnemann and Tversky have shown that people are much more concerned about losses than about gains of an equivalent amount. This helps explain the so-called 'endowment effect'. If students are randomly split into two groups, and one half given mugs worth about five dollars and the other half not, those 'endowed' with a mug will typically set a median value on them of roughly seven dollars whereas those without mugs value them at three and a half dollars (Kahneman, Knetsch and Thaler, 1990). The explanation for this is that those given the mug incorporate it into their possessions and so 'having a mug' is their reference point. To leave the experiment without it is a loss, for which they need to be compensated. Reference points are also crucial to the issue of framing, where people confronted with mathematically equivalent situations take different decisions depending on how they are described. So people react quite differently to situations that are framed as losses to those that are framed as gains, even when the underlying realities being described are exactly the same.

The idea of mental accounts, whilst not so well known outside the area of economic and consumer psychology, is based on similar ideas and has also been used by Tversky and Kahnemann. The term was introduced by Thaler (1980, 1985, 1993), though he first used the phrase 'psychological accounts'. It is best understood through analogy with the behaviour of organisations. Thaler points out that all organisations (beyond a certain minimum size) have accounting systems within which there are a number of accounts and budgets. These enable the chief executive to devolve spending decisions to separate departments and to monitor and control activities. The price paid for this arrangement is a certain amount of inefficiency: some departments will spend money at the end of the year on rather marginal activities (as otherwise they will lose the money and their future budgets will be cut) whilst at the same time others are unable to make vital purchases. Mental accounts function in much the same way, and enable individuals to monitor and control their own spending. In their behavioural model of saving, for example, Shefrin and Thaler (1988) propose that people have three mental accounts: a current income account, a current assets account and a future income account and that the marginal propensity to spend is very different across these three accounts. Extra money that is seen as in the current assets account is, for example, less likely to be spent than if it is perceived as being in the current income account. Similarly, in the lost ticket scenario described by Tversky and Kahnemann (1981), people are less willing to buy a replacement theatre ticket if they have just lost one than they are to buy a ticket if they have lost an exactly equivalent sum of money. Lost money is probably seen as coming from a mental 'general' account whereas the lost theatre ticket may be seen as impacting on a mental 'leisure' account, which, since it is smaller, is then more depleted. There is considerable evidence that people use mental accounts (Thaler, 1993) though there is some debate over how they function and how they are configured (Webley, 1995). So Kojima and Hama (1982), from their study of Japanese housewives, proposed that there are nine 'psychological purses' whereas Winnett and Lewis (1995) claimed that the evidence suggested the existence of three mental accounting schemes: asset/income, capital/labour and windfall/regular.

Etzioni's 'socio-economics' is rather different from the approaches described above and is really concerned with creating a new kind of economics, based not on self-interest and rationality but on communitarianism and morality. Etzioni (1988) is fiercely critical of neo-classical economics, arguing that it is individualistic, amoral and unrealistic. In his view, people have mixed motives: they are selfish but also have moral concerns. They should not be thought of as individual units but as members of a culture which creates and sustains different value systems and different identities. So the ideas of rationality and self-interest are not neutral but are themselves values: neo-classical economics, from this perspective, is not describing reality but is contributing to legitimising a particular kind of approach to economic life (which may be why in certain experiments, for example, students of economics act more rationally – that is more selfishly – than students of other disciplines: Frank, Gilovich and Regan, 1993). Etzioni even claims that a society made up of the truly self-interested would not survive.

Socio-economics is long on rhetoric but short on data. Nonetheless, it does provide a corrective to the very atomised approach of economics and fits better with many of the models of behaviour developed within social psychology.

The same cannot be said of notions derived from behavioural psychology, although these seem to us to be of great importance. The application of these to consumer behaviour is considered in great detail by Foxall (1990); here we will just consider two specific notions – melioration and myopia. To understand melioration, one needs to be familiar with Herrnstein's (1990) 'matching law'. This is derived from studies of pigeons (and other animals). The matching law can be seen when pigeons are given access to two simultaneously available, and different, variable-interval schedules. These are reinforcement schedules where a variable length of time must elapse before the next response is rewarded. Here the ratio of the response rates on the two schedules is roughly the same (that is, 'matches') the ratio of the two reinforcement rates. One could imagine, for instance, a person who has two separate email accounts (with no forwarding arrangement from one to the other) and who gets three times as much mail on one as on the other. Which one should he or she log in to? To maximise in this situation (that is, to minimise the amount of time wasted), one should just log onto the first account: in fact what people (and pigeons in comparable situations) do is to is use both but use the one that gets more frequent messages (or food) more often. The process that leads to matching is melioration. What this means is that at any given time an individual chooses the option which leads to the greater local reinforcement. So Herrnstein and Prelec (1992), for example, have shown that, when making choices between options, people tend to ignore the effect a current choice has on the utility obtainable from later choices and simply choose the option that gives the best immediate return.

That people are myopic in their choices is perhaps no great surprise, but behavioural approaches have given us a great deal of insight into the form that this myopia takes (Ainslie, 1991, 1992). Let's start with the useful concept of the subjective discount rate. This is the rate at which future income or consumption should be 'discounted' to make it comparable with current income or consumption.

This has been suggested to be as high as 50 per cent or as low as 5 per cent. Either way, in order for an individual's choices to be consistent over time, the discount rate has to be constant (which means that the discount function is exponential). However, the evidence suggests that, in fact, people's choices are not consistent over time: a preference for an immediate reward can be reversed simply by adding a constant amount of time to each delay. In other words, if you prefer five pounds now to ten pounds in three months' time, you may nonetheless prefer ten pounds in fifteen months' time to five pounds in a year's time (Ainslie suggests, on the basis of data and matching law considerations, that the discount function is hyperbolic). Overvaluing immediate and impending events makes us vulnerable to temptation (as we underweight the consequences in the future of our actions now) and to exploitation by others, but we can try to overcome this by choosing *patterns* of behaviour over time rather than individual acts. So we can choose a pattern of drinking (every Saturday but not more than four pints except on very special occasions) and follow this as a self-imposed rule.

We'll end this section by very briefly discussing the role of attitude theory in economic psychology. Attitudes are the most pervasive construct in modern cognitive social psychology. They feature regularly in accounts of economic behaviour (e.g. as predictors of debt, tax evasion, saving, buying, ethical investing) and are studied in their own right (e.g. national variations in attitudes towards money). In many cases, standard models of the attitude–behaviour relationship are used, in others attitudes are incorporated as part of more complicated models. This work adds three things to our general understanding of attitudes. First, by recognising the many constraints on people's behaviour it puts the impact of attitudes in perspective. In many areas, attitudes simply do not seem to be very good predictors of the related behaviour, as is the case with saving (Wärneryd, 1999). Second, many economic behaviours are not individual but are the end-result of discussion and negotiation within the household. Whilst it is possible to combine attitude scores from two or more household members to try to understand their investment decisions, for example, without some understanding of the collective decision process this is not a very sensible way to proceed. And finally, some studies of economic behaviour reinforce the view that changes in attitudes are a consequence rather than a cause of changes in behaviour (Davies and Lea, 1995; Webley and Nyhus, 1999).

How Can We Study the Economic Psychology of Everyday Life?

It is possible to study to study the economic psychology of everyday life with the full range of methods in use in the social sciences. We have not attempted a complete listing, since this would itself be of book length. Useful overviews of methods in economic psychology can be found in Lea, Tarpy and Webley (1987), MacFadyen and MacFadyen (1986) and Antonides (1996). Here we want to focus on three characteristic methods or approaches of economic psychology that are relatively unusual within mainstream social psychology. For these, we have tried to give sufficient information to give a flavour of an approach with some references that can be followed up.

Experimental approaches

The experimental approach has for long been seen as the approach that distinguishes social psychology from most other social sciences (see for example Tajfel and Fraser, 1978) and its advantages and disadvantages are well known. The main advantage of well-designed laboratory experiments is that they allow us to investigate the causal effects of particular variables, confident in the knowledge that they are not the result of extraneous factors. There are also some real practical advantages: it is much easier to manipulate variables in the laboratory than in real-life situations; people's behaviour in situations where they cannot usually be observed can be studied; complex tasks can be simplified; and it is usually a (relatively) efficient way of gathering data. The disadvantages are by now equally well known: the experiment itself is a social situation and people do not just passively react to it – they may alter their behaviour because they construe the experiment in a certain way. In particular they may try to behave in ways that show them in a good light and they are generally sensitive to what Orne (1962) called the 'demand characteristics' of the experiment (the social and physical cues that guide people's behaviour). They may do what they think the experimenter wants them to or they may, alternatively, sometimes be uncooperative or even malevolent. All these things may undermine the ecological validity of a laboratory experiment.

Experimental economics has evolved independently and has developed rather different ground rules (see for example, Cox and Isaac, 1986). Although experimental economists and psychologists often carry out research in the same areas (e.g. social dilemmas and public goods) their approach is quite different and, as Hey (1992) has observed, 'one particular area of almost complete incomprehension between economists and psychologists is connected with the running of experiments – and most notably with the question of payments to subjects' (p. 85). Economists generally believe that it is absolutely essential that those participating experience a real gain or loss as a result of decisions that they take during an experiment. This may involve a summative payment at the end of an experiment or a payment that depends on their performance in just one period of the experiment. In other words, the incentive structure of the situation must be clear, open and real. Loewenstein (1999, p. F31), in a very useful discussion of the external validity of experiments in economics, sums this up: 'of all the "rules" of experimental economics, perhaps the most strongly enforced is the use of monetary payments that are contingent on behaviour'. They also believe that it is essential that experimenters are completely honest with their participants. Social psychologists, on the other hand, are usually happy to use deception where it is felt to be necessary and generally hold that it is a participant's *involvement* in an experiment that is crucial (Aronson and Carlsmith, 1968). If participants are involved or psychologically engaged in a situation, their decisions will be meaningful. They do not need to be taking decisions about real money. According to this view it may even be counterproductive to have people taking decisions in terms of pennies or cents, as this emphasises the relatively trivial (in financial terms) nature of the decisions being made. These differences in approach create considerable potential for misunderstanding. Economists' traditional distrust of what people say is still evident in experimental economics (for instance, participants are not usually debriefed, and their construal of the experiment is not elicited) and they pay scant attention to the social psychology of experimentation (which, remarkably, is nowhere discussed in the bible of the sub-discipline, the *Handbook of Experimental Economics* – Kagel and Roth, 1995).

What may come as even more of a surprise to the reader with a background in psychology is that economists generally (as opposed to the rather special breed of experimental economists) are not very sympathetic to experimental approaches. As Cowell (1991) put it 'I am not sure that Economists trust experiments . . . experiments appear to be used only in situations when all else is seen to fail' (p. 124). But we will make considerable use of experimentally gathered data in this text, since we believe that good experiments are informative, and often give us insights and surprises.

Survey research

Those interested in economic behaviour and relevant attitudes and opinions have made extensive use of large-scale survey work. There are many good examples of this. The most famous economic psychologist of all (George Katona) made extensive use of large-scale surveys of consumer confidence, using what became known as the Index of Consumer Sentiment (see Chapter 5): other economic psychologists have carried out smaller-scale surveys to investigate debt, ethical investment and tax evasion (Lea, Webley and Levine, 1993; Lea, Webley and Walker, 1995; Lewis *et al.*, 1998; Wärneryd and Walerud, 1982). There are obvious advantages to using large representative samples to investigate economic behaviour, most obviously that it is easier to generalise the findings than with experiments. But there are some serious and well-known problems with surveys. First, they assume that people are willing and able to provide accurate information on their background, knowledge, opinions, attitudes and behaviour (actual and hypo-thetical). This assumption is often reasonable: people can and will properly report demographic information (such as their gender) and some psychological and behavioural information (such as their beliefs about the causes of unemployment or their attitudes towards mobile telephones). But we cannot always be so confident about self-reported economic behaviour: people are reluctant to give information about their savings and investments (as these are seen as a private matter) and may in some cases not even know themselves. They are similarly reticent about certain forms of economic activity (tax evasion, debt, drinking alcohol) which may be illegal or perceived negatively (the evidence suggests that respondents understate spending on alcohol by about 60 per cent – see Branch, 1994). And they may even mis-report some demographic information, such as the level of schooling they received (Grubb, 1993). With hypothetical questions ('what would you do if you received a lottery win of £1,000,000?') it is even harder to be certain as to the status of the answers. These kind of concerns (and perhaps, more fundamentally, Milton Friedman's view that the appropriate way to do economics is to observe behaviour) have led to what Boulier and Goldfarb (1998) call 'the historical "bad rap" among economists of questionnaire surveys'. As McCloskey (1983, p. 514) put it, 'one can literally get an audience of economists to laugh out loud by proposing ironically to send out a questionnaire on some disputed point. Economists are so impressed by the confusions that might possibly result from questionnaires that they abandon them entirely.' In fact, the view of economists of surveys is more complex than is portrayed by McCloskey, and they make considerable use of regular questionnaire surveys involving economic 'facts' (incomes, expenditure, work) and some use of questionnaire surveys on expectations (see Chapter 5). The kind of questionnaires that attracts opprobrium are those focusing on the hows and whys of behaviour, such as an interviewee's explanation of how and why she chose a particular savings account (Boulier and Goldfarb, 1998). We have our own reservations about questionnaire surveys, but believe them to be extremely useful and so will make much use of questionnaire data.

What is particularly interesting and distinctive within economic psychology is the use of panel studies and secondary data analysis. Both of these are rarely used in mainstream social psychology, although the second is commonplace in sociology. In a classic panel study, the same group of households or individuals are surveyed at regular intervals (which may be as often as each week, as in some market research studies, or each month or each year). This kind of survey has real advantages, principally that changes in attitudes and behaviour can be accurately tracked, that stronger causal interpretations are possible and that cohort effects can be taken into account. There are problems, of course: belonging to a panel can change the reporting of behaviour or the behaviour itself, and panel studies often suffer from attrition (respondents simply leave the panel). Two good examples of panels which have provided useful information for economic psychology are the British Household Panel survey, which has a sample of over 5,000 households and provides valuable information on social and economic change in the UK, and the somewhat smaller CentER panel, which was set up in the Netherlands specifically to investigate household savings and financial decision-making. This is unique in including a large number of economic and psychological variables, with questions having been specifically devised to look at, for example, income expectations, attitudes towards saving and money management techniques.

By way of contrast, in secondary data analysis, the researcher makes (hopefully) good use of data that has been collected with other purposes in mind. This involves the re-analysis of existing data sets and the combining of information from a variety of sources. The difficult task facing the researcher is matching the concepts he or she wishes to explore with the measures that are actually available. Thus one might try to use the annual Family Expenditure survey to investigate some of the factors influencing charitable giving but then find that the way respondents are asked about giving does not give enough information to differentiate charitable from other giving (Elliott and Halfpenny 1994).

The comparative approach

To understand the impact of differences in economic systems on people's behaviour, attitudes and understanding, we need to compare whole economies or compare economies before and after large-scale economic change. Cross-cultural and cross-national studies have had a growing impact on social psychology in recent years (see, for example, Smith and Bond, 1998) and they have also come to play a very important role in economic psychology. Two good examples are the study of psychological aspects of the introduction of the euro (Müller-Peters, Pepermans and Burgoyne, 1998) and Leiser, Sevón and Lévy's (1990) study of children's understanding of economic issues. Müller-Peters et al. found that member states of the European Union differed in their attitudes towards the euro along a number of dimensions, the most important of which was 'national economic pride and satisfaction'. This was expressed in the southern European countries (such as Italy and Spain) as pride in their culture and history, and such countries tended to be mainly pro-euro. In contrast, the northern countries (such as Germany and Finland) were more likely to express pride in their national currency and economic achievements, and were consequently less in favour of adopting the euro. However, nowhere was there such antipathy to the euro as that found in the UK. Leiser et al., by contrast, found evidence of remarkable consistency of the pattern of the development of economic understanding across ten different countries. Although there were some cross-national differences, for example, the Danish and the Finnish children had a more sophisticated understanding of banking than their counterparts in Algeria, Yugoslavia, Norway and Austria the similarity of responses across countries was striking.

The effects of economic change studies are well exemplified by studies in Poland (Tyszka and Sokolowska, 1992; Tyszka, 1999) and studies of East Asian transitions. The wide-ranging Polish studies show that the transformation from a state-controlled to a market economy was a difficult one: initially the quality of life deteriorated, unemployment and poverty increased, and in many Eastern European countries life expectancy dropped. This transition stage is now over in Poland (which opted for a 'shock therapy' approach) and all these indicators are now improving greatly. More interesting from a psychological point of view is that the drop in the quality of life (which was also marked by an increase in crime and drug addiction) went hand-in-hand with a general improvement in psychological well-being: so that although, for example, the material situation of young families worsened, they were more hopeful about the future. Perhaps more surprising is the finding that people's cognitive representations of economics were not very different between former communist countries and market economies: as Tyszka (1999, p. 572) says, 'cognitive representation of the economy seems to be quite general and insensitive to past experience'. Experience of the transition has had an impact on people's views though. In 1990, the socio-economic preferences of the Poles were closely in line with socialist ideology (e.g. there was strong support for medical care, a high minimum wage and unemployment benefits and no clear preference for privatisation), though this was coupled with support for the transition programme announced by the government. As Poles experienced the difficulties of the transition, there was an overall decrease in pro-market preferences. Pro-market preferences seem now to be based more on personal experience: those who are pro-market tend to be better educated and have higher need-for-achievement.

Psychology, Economics and the Economic Psychology of Everyday Life

Some (otherwise open and sympathetic) scholars feel that psychologists can shed little light on economic behaviour. Fine and Leopold (1993), for example, deride the approach as a form of commodity fetishism. Others claim that the interaction between social psychology and economics is difficult and may ultimately not be fruitful as their agendas are so different (Lunt, 1996). We think otherwise: while recognising that we need considerably more integrated theoretical development we believe there have been great strides in understanding since the publication of the first flush of texts in economic psychology in the mid-1980s (Furnham and Lewis, 1986; MacFadyen and MacFadyen, 1986; Lea, Tarpy and Webley, 1987; van Raaij, van Veldhoven and Wärneryd, 1988).

The aim of this book is to enhance our understanding of the economic problems people have to solve across their life-span. So the book is organised chronologically. In the next chapter we will look at economic socialisation and how children become active economic participants. Though we will consider the extensive research on children's understanding of the adult economic world, our main concern will be with the problems they face. How do children make sense of commercial communications? How do they get hold of money? How (and why) do they learn to save? What do they learn from the autonomous economic world of the playground? In Chapter 3 we look at a neglected topic in economic psychology, the transition from childhood to adulthood. Four routes of transition from school to adulthood are described: the worker remaining in the parental home, the student, claimants (young people who leave school and then derive an income of sorts from the social security system), and marginals, those young people who engage, for example, in property crime, prostitution or drug dealing. Chapter 4 focuses on economic behaviour in the family: here we are able to give a reasonable account of *what* people do, but cannot say too much about the processes underlying people's economic decisions in the family. The pervasive influence of gender is placed at the heart of our account. In Chapter 5 we attempt to deal with economic behaviour in maturity. Here we concentrate on expectations and individual differences, and consider some of the issues involved in buying and working. Chapter 6 considers the economic problems of the elderly, from retirement through to death, and in Chapter 7 we try to provide a round-up of some of the themes that emerge.

Throughout the book we will be eclectic in the theories we use and will cite studies of a variety of types. We hope that the resulting pot-pourri has a distinctive, complex yet satisfying scent.

2

The Early Years – The Economic Problems of Childhood

Economic Socialisation

In this chapter we shall be looking at economic socialisation. As children grow and develop from infancy through to adolescence, they learn about different aspects of their world. They learn, for example, that objects still exist although they are hidden behind cushions and that there is still the same amount of water to drink in a glass even though it's been poured into a tall thin container where the level is much higher than before (Piaget, 1970). Both of these achievements reflect significant changes in cognitive development. More recently psychologists have been interested in how children understand the beliefs, desires and intentions of other people (e.g. Damon, 1978) and how and when children understand that someone is lying or can have false beliefs. All of these strands of development, how children understand the world of inanimate objects and the motives of other people, are important, but there seems to be something missing. Children live in a world of goods and services where things have to be bought and sold and where people work, save, invest and pay taxes. This world is full of brands that are advertised from billboards, on television screens and also on the World Wide Web. It is probably not water that is being poured in real life but Coke and the objects that are hidden behind cushions are members of the Polly Pocket family. And yet psychologists have paid little attention to the world of goods and services although it is present and pervasive in practically all cultures and is an important part of the life of most children. Before we explore the research and theories in this area we have to consider why this is such a neglected area in developmental psychology. We shall see that not only has economic socialisation through childhood suffered from relative neglect by academic psychologists but that when the issues and problems in this area are tackled, they are approached in certain predictable ways that preclude other methodologies and theories.

Children and Commerce – An Uneasy Relationship

There are several reasons why developmental psychologists, on the face of it, have paid scant attention to children as they grow and develop in the economic and commercial world. For many years developmental psychology was preoccupied with general theories of cognitive development. For example, the principles of sorting and classifying objects, questions of similarity and differences, were investigated by using formal objects such as pieces of plastic cut into different triangles, squares or circles, and coloured red, yellow, white or black. The assumptions underlying investigations like these were that if general principles or ontogenetic laws could be established, then, just because the material used was culturally neutral and stripped of cultural meaning, the principles were applicable to all and any cultural setting with the addition of local cultural rules. In addition there was an implicit assumption that cognition *per se* is independent of the domain within which thought operates, and this now appears increasingly implausible. There are alternative approaches to studying children as they grow up, however, and the one that we have great sympathy for is a conception of childhood as a time of change when the environment poses real challenges that have to be coped with and problems that have to be solved. The adaptive responses of children to these issues and a description of their ways of coping and what can consequently be inferred about their levels of understanding constitutes a natural history of childhood. One can enter different worlds of childhood. Is this person my friend or my enemy? Why is this person being nice to me? What does my best friend know about me? Why is that teacher being sarcastic? In this way a psychology of the child's understanding of people and how they communicate emerges from the real problems the child faces and the adaptive strategies that he or she deploys. It is our contention that the varieties of economic experience and the way children cope with them constitute a valid and important world of childhood simply because the problems are there in every culture and at most stages of development. In addition the problems in themselves are non-trivial and the inability or ability to cope with and solve them depends on quite general developmental achievements such as being able to recognise agency and motive in institutional arrangements and taking the perspective and adopting the role of another. The extent to which children differ in their economic socialisation will also provide a range of different styles of coping with these problems and issues. Cultures will differ on the incidence and acceptability of 'economic personalities' that emerge during socialisation with some, for example, encouraging and rewarding the risk-taking behaviour that characterises entrepreneurial behaviour.

Approaching economic socialisation in this way allows the researcher to treat and analyse the children's performance in an economic world on their own terms rather than viewing economic socialisation merely as an interesting testing ground for the theories of mainstream developmental psychology. We do not accept the idea implicit in this latter approach, which is that there is a one-way traffic between the core of a discipline (where theory is developed and tested) and applied contexts on the periphery, where the theory is used. On the contrary, we believe that applied contexts are ideal places to develop and test theories and to feed ideas back to the core. In our approach we acknowledge both the transactional nature of the cycle of theory and results (where theory predicts results but, more importantly, the results inform theory) and the increasingly contextual nature of theory (as opposed to an overarching general theory of development).

We would argue that there are also deeper, historical reasons why researchers and theorists in developmental psychology have rarely investigated the world of economics and commerce. Kessen (1979) has argued that one of the effects of large-scale changes in the world of work in the United States in the nineteenth century was the separation of the workplace from the home. Such changes were not unique to the United States. They occurred rather earlier in Britain with the rise of factories during the Industrial Revolution and are still happening in parts of the developing world. The world of commerce at this time was a predominantly male world where wheeling and dealing occurred in smoke-filled rooms and families were excluded. It was the world of the bar and the brothel. This urban world, the world of downtown, was consequently defined in opposition to the world of domesticity, the world of home. Home became sentimentalised and motherhood and childhood were romanticised. The concept of childhood, although rooted in biological change, has always been amenable to social construction and there are several images of childhood available that have been used by different cultures at different times in history to suit their own needs (Aries, 1973; Pollock, 1983). One aspect of what we expect from children and childhood is based on the essential nature of children. Are they imps who need control and discipline in order for them to fit into the norms of the adult society? Or are they angels, unsullied as yet by the temptations of the adult world and in need of protection against this world? Given the nature of the adult world of work it is not difficult to see why 'the child as innocent in need of protection' became the dominant image in the context of economic and commercial influence.

The child as a consumer of goods and services

When do children become aware of this economic world? Let's take a typical child in England whom we shall call Laura and look at how she copes with and understands the very common, everyday economic activity of shopping. In this way and with this narrative we can introduce the reader to some of the issues surrounding the child as a consumer of goods and services.

Probably her first experience of this activity will be from a supermarket trolley as she is wheeled around sitting facing her mum who's doing the shopping. A particular version of the world of goods and services consisting of fast moving consumer goods (fmcg) is presented to her, at least once a week, with an enormous variety of heavily branded items in colourful, different-shaped packages. Supermarkets encourage family shopping because families tend to shop for regularly consumed items in this way and would want facilities that are child friendly, because children play an important role in the family consumer decision-making process (Moore-Shay and Wilkie, 1988; Lackman and Lanasa, 1993), and because children need to be cultivated by supermarkets as future consumers (McNeal, 1992). Much of the mother–child interaction in the supermarket will focus on the activity of shopping and some of it will involve the child wanting and demanding and the mother either complying or arguing. As well as seeing the real thing in the shops children from an early age become aware of representations of goods and services through the media in TV commercials for products. In addition, branded goods are common in the home. Consequently from a very early age children are exposed to this facet of the economic world, which we can call economic display or 'shop window'. There is evidence (Derscheid, Kwon and Fang, 1996; Haynes *et al.*, 1993) that children of 2 to 3 years of age can recognise familiar packages in supermarkets and familiar characters on toys and clothes and that brand awareness and recognition develops rapidly throughout childhood. The results and consequences of economic activity are very visible from an early age. What is still to come, however, is an understanding of the processes that precede production and the ability and resources to interact as a consumer or economic actor in this world.

The transition from observer to participant is driven by development within the child as well as by the child's experience of her own economic behaviour. The cycle of socialisation is an interaction between the parents' views of what is expected of the child at different ages and stages of development and the child's own growing skills with money and her ability to negotiate within the family for goods and services. The journalistic expression 'pester power' is often used to describe this part of the interaction.

'Pester power' is an unfortunate term with inappropriate connotations but it does reflect that, with age, the child will take an increasingly influential role in family decisions about what to eat, where to go on holiday, and even what car to buy (Foxman, Tansuhaj and Ekstrom, 1989; Williams, 1993; Carlson *et al.*, 1994). According to John's (1999) review of the literature, children's influence is greatest for purchases of child-relevant items such as cereals, toys and clothes, followed by family activities (holidays and restaurants, for example) and is least for purchases of consumer durables (so-called 'white' and 'brown' goods) and expensive items. Although purchase influence is an important aspect of the child's developing role as a consumer, the term 'pester power' also reflects the fact that many concerned consumers feel that the commercial world impinges on their children in a negative or malign way, getting children to buy things that they do not want or their families do not want them to have (Young, 1999). Most of the academic research in this area has used only two methodologies: supermarket observation and questionnaire self-reports or diary studies where mothers record incidents over a period of time. For example, Wiman (1983) interviewed 222 children aged between 8 and 9 years and their parents in order to establish how different forms of parental influence within the family affected children's responses to television advertising. He found that children whose parents see themselves as strictly controlling their child's viewing behaviour have more negative attitudes toward television advertising. Such children tend to come from a higher socio-economic level and have better-educated parents. They make fewer purchase requests to their parents and understand the purpose and nature of advertising better. This would seem to suggest that parents have an important role to play in mediating advertising and its influence on children. Style of socialisation has a role to play in purchase-request behaviour. Crosby and Grossbart (1984) sampled over 500 mothers of children in a Midwestern state of the United States and, using self-administered questionnaires, found that parents who claimed authoritative characteristics also displayed most concern about television advertising to children. This would be expected. Given the authoritative parental style, much television advertising to children would be seen as potentially subversive to this control by parental authority. Crosby and Grossbart, in a message to advertising managers, suggest that parental style might serve as a suitable market segmentation criterion. What this means is that the advertiser may have to pitch differently if the audience consists predominantly of families who are authoritative and consequently concerned about television advertising to children. Permissive families, on the other hand, will not bother so much and a different message can be delivered without the risk of rejection.

During the pre-school period, as the child grows and matures from an infant to a toddler to a young person, there are biological and cognitive changes occurring that will enable Laura to walk round the supermarket, remember aisles and where products are, categorise and recognise brands, develop preferences and make informed choices. The environment of the supermarket becomes structured and familiar: a place that the pre-school child can explore and understand.

By the time Laura is about to go to school, between 4 and 6 years of age, she will understand that there are notes and coins and cards called 'money' and that money is involved in a social process called 'buying'. When mum goes to the checkout and hands over cash or a card then we can all go home with the shopping. She will also understand that mum buys goods that have names on them (brands) and that these brands often appear on TV in short interludes between long programmes. She thinks these commercials or advertisements are just there for fun. Although she associates them with shopping where people buy things she probably has no idea at this age that advertisements are there because advertisers want you to buy things. Laura will also be noticing the influence of socio-economic variables. Perhaps she has some friends who don't have as many toys as she has and live in a small house or there are people in the supermarket who don't buy so much or are dressed differently from her. Class, inequality between rich and poor, ownership and possessions are all aspects of the consequences of living in an economic world that impact on children at this time and will have an effect on their understanding of and participation in economic life from now on until adulthood.

By the time Laura is 8 or 9 years of age she is an active participant in the economic world. She will probably get regular pocket money together with any extra she makes from doing chores around the house or in gifts from friends and relatives. Although she doesn't earn money by working, as the law in the UK precludes that until 13 (except under special circumstances), she does have a certain degree of financial autonomy and can go to the shops and buy sweets or toys on Saturday morning. Perhaps she has a savings account with a bank – maybe as a result of a local branch of a national bank coming to an arrangement with a local school. The local school is not now a refuge from the commercial world and in all likelihood some of the resources teachers have available will have been distributed free by an agency specialising in marketing to children in schools. These resources will of course mention particular brands. She will have a well-developed sense of what clothes she wants to wear that are appropriate for her age and gender and will negotiate within her family for them. She will make an informed choice of the gifts she wants at Christmas, not, as many people believe, by being dominated and swayed by toy advertising in the period before Christmas but by poring over catalogues issued free at a well-known store in the UK! Laura will have a good understanding of why advertising and promotion are in the media and realise that advertising only tells you about the good qualities of a brand and that they're there in order to get people to buy the products.

We'll leave Laura as a young teenager, capable of earning a regular sum of money on a paper round. By now her shopping will probably be done with friends and the 'mall culture' will dominate much of her life as it is a social arena for hanging out, meeting friends, dating, eating, leisure, and challenging adult authority (see, for example, Miller *et al.*, 1998). She will have a well-developed sense of the social meaning of goods and services and will use clothes, make-up and brands in general to cultivate her own personal identity and to maintain her social identity as a member of one group ('us') against other groups ('them'). Her patterns of consumption may be driven by an emerging political identity. She won't eat meat that's intensively farmed and might not eat meat at all. Her cosmetics will not have been tested on animals and fur is definitely out. She may earn with casual work and with her allowance and gifts from family and friends she might save for special occasions like Christmas and annual holidays (Ward, Wackman and Wartella, 1977). Advertisers will target her intensively but she will have a cynical mistrust of advertising and claim to be able to see through its rhetoric.

Of course, what we have described is very Western and in some ways peculiarly British. Supermarkets, for example, whilst commonplace in the UK, are not so common in some European countries, and in other parts of the world do not exist. A Laura brought up in Zimbabwe may well have early experience of selling things in the vegetable market (Jahoda, 1983) and a Laura in many parts of the world may be working from 6 years of age. Both the nature of the economic world and the opportunities children have to observe, participate and learn about it, differ widely from culture to culture. We will concentrate on the experience of Western children here (as this is what most research tells us about). It is important to describe the Western experience not just to clarify the processes in a Western society but also to establish just those important differences between our society and other cultures with different economic experiences. It is vital to recognise the potential biases in our descriptions and comments.

Making sense of commercial communications

One of the main economic problems that the growing child has to face is how to make sense of what are euphemistically called 'commercial communications'. These include point-of-sale displays, brand logos, packaging, various discounting devices (such as '10 per cent off!' or 'one-third more!'), billboard posters, television commercials, character merchandising, sponsored TV programmes, branded resource packs in schools, and so on. The list is not comprehensive but the term covers all the communicative aspects of the commercial and economic world that bombard us every day whether we are children or adults. There is an academic literature on the subject (Young, 1990) that tends to focus on the child's understanding of television advertising. There are at least two reasons for this emphasis on TV spot advertising. One is the simple fact that most of the advertising children are exposed to is on TV, both between and within programmes. Adler and Faber (1980) report that in the US children see the equivalent of three hours of commercials a week. The other is that many people are worried and concerned about advertising to children, especially on TV. Flurries of concern that on occasions seem like waves of moral panic occur at regular intervals. When advertising to children gets to the top of the agenda then research money is often found to 'get at the truth' and research is published. For example, the research that was published in the 1970s in the USA was preceded by a campaign and a federal government inquiry into advertising to children (see Young, 1990; Chapter 2). Why should this be? Why is there such concern with television advertising to children?

Advertising has always had a bad press. The parody of advertising presented by popular writers such as Packard (1957) suggests that advertising is akin to black magic with the psychologist as master of these arts. The main aim of advertising by all these accounts is the subversion of reason with the imposition of false wants and desires in a public who don't really want the majority of goods and services on sale. The considered evaluation of costs and benefits of purchase and consumption is distorted by the techniques of the 'hidden persuaders' with their rhetorical devices. If children are viewed as innocent (and this is a common image that emerges when commerce and children are put together) then theories of child development that reinforce this image of inadequacy will be preferred and adopted in contrast to those that emphasise the adaptability and skills of children coping with a new and different environment with unexpected and strange contingencies. Children who are 'unable to erect cognitive defences' against the 'onslaught' of commercial messages should therefore be protected and one way of protecting them is to remove the source of problem by banning or seriously limiting their access to advertising.

There is, however, a more sinister reason why advertising to children evokes such concern with members of the public. One of the chapters of Packard's book is called 'The psycho-seduction of children' and this relationship between the advertiser as seducer and the child as innocent is one that evokes deep anxieties in many people, dealing, as it does, with a fundamental and widespread taboo. If advertising is carried on television then we have to consider the ambiguous relationship television has with the home. When television was first introduced as a home purchase it was promoted as a new hearth, a window on the world round which the family would cluster for information and entertainment at set hours in the evening. In the UK, television broadcasting was under the control of the BBC until 1955 when channels with advertising were introduced (Henry, 1986). Television came to be perceived as a threat to family life as the commercial world was allowed to invade the sanctity of the home. There is a resonance with the present desire to keep the world of commerce and business at a distance and away from children with advertising on the World Wide Web and the rapid growth of sponsored and branded resource packs in schools.

In order to make sense of children's understanding of advertising we need to identify what makes advertising unique and different from other forms of communication that the child is exposed to and participates in. It soon becomes apparent that there is no unique defining characteristic of advertising but rather it is a communicative form that has many characteristics and each one shares common features with other kinds of communication. For example:

- Advertising is entertaining. Advertising is not alone here. *The Simpsons* is fun for most children and much of children's TV is designed to entertain.
- Advertising is involving and attracts the child's attention. There are many communicative forms that have this quality, such as telling ghost stories or listening to a good teacher.
- Advertising provides information. So do encyclopaedias, or instructions on how to make paper cut-outs.
- Advertising is about goods and services. Holiday programmes on TV or consumer reports are also about goods and services.
- Advertising is promotional. That is, it only tells you about the positive aspects of the brand advertised, never the negative qualities. People are promotional when they present at interview or show off.
- Advertising is rhetorical. Advertising uses visual and verbal rhetoric in order to communicate propositions about brands. Lawyers and poets use rhetoric too, to achieve different ends.

What distinguishes advertising is that it is all, or most of these, at once. Although adults will recognise advertising as a unique form defined as the fuzzy intersection of all these categories, children understand these various features of advertising at different ages. So, rather than defining a particular age at which children are 'capable' of understanding advertising, it is more appropriate to identify several strands in what has been termed 'advertising literacy' (Young, 1986; O'Donohoe, 1994; Ritson and Elliott, 1995) and examine the evidence of when these understandings emerge. It should be pointed out that much still remains to be done in researching advertising literacy and that little is known about the later stages of understanding when there is evidence for an appreciation of rhetoric and cynicism with the aims and intentions of advertisers emerges with a vengeance.

There is some evidence that an understanding of the world of brands emerges in infancy. Meltzoff (1988) found that even 14-month-old babies were capable of deferred imitation as well as immediate imitation of what they've seen on TV. Very young children aged from 14 months to 2 years saw an adult manipulating a novel toy in a particular way on television but were not presented with the real toy until the next day. A significant number of children, including the youngest group, imitated what they had seen 24 hours previously. This would suggest that infants are capable of watching television commercials and imitating what they saw, thus establishing a link between watching TV and subsequent behaviour. Jaglom and Gardner (1981), in a longitudinal study that assessed three children over three years, established that one child as young as 2 years of age was capable of making a distinction between TV commercials and the 'rest' of television. This was the first distinction made, before kinds of programmes were seen as different. Of course, commercials are short and TV programmes are longer and it's probably this clear-cut structural difference between these two kinds of televisual experience that will account for the early appearance of this distinction. In addition, infants are quite capable by the end of the first year of communicating two basic kinds of information by pointing or gesturing (Bates, 1979). The proto-declarative is where the baby touches an object, holds it up, or points to it while looking at others to make sure they notice. Proto-imperative gestures are when the infant gets another person to do something by pointing, reaching, and often making sounds at the same time. These are pre-linguistic ways of communicating the intentions of 'there is . . . ' and 'gimme . . . !' Although no research has been done at this age using branded goods and services, these results would suggest there is every reason to suppose that, even during infancy, children are capable of gesturing from their seat in shopping carts for things they want or recognising them either on shelves or on the TV screen. John (op. cit.) cites Langbourne Rust Research (1993) who observed that toddlers and pre-school children exert their influence by pointing at products and occasionally grabbing them off supermarket shelves and putting them in their parent's shopping trolley. The link between the world of goods and services and the child as an emergent economic actor has been established.

By the time the child is 2 or 3 years of age he or she is aware that there is a world of goods and services, packaged in shops and supermarkets, existing in the kitchen and in the home, and appearing on television. No studies have been done, however, on how these different cultural representations of brands are understood by the young child. Brands as represented in the media in the form of television commercials are brands in a very different kind of context from brands in shops, on kitchen shelves or hidden inside school bags, and we don't yet know whether children identify them as the same or different. It is recognised, however, that children respond to branding at a very early age.

Hite and Hite (1995) investigated brand choice and product preference in children as young as 2 years of age. Using an analysis of variance design they investigated whether children would prefer, by rating on a five-point scale from 'tastes really good' to 'tastes really bad', two kinds of foods, viz. peanut butter and breakfast cereal. These foods were presented in two kinds of package. One was the nationally advertised brand and package and the other was the local store's brand and package, which was not advertised. Half the children were offered the products in the right package and the other half had the products in the wrong package, where the local and national peanut butter and cereal had their packaging swapped about. Samples from the familiar, nationally advertised brand packages were reported by children as tasting better than samples from less-familiar, unadvertised store-brand packages and were significantly more likely to be chosen. Interestingly, children actually rated the store product as better tasting when tasting blind, a fortuitous result that makes the findings more convincing, since it must be that they were influenced by a memory of preferred taste in the national brand.

What makes a child develop such loyalty toward a particular brand? Brand loyalty can be seen as a psychological state involving trust, affection, familiarity and intent to repeat-purchase a brand. Children are risk-averse and if something tastes familiar or provides satisfaction then it is likely to be chosen again. The origins of brand loyalty are found in brand preference and repeat purchase and the evidence from Hite and Hite's findings is that these are in place at a very early age.

Returning to the child's understanding of commercial communications there is almost a consensus in the literature that children in the pre-school period (until 5–6 years of age) see advertising as just there for fun and entertainment. In that sense it's like *The Simpsons* with brands rather than the adventures of Bart or Lisa. At this age there is little evidence that the commercial, informative, or promotional functions of advertising are recognised. There is one piece of research, however, that goes against this trend. Gaines and Esserman (1981) sampled 104 children ranging in age from 4 years to 8 years. Two thirty-second animated commercials for a breakfast cereal aimed at children were embedded in a six-minute *Mighty Mouse* cartoon programme for children and the videotape was shown to each child. Children were asked what a commercial was for and why it was on television. Almost two-thirds of 4–5-year-olds were able to produce responses that were categorised as showing an understanding of the purpose of the commercial such as 'getting you to buy it' and over half this group, when asked how they felt about the cereal they had just seen on television, gave a sceptical response such as 'might not be as good as they say' or 'can't believe what they say because they want your money'.

Young, van der Valk and Prat (1997) investigated the child's understanding of promotional communication by taking several commercials that adhered to the narrative convention that Berger (1974) called the 'pain, pill, pleasure' model. The pain is an everyday problem either discovered or created from market research. Examples would be shirt collars that are never white after a wash, or an irritating cough, or body odour. The pill is the brand, and the pleasure consists of the results ensuing from consuming the brand. The commercials were edited so that only the first two stages were shown. Three alternative endings were prepared on cards and shown to the child with the instruction to choose the best one to use when the commercial is shown on TV. One ending was a control with little or no expression on the actor's face. The other was the promotional ending with the problem cured and the actor smiling and happy. The final ending was the most entertaining but it showed the brand in a negative way. For example, in an ad for cough sweets the actor was shown looking ill and vomiting and in a commercial for face cream the actress was shown with her face covered in spots as a result of putting on the cream. The majority of 4-year-olds chose the funny ending that showed the brand in a negative way – a result that is predicable from our knowledge of how this age group understand advertising. From 5–6 years of age and older, the majority of children chose the promotional ending.

Robertson and Rossiter (1974) found two types of attribution of intent to commercials by children. One, that they called 'assistive', is where the child sees commercials as informative, as in 'commercials tell you about things', and the other, called 'persuasive', is where the child sees commercials as 'trying to make you buy things'. Although both types of attribution of intent can co-exist in the individual child, there is a trend towards persuasive intent attribution, as compared with assistive intent attribution, becoming more frequent as the child gets older. By 10 to 11 years of age, practically all children are able to attribute persuasive intent. Also, children of parents with higher educational levels will tend to attribute persuasive intent at an earlier age than children of parents with lower educational levels. Another function of advertising is its commercial intent, the role that advertising plays within the world of exchanging goods and services. The fact that television advertising is to 'do with' brands, goods and services emerges early in development and, as we have seen (e.g. Hite and Hite, 1995), brands are an important part of the child's life from an early age. Commercial intent means more than this, however. To understand that commercial communications are part of the economic and commercial world presumes that the child is aware of a source *behind* the message that is there for a particular purpose, and is aware that the purpose is promotional. In other words, messages are designed to get people to purchase that brand and all the rhetoric and the puffery is there for that reason. Robertson and Rossiter (1974) found that this essential ability to be aware that there is a source behind messages and an intended audience for them was common to those children who attributed assistive intent as well as those who were able to attribute commercial intent. Being able to attribute commercial intent, however, was identified with other abilities such as being able to understand the symbolic nature of advertising. The 'symbolic' nature of commercials means that advertisements use devices such as idealised settings or dramatised character emotions and that these devices symbolise or represent 'real' situations or 'real' emotions. Adverts represent reality and a full understanding of this representational nature seems to be necessary to achieve understanding of commercial and persuasive intent. Roberts (1982) identified metacognitive skills as the key to a mature understanding of television advertising where the child is capable of effectively monitoring messages in order to adopt different strategies where appropriate.

Children understand the language and processes of buying and selling at different ages. In a classic study, Gentner (1975) asked children to act out the economic transactions of 'buy' and 'sell', as well as several others such as 'spend', 'trade', 'give', 'take' and 'pay', using a couple of toy dolls, some small objects, and coins. He found that 'give' and 'take' are understood first between 3.5 and 4.5 years, followed by 'pay' and 'trade' (5.5–6.5 years) and 'spend', 'buy' and 'sell' (7.5–8.5 years), and that within this last age range there was a significant lag between 'buy' and 'sell'. One common error for younger children was to omit the monetary transaction so that children responded to 'buy' as if it was 'take' and to 'sell' as if it was 'give'. This result suggests that economic transactions are understood as two developmentally distinct processes. The idea of exchange together with the direction of exchange is common to the pairs of 'buy'/'take' and 'sell'/'give' and this emerges first. The concept of monetary compensation emerges at a later point in development. The lag between 'buy' and 'sell' was not satisfactorily explained until a paper by Henriksen (1996) uncovered a relationship between 'perspective taking' and the understanding of selling. Perspective taking is being able to take the role of another person and see from his or her point of view, or understand his feelings, or infer her thoughts. Children who are unable to do this are termed 'egocentric', and egocentrism has an important role to play in explaining various cognitive limitations at different ages. Henriksen assessed perspective taking using a moral judgement task, where successful reasoning presupposes that the respondent can infer that two of the actors in the scenario had different information about the action. The child's understanding of selling was significantly correlated with the ability to take the perspective of the other.

So far, the approach taken to the child's understanding of commercial communications is one that emphasises the processes occurring within individual children and how they process information according to their different levels of comprehension. An alternative view of advertising literacy was proposed by Elliott and his colleagues (Ritson and Elliott, 1995; Ritson, Elliott and Eccles, 1996; Elliott and Wattanasuwan, 1998). The basic assumptions here were that consumption in general and advertising in particular had an important role to play in the construction of individual and social identity (see pp.7–9). People often use their material possessions and the representation of material possessions in their self-definitions, both as individuals and in their relations with others (see, for example, Dittmar, 1992). However, this construction is often done collectively: the meaning is deliberately manufactured in discourse by a group, using the raw material of the collective experience of the brand and the various media representations of the brand, including advertising. Groups of young people in particular would laugh, joke, gossip and parody what they have consumed in order to produce meanings that were often not at all what the advertiser had intended.

Buckingham (1993) led group discussions with children from various schools in London about television, including their talk about advertising. Using this methodology, they provided evidence that by 9–10 years of age children are quite capable of taking an interpretative position that is objective to the extent they are interpreting why certain techniques are used and to what purpose the ad is constructed in a particular way. For example, they are aware of techniques that are designed to attract the audience. In other words, they have a grasp of the rhetorical devices used in advertising, and can discuss advertising and mock and scoff amongst themselves. They can adopt and maintain a metacommunicative stance where the ad is watched and listened to and then the collective experiences are examined and analysed.

In summary, the evidence indicates that a mature understanding of advertising emerges in middle childhood. One of the major achievements is the ability to stand outside the flow of advertising and critically examine the promotional communication. There would seem to be (at least) three aspects to this. One is an acknowledgement that there is a source behind the communication and that this source has interests that are not the same as the consumer's. The reciprocal relationship between buying and selling is intimately related to this understanding of the commercial function of advertising. Next, there is an appreciation of the representational nature of the medium of advertising, what Robertson and Rossiter (1974) called the 'symbolic nature of commercials'. Last to emerge is an understanding of the rhetoric of advertising, including how it is produced and how it is designed to woo audiences. All of these understandings can be detected in other areas of development and there is every reason to suppose they are very general abilities that emerge in different contexts. The general principle of metacognition – of being able to think about thinking – is well known (Gombert, 1992) and monitoring and evaluating one's communication and the communication of others is a feature of metacognition. Acknowledging that there is a communicative source with beliefs and intentions that need not correspond to one's own beliefs and intentions first emerges in social interaction between 3 and 5 years of age (Mitchell, 1996). The awareness of a difference between reality and representations of reality also has its precursors early in development (Flavell *et al.*, 1990; Wellman, 1990). A knowledge of the tactics and strategy of media representations is part of the process of becoming literate with media, whether it is audiovisual or written, and the parsimonious assumption is that advertising literacy is but one part of this process.

'The Wherewithal'

Getting hold of the wherewithal

One of the main economic problems children face is getting hold of money in order to buy the things they want. Ideally they would like an income that is regular, large enough for their perceived needs and has no strings attached. Parents often have other ideas. They may only hand out money irregularly, and often use money as a reward or withhold it as a punishment. Newson and Newson (1976), for example, found that some parents introduced regular pocket money for the sole reason that it simultaneously allowed them to introduce a system of fines. In addition, pocket money is seen by many parents as a way of socialising children and providing them with training in money management. Children may be given money which is tied to a particular purpose (money which has to be put in a savings account for example, or money which must be spent on parentally approved goods or activities), or money that is linked to the satisfactory completion of work around the home (Sonuga-Barke and Webley, 1993).

So where do children get their money from? Good-quality information is available from Britain (Furnham and Thomas 1984; Furnham, 1999; the regular *Bird's Eye Wall's Pocket Money* monitor), France (Micromegas, 1993; Lassarre, 1996), America (Miller and Yung 1990; Mortimer *et al.*, 1994; *Kids' Money*, 1999) and Holland (for adolescents, Warnaar and van Praag, 1997; de Zwart and Warnaar, 1997). This research shows that parents usually introduce pocket money (in the sense of a regular standard sum of money) when a child is between 5 and 7. The amount of pocket money is linked to age. In the UK in 1996, 8–10-year-olds got on average £1.69 per week whereas 11–13-year-olds received £2.73 for the same period (cited in Waterson, 1998). In the USA, in 1997 a third of 9–11-year-olds received no allowance and the most common amount given was $5 (*Kids' Money*, 1999). In the UK pocket money has, on average, gone up more than inflation over the last twenty-five years and the findings of French surveys describe a similar trend. The French surveys give an indication of the extent to which different age groups rely on pocket money as a source of income. It makes up 100 per cent of the income of French 7-year-olds but only 15 per cent of the income of 13–14-year-olds, as half of children in the latter age group have part-time work of one kind or another. A similar picture is painted by the pocket money surveys that have been carried out by various schools and disseminated using the World Wide Web (e.g. European Schools Project, n.d.). One of these, for instance, reports that mean income from pocket money in a school in the UK for 14–15-year-olds is £3.86 per week and mean income from work is £11.50 per week, although the quality of this data may be a little uncertain. Thus many children solve the 'wherewithal problem' by taking part-time jobs or by doing extra work for their parents or others on an informal basis. Of course there are legal restrictions in all Western countries on employing children, but it should be recognised that there is also a flourishing informal economy that allows children to increase their income above and beyond the limits of parental contributions through pocket money. McKechnie and Hobbs (1999) have argued against the idealised stereotype of children's work as involving only light tasks such as newspaper delivery and have gathered evidence that children are involved to a significant extent in low-paid work in areas that may be more associated with adult employment.

Pocket money is only one source of money even for young children. Webley and Plaisier (1998), in a small-scale study, identified three important sources of money for children aged from 5 to 12 years in the UK. These were pocket money, holiday money and birthday money. Holiday and birthday money often consisted of quite substantial amounts (up to £45 for holiday money and £75 for birthday money) and could constitute a significant part of the child's annual income. One 11-year-old boy, for example, received £1.50 a week pocket money but £74 birthday money and reckoned to be able to earn £16 from a couple of evenings' carol singing before Christmas. Money from these sources was perceived as different and used differently. Despite the fact that parents tend to see pocket money as money for spending (Sonuga-Barke and Webley, 1993), quite a lot of pocket money is in fact saved, although sometimes only for short periods of time. Holiday money is seen as spending money and is used for entertainment, souvenirs and presents. Birthday money was used to buy clothes, shoes and toys with any money left afterwards being saved.

The information we have at the moment provides only the sketchiest outline of how children solve the problem of getting hold of money. It is clear that young children rely almost exclusively on their parents and relatives to provide money, and that this dependence declines with age, but how exactly older children fund their activities is less clear. They may get money (as a gift) for birthdays and for Christmas; they may get holiday money (more than once a year); they may earn it (legally or illegally, formally or informally); they may trade; they may gamble (Ide-Smith and Lea, 1988; Pugh and Webley, 2000); and they may steal. We need to know a lot more, but our guess, for what it is worth, is that we will only do so when we adopt an ethnographic approach, and make use of children as researchers (cf. Webley and Lea, 1993b).

Children's understanding and use of money

In the previous section we saw that children have various different sources beyond the regular instalments of pocket money for obtaining money. Children also need to understand the functions of the money they have acquired. It is clear that children pass through a number of stages in achieving an adult understanding of money and that the order of acquisition of these stages is the same across cultures. Different researchers have identified different numbers of stages, however. Also, the number of stages the child passes through is not necessarily the same for money and other related concepts like pay, bank interest and debt. For example, three to nine stages have been identified in the case of money whereas children go through between six to eight identifiable stages in understanding the concept of banking. Furnham (1996) has pointed out that these stages can usually be summarised into three basic levels of comprehension. The first stage involves little or no understanding, the second stage consists of understanding some isolated concepts, while in the third stage these isolated concepts are linked into a full understanding. But it seems to us that this could be said about the child's understanding of almost anything, from cognitive maps to moral principles, and at this level of abstraction some of the vital detail contained in the original descriptions is lost.

As examples, we will now describe briefly the development of children's understanding of the two economic concepts of buying and selling, and banks. In addition, the child's understanding of money was briefly examined in Chapter 1. A fuller review of the development of other kinds of economic understanding is provided by Furnham (1996). In order to grasp the transaction of buying and selling, which is one of the central economic activities, the child has to understand a large number of related concepts and activities. Some of these the child can experience directly (such as buying sweets in a shop) whereas others can only be observed (such as the delivery of newspapers to a retailer). A third group are activities which are rarely observed or experienced, and as such have no direct visibility, although they can be inferred: an example would be a factory buying products from farmers. It is perhaps not surprising that children are able to understand the idea of payment by a customer, which they can both experience and observe, before they can understand the idea of payment by the shopkeeper, and can understand both forms of payment before they can understand how profit works (Furth, 1980). Leiser, Sevón and Lévy (1990), in their large-scale cross-cultural investigation, also report that 8-year-olds understand the exchange of money for goods and the exchange of money for work but not until the age of 11 years do children understand how these fit together into a system. As with the understanding of advertising, the visibility of the activity as well as the ability to take the perspective of the other is important (Henriksen, 1996).

A very similar kind of progression can be found in studies of children's under-standing of banks and banking. This is a particularly intriguing area, as although children use banks and see banks being used by others, the position of banks in the economic system is largely hidden and what exactly it is they are selling is rather hard to grasp. Jahoda (1981) describes Scottish children's understanding of bank profit as consisting of four developmental stages. He reports two interesting findings. First, interest on deposits, which is something the child has direct experience of, is understood before interest on loans. Secondly, the false belief that deposit interest is higher than loan interest precedes the recognition that interest is higher on loans than on deposits and that this difference is in fact the source of bank profits. Ng (1983) found a similar developmental progression with a sample of Hong Kong children though the latter were considerably more advanced in their understand-ing than their Scottish counterparts. Although he concluded that the maturity of the Chinese children reflected their high level of economic socialisation and the business ethos of their society this explanation seems unlikely since Takahashi and Hatano (1994) found that the understanding of banking amongst Japanese children lags well behind that of both European and Hong Kong children. Bonn and Webley (1999) found that black South African children's conceptions were as unsophisticated as those of the Japanese children. The most popular misconception in Japanese 11–16-year-olds was that the bank was a kind of safe-deposit box and these South African children also saw the bank essentially as a place of storage. Takahashi and Hatano (op. cit.) attributed the Japanese children's relative lack of understanding to the fact that they were sheltered from economic activities. The South African children were not so sheltered but do live in a society where economic activities do not flourish generally. It would appear from these results that both a business ethos and involvement by children in economic activities are envi-ronmental requirements for the development of an understanding of banks and banking by children.

Leiser, Sevón and Lévy (1990) conducted the Naive Economics Project which was designed to explore children's understanding and reasoning about various economic concepts. The results consisted of 900 interviews from ten different countries and the resultant information constitutes the largest database in this area. They categorised the sample into three groups based on the sophistication of answers on banking. It is not easy, however, to make sense of these inter-group differences on the basis of the different countries sampled. The most advanced children were from Scandinavia (Denmark, Finland), followed by those from France, Poland, Israel and West Germany. The least sophisticated consisted of the samples from Algeria, Yugoslavia, Austria and another Scandinavian country (Norway). As there is no information about the level of economic activity by children across these countries, it is not possible to draw conclusions about the economic status of a country and the emergence of understanding about banking.

A consistent picture seems to emerge from this research into children's understanding of money and related economic concepts. Although some differences between and within countries exist, these are fairly minor in comparison to age. This variable appears to be the biggest influence on a child's economic understanding. It is our contention, however, that this consistency is probably the result of researchers ignoring the social dynamics of transactions. In looking at both the understanding and the use of money (and other economic concepts) economic psychologists have been constrained by the definition of those concepts used by economists. So, for example, psychologists have investigated the development of the understanding of the standard economic definition of money considering it as a medium of exchange, a store of value, and a standard of value. It would be fruitful in future research to put different questions. Asking children why their parents give them pocket money might shed light on their understanding of the links between power and money and the tension between independence and control. Asking why money is not acceptable as a gift for one's mother (Webley, Lea and Portalska, 1983) may inform us of their understanding of the boundaries between the social and the economic. And asking why it is possible to buy gift tokens may give us some idea of their views of the limitations of money.

Saving

Money rarely arrives at just the right time and in just the right amounts. A problem children (indeed all consumers) face is adjusting the flow of income to expenditure. Saving can be the solution. A child can save in the short term in the sense of spending 30 pence of the £1 pocket money they receive on Saturday and the remaining 70 pence on Tuesday, in the medium term where they save all their pocket money for a month and then spend £4 on a toy, or in the long term where savings are accumulated over months and years. Though we might not usually call the first of these 'saving', we have to recognise that the definition of saving is essentially arbitrary and depends upon the accounting period.

The first thing to note is that saving does increase with age, even when the effect of increases in income is taken into account (Ward, Wackman and Wartella, 1977; Furnham and Thomas, 1984). In Furnham and Thomas's study older children reported that they saved because they expected to need money in the future whereas younger children tended to have concrete targets such as a toy or a Christmas present for their mum, in mind. Older children were also much more likely to save using saving accounts in banks or other financial institutions. The age difference could be a consequence of older children having easier access to bank accounts, but we believe that something different and more interesting is going on here.

Partly this is an increased understanding and use of strategies that help children delay gratification. If children are given a choice between a small immediate reward (10 pence now) and a larger delayed reward (20 pence in five minutes), there is a marked tendency for younger children to choose the immediate but smaller reward and for older children to wait for the bigger reward (Mischel and Metzner, 1962). This improvement in the ability to delay gratification seems to depend, in part, on a better understanding of the problem and effective strategies to solve it (Mischel and Mischel, 1962). These include things like thinking about other things rather than the reward, and hiding the reward. But this is not the whole story, as the experiments into delay of gratification test children's ability to wait, rather than their ability to save (the price you pay to get the bigger reward is the time you have to sit and wait). In saving, a child does not have to wait in the same way and has to make a whole series of decisions (to add to savings, to withdraw) over time. But some of the things children are learning, such as how to deal with temptation by distraction, may be helpful in learning how to save.

A broader picture of the processes underlying saving by children can be found in the series of studies of saving carried out by Sonuga-Barke and Webley (1993) and Webley, Levine and Lewis (1993). Sonuga-Barke and Webley carried out a number of studies using a savings board game. Children would first earn tokens on an operant task and then play a board game designed to present them with problems similar to those that they might experience in the real world. For example, in one of the board games children were faced with temptation in the form of a sweetshop and threat, where a robber steals, but only one token at a time, in order to prevent the children from bursting into tears! Possible solutions to these problems were made available, including a bank, where money could be deposited to keep it safe, and a detour, so that the robber could be avoided. The exact problems and solutions represented on the board game varied from one study to the next, but in each case there was a toyshop, where the child chose the target toy to save for, and a bank. In these studies the problem of saving was operationalised spatially, as children moved from one square on the board to the next, and encountered problems and possible solutions in turn.

By contrast, Webley, Levine and Lewis (1993) operationalised the problem of saving temporally. They used a play economy set up in a suite of rooms, where a range of activities were available. Some activities such as the library and resources for drawing were free, but others, where the child watched a cartoon film or played a computer game, cost a fixed amount. Finally, there was a sweetshop and café, where costs varied. The experimenter explained to the children that the experiment lasted a 'speeded-up' week, where each day lasted ten minutes. During each 'day' each child would be given ten tokens and spent ten minutes in a room where a free, a fixed-cost and a variable-cost activity were available. In order to obtain their target toy, which they had chosen at the beginning of the study, children had to save seventy tokens out of the ninety they were given in the course of the game. Sixty tokens were given out as pocket money and there was an initial endowment of thirty tokens in a bank account.

Although these studies operationalised saving differently from the Sonuga-Barke and Webley studies, the results are very similar. By 6 years children have learnt that saving is a 'good thing'. They have learnt that to be patient, to be thrifty and to exercise self-control is to be virtuous. They do not like it very much and they are also not very good at it. In one of the board games, for example, children could deposit their tokens in the bank before they encountered the robber or the sweetshop and then take them out again when they had passed the danger. The 4-year-olds used the bank randomly. Six-year-olds used the bank but not consistently, whereas 9-year-olds both used and understood the function of the bank. For example Mary, aged 9 years, said 'I won't take it out of the bank as I don't want to be tempted'. In the play economy 6-year-olds also showed a limited ability to save, and half of them did not manage to save at all. Many children at this age saw money saved as money lost. By the time children are in the age range 9 to 12 years they will seem to understand the problem that saving helps to solve. However, they will also have developed a range of other strategies for getting hold of money when they need it. These strategies are nearly all techniques for getting money out of their parents and other relatives. One example would be spending all your pocket money and then appealing to parents for cash so that one could buy a birthday present for a sister. One very clear conclusion from these studies is that saving is not the only possible way of solving the child's financial 'wherewithal problem', and that it may not in fact be the most efficient one. Negotiating, arguing with, and even the emotional blackmailing of parents may, in some families at least, be more effective.

Autonomous economies

There is a tendency for us to assume that the central economic problem children have to face is coming to terms with the adult economic world. Clearly children do have to understand and learn how to function effectively in adult society. They have to learn, for instance, how to buy and then how to be proficient and then sophisticated shoppers. But there is also an autonomous economic world of childhood, which while remote from the adult world is important in a variety of ways and presents children with challenges. Webley and Lea (1993b) and Webley (1996) describe a number of studies of what they call 'the playground economy'.

Under close examination this natural economy displays a surprising degree of sophistication. For example, when there is a marble 'craze' children between the ages of 8 and 12 years play marbles in the playground. But marbles are not only used to play games: they are also traded. In this market, the value of the different kinds of marbles (oilies, emperors, etc.) is determined by local supply and demand and not by the price of the marbles in the shops. So a locally rare emperor marble may be worth five 'ordinaries' even though in the shops it only costs three times as much. The children are good at explaining how this market functions and indeed seem to understand it better than the adult economy, which for them is less important and more abstract. Children can learn the art of negotiation and bargaining, not only in trading marbles but also in 'working' in the playground economy. A child who is a skilled player (the 'worker', with human capital), but who, on a particular day happens to have no marbles, may 'work' for another child (the marble capitalist) who owns lots of them. If the worker wins some marbles, the proceeds are shared between the two of them. If an adult researcher asks about this, he is told that the proceeds are shared equally. A child researcher on the other hand, operating like a local informant in ethnographical studies, is told that the marble capitalist always gets a bigger share than the marble worker. Studies of swapping reveal a different side of the playground economy. Swapping is a curious twilight activity that is often banned in schools because of complaints from parents stemming from incidents of older children exploiting younger children. Put simply, it seems to be an economic act with a social function. Its purpose is not really to acquire a toy car, a penknife or a sweet but to cement friendships. So children will make swaps that are clearly unequal, but will always have a good reason for doing so, as an overture to friendship, for example.

Although the research reported here on the marble economy is interesting ethnography, the description we've given only applies to one school, in one country, at one particular time. We do not, in fact, really know how important this domain is. We believe that for some children, at least, it is important in developing skills that they will use later in the adult economic world.

The Broader Picture

How children understand the institutional arrangements that constitute the economy at large

In much of this chapter we have concentrated on how children deal with the practical economic problems they face on an everyday basis. We have looked at how they understand and take action on the basis of commercial communications, how they make sure they have sufficient money, and how they swap with others to get what they want. But they also need to develop an understanding of the functioning of the wider economy, as this is part of making sense of the world and their place in it. So the ideas children develop about why some people are poor and why others are rich, about why some have highly paid jobs whereas others have no job at all, and why some services are provided by the state whereas others are provided through the market, are all issues that matter. They may not have immediate direct effects but they provide the context within which important decisions such as later career choice are made. In short, having these ideas and knowing about them enable the child to navigate his or her way through society more effectively. So a general understanding of how prices are determined can help when buying or selling a second-hand bike and views about the determinants of poverty may influence charitable donations.

Here we will consider aspects of children's macro-economic understanding, particularly wealth, poverty, inequality and unemployment, from a cross-cultural perspective. Studies in this area have been particularly valuable as they provide evidence relevant to two models of socialisation. Functionalist models (e.g. Parsons, 1960) predict that socialisation produces uniformity of beliefs across groups in society about the nature of social stratification. The social consequence is a stable society as these beliefs provide a justification for inequality ('he deserves to be rich, I deserve to be middling and he deserves to be poor'). Dialectical models of socialisation, on the other hand, predict that children's beliefs are constructed from their dealings with the environment. Since these experiences differ between different social groups, so too should the beliefs that children hold. This might imply that, for example, children from affluent backgrounds in meritocracies would attribute being rich or poor to individual effort (since they see people being rewarded for hard work) whilst children from poorer backgrounds attribute poverty and wealth to bad or good luck (since in their experience being in employment or not seems largely a matter of chance).

There is evidence for both of these models, but perhaps more support for the dialectical approach. On the functionalist side, Connell (1977), for instance, investigated Australian children's views of whether income inequalities were fair, and found that whilst young children saw them as unfair, adolescents tended to regard them as justified. Similarly Leahy (1981) found few class differences in children's descriptions of rich and poor people. However, in Emler and Dickinson's (1985) Scottish study of children's understanding of economic inequalities, substantial class differences but few age differences were found. Middle-class children not only believed that inequalities in income between the classes were greater than did working-class children, they also felt that these income differences were fair. Emler and Dickinson accept that, although there is a dominant view of inequality in society (the meritocratic view that differences are justified and reflect mainly individual differences in ability and application), there are other culturally available views, and children will tend to accept those that are prevalent in their community.

For macro-economic phenomena, therefore, the balance of the evidence is that there is not one form of adult understanding that children will achieve (as is the case for money and banking, for example) but a number of possible ways of understanding are available. These explanations can be broadly categorised into personal or individualistic, structural or economic and fatalistic (Feather, 1974; Feagin 1975). Typically the middle classes favour individualistic explanations and lower-income groups structural and economic explanations (Lewis, Webley and Furnham, 1995). But this neat summary is not universal, as cross-cultural studies have shown. Roland-Lévy (1990), for example, found that the dominant explanation for both poverty and wealth in Algerian children was individualistic, whilst French children saw poverty as mainly the responsibility of the socio-economic system. Although Algerian children saw poverty as due primarily to an individual's lack of effort and abilities, they were more aware than the French children of the power of the government to influence unemployment. Bonn *et al.* (1999), in a study of Black South African children from three different backgrounds, found that while social milieu was important, age had a much more powerful influence on children's explanations. Rural children were fatalistic and held God nearly as accountable as unemployment for inequality, while semi-urban children regarded lack of education and individual characteristics as more responsible. But the complexity and sophistication of the children's explanations depended mainly on their age. Indeed, cross-cultural studies in economic socialisation have shown that there is a remarkable consistency across countries with varied socio-economic systems and at different stages of development. In the Naive Economics Project described above, wealth differences were attributed by the children mainly to personal factors at all ages (Leiser, Sevón and Lévy, 1990). The socio-economic system was seen as the second most important explanatory factor, but its perceived importance diminished with age.

Summary and Conclusions

It is never surprising to find that age is the leading factor in differences between children, in any domain. It is a truism that children tend to get better at many things as they get older and, if apparent anomalies such as inverted 'U' trajectories of development occur they provide opportunities for an explanation of the underlying processes involved in such apparently anomalous behaviour. Much of the research reported in this chapter is summarised in terms of age-related trends but we would hope to go further. The real work in developmental psychology is not just to discover what the age differences are but to understand the processes by which children develop from their understanding or behaviour at one age to a different understanding and behaviour later. The study of economic socialisation has made more progress with the first of these tasks and less with the second one. Our view is that it is unlikely to advance until certain assumptions, which have been taken on board within mainstream psychology, are critically examined.

One of these assumptions is that children are mere learners of the adult economy. The world of childhood is seen as preparation for adulthood and children are regarded as being inadequate to the extent they have not achieved these adult skills. In cognitive development the work of Cole (1996) has emphasised the importance of culture in determining what skills are seen as important and valuable and how the course of cognitive development is not universally shaped but can assume a variety of cultural forms. And yet research in economic socialisation tends to adopt the model that assumes there is a level of 'adult-like' understanding and children are progressing towards it. There is a relative neglect of the child's own experiences of the varieties of economic life that he or she encounters, and how these experiences influence the understanding children have of the workings of aspects of the economy within their own friendship groups. What we have called 'autonomous economies' require more research.

What are some of the changes that occur during economic socialisation? Cognitive development is crucial as it underpins children's progressive understanding of economic concepts, advertising, and other aspects of the adult economic world. Cognitive development is also important in the child's own economic behaviour. Economic activities such as setting a budget, making decisions about how much can be spent and when, deciding how much money should be put aside for Christmas presents, all require some mathematical competence. A full understanding of commercial communications requires an ability to mentally represent the communication, adopt a metacommunicative stance, together with a knowledge of the rhetorical tactics and strategies that are used in the world of business and commerce. There are other factors apart from cognitive development that are equally important. As we have documented, there is a marked increase in economic independence and economic opportunities during childhood. Income increases considerably from 5 years of age to 12 years and there is a parallel increase in children's opportunities to spend. The choices of young children are heavily constrained by their parents: older children and adolescents are generally able to make their own choices with fewer imposed limitations. From age 13 onwards, children's income can increase even more as they have the opportunity to participate as part-time workers in the adult economy. Active participation in the economy is very important in understanding it, and may account for the superiority over European children that African children show with regards to economic understanding. We have seen in this chapter how experience obtained through economic participation, as opposed to experience derived from passive observation or information that is merely inferred, can enhance the child's economic understanding. The child's self-concept also develops from infancy through to adolescence (Markova, 1987) and this will have an effect on economic socialisation. For example, the desire to obtain certain goods and present to others in particular ways will depend on aspects of the evolving self-concept such as identity, both personal and social, and self-esteem. As well as relating to children's wants to have particular goods the emerging self-concept will affect the range of self-control and money management strategies that they develop. Finally, children's representations of the economic world will become more sophisticated and functional in the course of development. One important feature of these representations is their organisation and how concepts are categorised and classified. For example, there is no reason to suppose that the world of goods and services will be classified by children into the same categories as those used by adults and certainly they need not correspond to those of economists (Young and Claessen, 1988). The term 'mental accounting' implies that income and assets should be categorised in some way and that this categorisation will affect spending and other decisions. Our guess is that this emerges from the way parents encourage children to spend money differently depending on its source. Further research in the area would be welcome.

3

Becoming an Economic Adult

Four Paths to Economic Independence

The transition from childhood to adulthood is a neglected topic in economic psychology. In much of this chapter, therefore, we shall be pulling together research from the parent disciplines and trying to make sense out of it from our own perspective. Furthermore, one of the parent disciplines, psychology, has also tended to neglect adolescents and young adults (except for the ubiquitous university student used as an experimental participant – but in these cases the person's life stage is rarely in the researcher's mind). On the old definition of developmental psychology as, essentially, child psychology, adolescence was the last and perhaps the least interesting stage of childhood, when children were perhaps least mysterious, least unlike adults. On the newer conception of development as a life-span process, it is again less interesting as being more like childhood than other adult phases. To an economic psychologist, however, the period of adolescence and young adulthood is critically interesting. Fortunately, to offset the neglect of adolescence by psychologists, there is a rich literature in sociological and educational research. Educationalists' interest is driven partly by the fact that in adolescence, for the first time in their lives, people become voluntary rather than conscripted participants in the educational process, so like other customers, their convenience has to be studied rather than taken for granted. As far as sociologists are concerned, the concept of transition is at the heart of much sociological theory, and the transition from child to adult is one of the most significant in any person's life.

Chapter 2 emphasised that even the youngest children are not economically inert. Nonetheless, as children become first teenagers and then young adults, they acquire greatly enhanced economic significance. This is the stage of life at which we become independent agents within the economy. We take up positions in the labour market which we may very well occupy for the rest of our economically active lives, and these in turn will determine much of the rest of our economic behaviour. We start to take our own spending decisions, spending money which we view as our own, and in the process we acquire consumption preferences and habits that are relatively unlikely to change. This is, in other words, a very important phase of economic socialisation. The choices we make at this time of our life are important to other economic agents, who are anxious to secure us as potential workers or customers;

and they are important to us, because good or bad decisions at this stage may have far-reaching consequences for our prosperity and happiness.

The transition to economic adulthood in fact involves several distinct transitions. Typically they do not all happen at once, and for some individuals, some of them may never happen. The age at which they each occur, the period of time over which they are spread, and the sequence in which they occur all show wide variation between societies, between historical periods, between classes and groups within a society, and between individuals. In modern 'Western' societies, which have been by far the most thoroughly researched, the most important transitions are acquiring paid employment, acquiring an independent income, and acquiring one's own home. We shall look at each of these in more detail later in the chapter. In this first section we shall consider the main pathways to economic independence that are commonly seen in our own present-day society, and some of the factors that determine which of them an individual will follow.

From school to adulthood: workers, students, claimants and marginals

In a modern society, there are four major economic routes of transition from school to adulthood. Most traditional is the 'worker' model: teenagers remain in the parental home while in compulsory education; on leaving this they get a job whose income is treated as theirs (though they may well contribute financially to the home); some time later, they set up their own household, either alone or, more usually, on marriage. This traditional model is in decline at almost every point (see, for example, Andrews and Bradley, 1997, Fig. 1). What is rapidly replacing it as the norm is the 'student' model: at the end of compulsory education, young people proceed to higher or further education, receiving a mixture of state and family grants which they treat as their own income. Often, especially in the UK and in countries with dispersed population, becoming a student also involves leaving home; however, this tendency is declining as higher education becomes more of a mass phenomenon, and consequently both available in more sites and funded at less generous levels. The high levels of unemployment that have existed in most Western economies since the 1970s have made it increasingly difficult for relatively unqualified school leavers to find jobs, and as a result the 'claimant' model has become common – young people who leave school and then derive an income of sorts from the social security system; this may or may not make it easy or advantageous for them to leave the parental home. Finally, there has always been a subset of young people who on (or before) leaving school take on one or another marginal economic role – property crime, prostitution, drug dealing and homelessness being currently significant examples. Some of these assimilate more or less to one of the other models (prostitutes, for example, may be considered as workers), but their marginal status is an important common factor.

Simply listing these four models is a sharp reminder of how culturally relative discussion in this area inevitably is. The proportions of people following these four routes show enormous variation between generations, nations, social classes, ethnic groups and genders, and so do the detailed implications of each route. But, for better or worse, we shall have to consider the transition to independence in the forms that we can currently see and the forms that have been researched. One of the tasks of this chapter will be to see whether any constant or universal factors can be seen among this diversity and cultural dependence.

The different pathways give different kinds of economic independence at different stages. Superficially, employment seems to offer the most genuine economic independence. In practice, however, it is often coupled with continuing to live at home, and many young workers have traditionally made substantial contributions to a collective 'housekeeping' budget, managed by their mothers. They thus do not, at least at first, have the responsibility for housing costs or food and utility bills, and are to some extent cushioned from the economic errors that students frequently make. Conversely, the student role implies continued financial dependence on parents (and probably also the state); but where students live away from home, there is probably much greater and much more sudden independence in managing all aspects of a household budget. The student role also has other special features, including relatively good expectations of future employment, at least in the UK (Vicenzi, Lea and Rumiati, 1999), and immersion in a rather specific 'youth' culture, associated with distinctive spending patterns. The claimant role implies possibly the greatest degree of continuing economic dependence, especially as changes in the social security regulations put increasing barriers in the way of young claimants setting up their own households; however, our own research with such young people suggests that they prize independence very highly, and succeed surprisingly well in maintaining it (Lea *et al.*, 1999). Finally, the marginalised are probably the most economically independent of the parental household of all, but the nature of their lives means that they can only be researched with difficulty.

None of these roles is immutable, and young people can and do move between them, or combine them, quite freely. Some of the transitions or combinations are conventionally expected, others attract various kinds of attention when they occur. For example, in the UK recent years have seen a major increase in worker–student transitions due to the expansion of the 'mature-student' sector, the virtual necessity for many young people to combine study and employment (see Bailey and Mallier, 1999), and occasional scares about student–marginal combinations such as claims that students are resorting to drug-dealing or prostitution to fund their studies. Furthermore, the four roles we have outlined do not exhaust all the possibilities. Traditionally, some young women moved directly from being a dependent in the parental household to being a dependent within a marriage, without any intervening period of employment, study or claiming; this is now much rarer, but not unknown. Young people destined to be students, or ceasing to be students, frequently take a 'year off' to travel or undertake voluntary work. Self-employment, and family businesses, will create a further range of variants. But, imperfect as this list of roles may be, the roles are distinctive enough and common enough for the list to be useful as a point of reference for the discussion in the rest of this chapter.

New households – individuals, couples, communes

One of the key steps on the road to economic independence is the formation of an independent household. In terms of conventional economic theory this is the only step that matters, since households rather than individuals are the units of analysis. As we shall see in Chapter 5, much of the work of economic psychology is to show that that approach is inadequate; however, in terms of the new tasks the individual has to undertake, household formation probably is indeed the most important step. We need to distinguish three ways in which it can happen. Some people set up a household on their own, others move out of the parental home to move in with partners (whether through marriage or not), while others move into various forms of communal household. The last group consists not only of the idealistic communes that received much attention in the 1960s and 1970s, but also such arrangements as groups of unrelated students sharing a house and paying a significant proportion of costs in common. Even with this addition, communes may seem unimportant in numerical terms, but they are potentially important because they can offer useful test cases for theories about the economic organisation of the household. Sadly, there seems to have been little research on them so far.

New household formation will rarely occur in isolation. Normally it will be associated with other life events, very probably stressful ones – a quarrel with parents, a change of job, a new stage in study, marriage or the decision to cohabit, pregnancy, or several of these. In the UK, a particularly important special case is the new student moving in to university-provided accommodation, in a hostel or hall of residence. In many cases, therefore, the new household starts its existence in a difficult or exciting situation, both interpersonally and financially. This means that important economic choices may be taken, or habits set in place, with relatively little consideration, because people's minds are on other problems.

There have been many changes in the pattern of new household formation in recent decades. Berrington and Murphy (1994) provide a useful overview of the UK situation, showing that it is not a simple matter of staying at home or leaving. Increasing numbers of teenagers, but decreasing numbers of young adults, now live outside the parental home. Increasingly, and especially in more prosperous socio-economic groups, people now leave home in order to live independently; leaving home to form new families is becoming the prerogative of poorer groups within society.

Class, gender and race

We have already stressed the variability of the routes to economic independence as a function of nations, generations and classes. This book is being written in the UK at the end of the twentieth century, and inevitably our discussion will focus on our own period and society and others rather like them, with only occasional forays into historical or cross-national comparisons. But we cannot afford to focus on a single social class, or to be blind to the effects of gender and race. In the UK at least, it is impossible to consider any of the points raised so far in this chapter without taking class into account, and there has never yet been an economy that offered the same economic opportunities to young men and young women. Virtually all economies also contain relatively advantaged or disadvantaged ethnic groups. The four major routes to economic independence have very different probabilities, depending on people's gender, race and class background, and they also have different meanings. For a young person from a working-class background, becoming a student often represents a conscious attempt to make a class transition; for a middle-class youngster it is more often simply what is to be expected. The experience of being a student, or a claimant, may be very different for people of different classes. If a household is formed by marriage or cohabitation, the expectations of the man and the woman involved are likely to be strikingly different. If a young person ends up at the margins of society, we need to ask whether he or she started from anywhere else. That does not mean that there are no universals at this stage of the economic life-span, but it does mean that we cannot assume that any trend is universal until we have investigated whether it varies with race, class and gender. Naturally these factors also interact. For example, in ethnically divided societies, members of minority races are almost by definition members of disadvantaged classes.

Challenges and resources

So far in this chapter we have argued essentially from first principles, looking at what it is possible for people to do. The rest of this chapter has a more empirical thrust, setting out what people actually do. It is organised around three important classes of economic behaviour – work, money management and buying. They correspond closely to the three transitions towards economic independence that we have outlined in this section, and this dictates the order in which we shall take them. Work maps closely into the issue of employment. The need for money management is what follows on from having an independent income, while buying is usually transformed out of recognition by the formation of a new household.

These three kinds of economic behaviour can be seen as three crucial challenges that a young person faces in becoming an economic adult. Ideally, we would like to consider the choices that are open to young people in each of these three arenas, the resources of experience, knowledge and rationality that they are able to bring to them, and the success or failure that they typically achieve. In practice, naturally, what we are able to say is constrained by the research that is available, and this is patchy.

A First Job

From the point of view of empirical research, work is much the best documented kind of economic behaviour, both in economics and in psychology. That is as true of young people as it is of adults. This section cannot offer a comprehensive review of the literature on young workers, a task that would require a book on its own. For each topic that we discuss, therefore, we will mention a few classic sources, and then draw quite selectively on recent research literature, aiming to bring in ideas from labour economics, the sociology of work, and occupational and organisational psychology. We will be looking at the behaviour of young people who are about to go into work, and young workers, especially those in their first jobs. In terms of the routes to economic independence outlined above, some of these will be 'workers', but others will be 'students', going into employment following a stage of advanced study. Some of the behaviour of 'marginals' also needs to be considered here, since criminal and other marginal behaviour is simply the form of work available to certain social or cultural subgroups within society. For example, in a study of Thai sex workers, Wawer *et al.* (1996) point out that prostitution is, after agriculture, the second source of employment for women in the country. Even against such a background, however, marginal activity cannot be treated simply as a form of work; Wawer *et al.* found that while young women from the North region of the country were more likely to enter prostitution as the only way of fulfilling quite conventional social expectations on them, young women from the North-east region were more likely to be individually marginalised – they tended to have suffered adversity or failure in conventional economic life.

Attitudes and work

Unsurprisingly, social psychologists have taken an enduring interest in attitudes towards work and employment among young people, and also on the impact that work and employment have on more general attitudes. Some of the most interesting studies stretch back into childhood, and trace both the understanding of work, and values and attitudes relating to work, as they emerge in childhood and continue into adulthood. Particular attention has been given to work values, including, of course, the 'Protestant work ethic' (Furnham, 1990), which is supposed to reflect the extent to which work as such is valued. Two general questions dominate the literature: what differences in work attitudes are there between younger and older people, and what differences are there between different groups of young people? Both these questions are problematic.

If there are differences between younger and older workers, that may be an effect of age in itself, or it may be because younger and older workers occupy different subcultures. The youth subculture idea occasionally generates moral panics in the media, with the suggestion that young people are no longer interested in employment – a proposition for which there is no evidence at all: employment raises the self-esteem of young people, and welfare dependency depresses it, just as much now as it always did, as was shown for example by Elliott (1996). Furthermore, the experience of young workers is not the same as that of their older colleagues, even within a single organisation: Warr and Pennington (1994) showed that there are well-defined age-gradings within employment roles, with different expectations about the kind of work that would be appropriate for younger and older people: younger people are expected to be more physically fit, for example, and to pick up new ideas and new techonologies faster, but also to be more literate. Nor will longitudinal studies necessarily enable us to abstract from such expectations, because secular changes in employment patterns confound the picture. For example, Winefield and Tiggemann (1993) point out that by the 1990s, studies of high-school leavers were showing anticipatory stress about possible unemployment, a tendency that was quite absent in 1980: in other words, even for a particular age-group, the culture of one decade is not the same as the culture of another, so as people grow older they do not only change in age, they also move into different subcultures.

Charting the differences between different groups of young people similarly poses problems. The most interesting cases from the point of view of economic socialisation are those that reflect different economic experiences – for example, the difference between direct entry to the labour market after school and entry after a period of further study or of unemployment. But all such differences tend to be heavily confounded by wider social differences, such as race, class and gender. Such factors are certainly not irrelevant to an economic-psychological analysis, but their impacts tend to be quite predictable, and not in any specifically economic way.

Granted these difficulties, however, what do we know? First, consider the differences between younger and older workers. Several studies suggest that younger people actually value work (or, more strictly, employment) more than their older colleagues. For example, Banks and Henry (1993) found that in young workers (aged between 16 and 20), employment commitment fell even across a two-year period.

As regards studies of differences between groups of young people, it is particularly interesting to compare people who have gone into work at the school-leaving age with those who have entered roughly the same career path after a period of study. Banks and Henry compared employment commitment in young people who had followed five distinct trajectories into the labour market, and found higher commitment among those who had gone straight into work, or who had alternated between unemployment and employment, rather than undergoing post-compulsory education. Rather similarly, Hagstrom and Gamberale (1995) reported that students, especially girls, attending more theoretical high-school courses tend to show 'post-materialistic' values (cf. Inglehart, 1990), ranking intrinsic work values higher than economic work goals. It is easy to see both these results as reflecting a somewhat less realistic attitude towards a career that is easier for those with a less immediate need to secure an income.

A particularly interesting comparison of attitudes in young people was carried out by Watts (1994). Watts compared young people from the former states of East and West Germany both before and after German reunification in 1990, and found that the most important differences between the two groups were in the area of work orientations and goals. East Germans put greater emphasis on authority, respect and high income, but also on some collective values. To some extent, however, these differences may simply reflect the economically disadvantaged position of the East Germans – theirs somewhat resemble attitudes found by Petterson (1997) among young black men in the United States, for example. Indeed, there is considerable consistency in work values across nations: Lebo, Harrington and Tillman (1995) found that good salary, job security and 'variety-diversion' were the most valued features of jobs across six different national samples, though there was more consistency among young women than young men.

Career choice

Choosing a career is an unmanageable task. There is an almost indefinite range of possible jobs; it can only be a guess how well one will do in any of them, and how rewarding it will be; and the benefits and costs of choosing are likely to be delivered far in the future. So career choice involves information overload, risk and intertemporal choice. The bounded nature of human rationality is likely to mean that choices are not made in an optimal way. And, on the other hand, for many young people, there may appear to be very little real choice, or no real possibility of a career at all, so the effort of making a careful evaluation of the alternatives will hardly seem worth while. How do young people in fact cope with this situation?

There is an extensive empirical literature in both psychology and economics about career choice. Both are of course concerned with the question of which young people will try to get into which careers, but each has its own set of explanatory variables (economic opportunities and wage rates on the one hand, family, personality, attitudinal and ability factors on the other). Even those variables that both recognise as important, such as gender and educational attainment, are handled in totally different ways in the two kinds of literature. Much of the psychological literature on career choice is practically oriented, aiming to assist the work of careers advisers. We cannot fully summarise either the economic or the psychological literature here, still less synthesise them, but we will try to draw out some dominant themes.

To talk about 'career choice' rather than merely 'job choice' is to emphasise how choice of employment is embedded in issues affecting the whole of one's life. Such a life-cycle approach has always been a key element in psychological theories of career choice. For example Super (1957) saw a career as a series of developmental tasks, and D. J. Levinson's (e.g. 1986) life-cycle theory has a similar emphasis while H. S. Astin's (1984) theory of career choice focuses on the special problems of embedding work within a woman's, rather than a man's life. Lopez and Andrews (1987) make the point that career choice is always confounded with the process of separation from the family. But psychologists have paid relatively little attention to the fact that career choices have an essentially intertemporal aspect: the benefits of some career choices are delivered far in the future, while their costs are incurred at once. The well-established age, intelligence and class differences in delaying gratification (see Lea, 1978) may therefore predict some of the consistent themes that are seen in the career choice literature. Choosing a career is very much an inter-temporal choice, and, as such, it needs to be seen in the contexts of the theories of such choices, such as life-cycle, mental accounting and impulse control theories, which we will discuss in Chapter 5; Hesketh, Watson-Brown and Whiteley (1998) have made a start on such formal consideration. But relatively little of the empirical literature on career choice is seriously informed by such theories.

One of the pervading themes of current empirical research on career choice is constraint. Young people are constrained in their possible career choices by their class, race and gender, by the educational opportunities they have had in the past and the extent to which they have used them, by the places where they live, and by the local economy. The force of these various constraints, and the extent to which young people can rise above them, have been investigated in detail, particularly by sociologists. It is important for both economists and psychologists, both using theories that emphasise individual choice, to recognise the importance of social constraint. Career choice is not a neutral matter in which undifferentiated individuals simply try to do as well as their natural abilities and educational attainments will allow. It is embedded in a class system, within which parents and families (not necessarily consciously) manipulate the educational system and the values of society to ensure that their children will have the best chance of occupying favourable positions in the economy of the future. 'Career choice' is thus partly a matter of how high a person can aim, in terms of social status or income or both. Bourdieu (1984) gives an extended discussion of how differences of 'social capital' (crudely, who you or your parents know) and especially 'cultural capital' (what you and your family know) influence the outcomes for young people of different classes; in particular he shows that there is not a single hierarchy from poverty to wealth, but differentiation within different groups within the dominant and middle classes. Education, often proposed as a social leveller, may instead be the means by which privileged classes in general pass their privileges on to their offspring, and those who have acquired economic capital seek to broaden the base of their advantages.

Perhaps the most extensively investigated constraint, however, is not class but gender. Not so very long ago, the question being asked was often whether young women would choose to make a career at all, rather than settling for early mother-hood (e.g. Jensen, Christensen and Wilson, 1985); more recent literature has focused on the extent to which they see all careers, and all levels of achievement, as open to them. But even in the past decade, a general lack of ambition among young women continues to be a concern, and escape from it seems to be dependent on the nature of a young woman's home life. McKenna and Ferrero (1991) found that most 14-year-olds were influenced in their career objectives by their same-sex parents, and rejected non-traditional possibilities. O'Brien and Fassinger (1993) investigated the career choices of high-social-class late teenagers, and found that those who selected the less traditional and more prestigious careers were characterised by high ability, but also by stronger 'agentic characteristics', i.e. confidence in themselves, their educational abilities and their career prospects. O'Brien (1996) found that the pattern of family relationships, and the progress of a young woman towards individuation as a person separate from her family, were good predictors of women's career choice orientations. Although O'Brien and Fassinger argue that the career choices of young women remain more complex than those of young men, there is a general trend in the literature for the differences in perceived opportunities between young men and women to decline towards nothing, especially among older students, those of better education and those of higher social status. By the 1980s, Dunne, Elliott and Carlsen (1981) were reporting no differences between male and female late teenagers in occupational aspiration (and in a rural sample at that), and such findings are more common in the more recent literature. In a longitudinal study in which Australian high-school students were followed until they were 27 years old, Poole *et al.* (1991) found that although family expectations were powerful predictors of outcomes, the effect was weaker for women than for men, suggesting that women's opportunities are undergoing a generational shift. Indeed, given the current concern about educational under-achievement by boys, it is no surprise that the trend is going further, and we are beginning to find reports of young men seeing fewer career opportunities available than young women (e.g. Wall, Covell and MacIntyre, 1999).

But it is not only in mediating gender differences that home and parents influence career choice. As has long been known, parental class and education are critically important to the jobs that young people take up (Blau and Duncan, 1967). A caricatured summary of the literature would be that the children of parents with higher incomes and more education are more likely to be found in more selective schools and colleges even when ability scores are controlled for, will gain higher qualifications even when ability and school choice are controlled, are more likely to get any job at all and in particular to get higher-prestige jobs even when ability, education and qualifications are controlled, and will rise to higher levels in their jobs even when ability, education, qualifications and occupational choice are controlled. Reality is naturally more nuanced, and no study has controlled every level of the process. Much attention has focused on entry to the 'service class' (Goldthorpe, 1979), the group of high-prestige, mostly government-funded occupations that command high social status, though not such high pay as commercial management. For example, in the UK Egerton (1997) found that having parents who belonged to the service class increased a child's chances of achieving a job within it, and the level within it the child would reach, even with cognitive ability controlled. Raudenbush and Kasim (1998) found that in the US, both class and gender gaps in earnings remained within each occupational group, even when literacy and education were taken into account. Such social inheritance of high-prestige positions can be found in relatively egalitarian communities such as in Scandinavia, where social origin has little impact on the initial pay that a person of given educational achievement will receive (Erikson and Jonsson, 1998; Hansen, 1996). Interestingly, however, Lee and Brinton (1996) found that in South Korea (a highly meritocratic society because of its recent history), educated parents' influence did not seem to reach beyond getting their children into the highest-prestige universities. In the less developed economy of Honduras, however, Bedi (1997) found that parental education predicted lifetime earnings even with education taken into account.

Parental influence is not only a matter of securing privileged positions, of course. In the literature we have just been discussing, there is a tendency for the offspring of the service class to prefer that kind of career, rather than the financially better prospects of the commercial world. Young people who perceive their parents to have jobs with a higher technological content are more likely to opt for technical careers themselves (Breakwell, Fife-Schaw and Devereux, 1988); interestingly, Breakwell *et al.* showed that this parental influence was not due to overt persuasion attempts. Lee (1984) showed that among disadvantaged racial groups in a rural United States sample, parental influence was more powerful than among whites. All these results, and there are many more like them, confirm the continuing force of what Jahoda (1952) long ago pointed out: most institutional intervention in career choice comes too late to make any difference, since by the time young people come into contact with careers guidance, family and friends have already severely narrowed the range of careers they will realistically consider.

Another recurrent question in the literature on career choice is the extent to which young people have the knowledge and maturity to make any effective choice at all. School students typically do not (e.g. Grotevant and Durrett, 1980), and, lacking these, there is an obvious risk that they may simply drift into the most accessible jobs, make wrong choices of subjects to study and foreclose what would be the best choices for them, get into inappropriate jobs, or fail to get a job at all because they had infeasible aims. Crites (1965) sought to capture this aspect of adolescent readiness to make career choices in his influential concept of 'vocational maturity'. However, attempts to devise psychometric scales of career choice ability have had only partial success (see, for example, Westbrook, 1976; Westbrook, Sanford and Waters, 1999). In any case it is not entirely clear how such ability should be judged. Hodkinson and Sparkes (1993) point to a mismatch between the formal rational choice paradigm within which careers guidance programmes are often conceived, and the more pragmatically rational approach of its clients, who often have a greater clarity about the real constraints facing them. Of course, young people do differ in the extent to which they explore different career possibilities, and those who explore a wider range are indeed likely to make choices that are a better fit to their interests and abilities (e.g. Grotevant, Cooper and Kramer, 1986). However, Poole and Cooney (1985) found that even when young people were aware of a wide range of career possibilities, social and environmental factors still led them to rule out many of them as irrelevant to themselves. Perceived career constraints, perhaps imposed by a particular social identity, may thus outweigh career maturity as a factor in determining the effective range of career choice.

Whatever the structural and social constraints, and the possible inefficiency of many career choices, to some extent, people's chosen jobs will reflect their long-held values. In a sample of UK university graduates Duff and Cotgrove (1982) showed that the level of 'anti-industrial values' correlated with career intentions towards the public or personal services rather than industry, even when their prior choice of degree course (also, of course, highly correlated with values) was controlled for. Indeed, some of the persistent class, ethnic and gender differences in career choices reflect corresponding differences in values between these groups; it would be no surprise to find that Duff and Cotgrove's anti-industrial values were more prevalent among the offspring of the service class, for example. Similarly, Marini *et al.* (1996), in a US study, found gender differences in work values, with young women more strongly attracted than young men to jobs offering intrinsic, altruistic and social rewards – though in keeping with much other literature on gender differences, they reported that the differences had declined over the period 1971–1990.

From a psychological perspective, it is one of the weaknesses of much of the literature we have cited so far that these backround differences in values have rarely been investigated, and where they have, they have not been put in the context of the sociological variables that are known to influence career choices and out-comes. Admittedly, in many cases what is measured as parental and family influence will be a fairly direct proxy for individual values. But values are not only a cause but also a product of young people's different work experiences. Claes and Quintanilla (1994) used the well-studied meaning of working value scales to study work values, as part of the Europe-wide Work Socialisation of Youth project. They identified six different early career trajectories, which were consistent across seven countries, and showed that they led to different clusters of work values, as well as to different levels of psychological well-being, as measured by the General Health Questionnaire, which has been widely used to measure the impacts of types of work and unemployment.

The work/study choice

What decides a person to continue in study rather than seek immediate employment? It may seem that this is a consequence of a prior career choice. For many young people, though, the choice to continue at school beyond the earliest legal leaving age, or to proceed from school to university, is taken well before they have fixed ideas about their career. It is a choice of a broad 'student' rather than 'worker' route to economic independence.

Working or studying is not, of course, an absolute choice, and many students combine the two roles. During the years of compulsory education, student workers do not face an altogether sympathetic environment: their teachers regard employ-ment as impairing academic effort, but are unlikely to be accommodating towards the problems they have in combining work and study (Bills, Helms and Ozcan,

1995), they have a poor choice of jobs, receive low pay, often suffer discrimination on grounds of gender or appearance within them and may damage their school achievement and attendance (see reviews in Dustmann, Rajah and Smith, 1997; McKechnie and Hobbs, 1999). Nonetheless researchers often claim that there is a widespread public view that working while studying is good for young people (e.g. Steinberg and Dornbusch, 1991; Wright, Cullen and Williams, 1997). Steinberg and Dornbusch challenge this popular belief, showing that longer hours spent working are associated with poorer academic and personal outcomes, while Wright *et al.* show that among young men who are on other grounds at high risk for delinquency, longer hours worked are associated with higher parental ratings of delinquency. A rather similar interaction was found by Barling, Rogers and Kelloway (1995), who found that whilst working while studying could be associated with poorer educational attainment, good-quality employment raised young people's self-esteem without harming their academic work.

Wright *et al.* (1997) comment that most of the deleterious effects of working while at school were indirect, reflecting mutual correlation with disaffection from school. For such students, work is an alternative, perhaps a preferred alternative, to the school environment. When university students seek employment, however, as most now do, they usually see it as subordinate to their studies – it is a way of enabling them to continue to study. In the traditional UK vacation work market, Bailey and Mallier (1999) showed that students can be treated as a single, largely unskilled, labour pool, though with the decline in state support for university students, attempts are being made to capitalise on students' abilities to secure them more profitable jobs (see 'Job prospects better by degree', *The Guardian*, 31 July 1999).

What, then, are the motivations for staying in education beyond the point where it is compulsory? The UK has particularly low levels of staying on at school after the end of compulsory schooling at 16. Moving straight into employment from school at this age is not, in the long term, an attractive prospect, for many entry-level jobs offer little chance of subsequent improvement: this was true of about 70 per cent of such jobs in the study by Lynch (1993), though he did find that post-school training could help young people escape from such dead ends. Yet it has often been suggested that many young people only stay at school because they cannot find jobs: they are really 'discouraged workers'. For example, in an area of east London with a particularly low rate of 'staying on' at school, Kysel, West and Scott (1992) found that the decision whether to leave at 16 (the end of compulsory schooling in the UK) was heavily influenced by perceived short-term employment prospects; as a result, non-white students were more likely to stay on, and to give enhancing their employment prospects as their reason for doing so. Although Paterson and Raffe (1995) argued that there was a decline in the formal 'discouraged worker' effect in Scotland, they recognised that much of the expansion in 16–18 educational participation was due to the lack of 'pull' from the employment market. Economic expansion is always likely to draw people out of the education system (e.g. Shanahan, Miech and Elder, 1998), and economic recession to keep them in it (e.g. Rees and Mocan, 1997).

But the availability or otherwise of the attractions of work are not the whole story about staying on. Local culture clearly plays a part: Paterson and Raffe (1995) report that there are big variations in staying-on rates between schools with apparently similar social and economic characteristics. Researchers with their eye on long-term factors like career prospects tend to forget that school can be a deeply unattractive environment for teenagers – Kysel *et al.* found that around a fifth of early leavers gave as the reason sheer dislike of school, and in an earlier study in inner London that gave a similar result, Varlaam and Shaw (1984) also found that the desire to be treated like an adult was also important (the move towards tertiary college education for British 16–18-year-olds may have met this demand to some extent since Varlaam and Shaw also found that the same reason influenced choice of a further education college rather than a school for post-16 education). Premature leaving is also influenced, perhaps more strongly, by individual factors such as early parenthood (e.g. Pirog and Magee, 1997), and so is the choice to stay on: for example, the choice to go to university by young women in Japan is affected by their confidence in their ability to make career choices, as well as more obvious factors like academic ability (Matsui and Onglatco, 1992).

If young people who stay in school longer than the law requires are not discouraged workers, what are they? An alternative view of the staying-on decision is that post-compulsory education is in micro-economic terms a normal consumption good. That is to say, it is something of positive value, which people will buy more of if they (or their parents, or government institutions) are better off and more able to afford it. The pioneering econometric work of Pissarides (1981) suggested that this analyis captures more of the variation in staying-on rates than the discouraged worker hypothesis. Econometric analysis has proved generally useful in understanding the details of why young people do, or do not, continue in education. Andrews and Bradley (1997) used a large cross-section database of all school leavers in Lancashire, UK in 1991, and attempted to predict their destinations six months after the end of compulsory schooling. They identified six outcomes (non-vocational continuing education, vocational continuing education, youth training, employment with on-the-job training, employment with general skills training, and unemployment) and they showed that these could not be grouped into a simple staying on/leaving school dichotomous choice. Not very surprisingly, destinations chosen were influenced by academic ability; less obviously, the lower young people's expected lifetime earnings, the more likely they were to leave school.

But what is it that young people are buying, if post-compulsory education is a normal good? One obvious answer is enhanced career prospects, but how does that work, considering that much post-compulsory education does not have obvious or direct vocational relevance? Economists have conceived of the impact of education on subsequent employment in a number of ways. At least since the influential work of Becker (1974) and Denison (1974), the dominant theory has been that to continue in education is to invest in one's own 'human capital', presumably in the hope of greater returns to that capital in the future (Paulsen,

1998). There are alternative accounts, however. A qualification may be a 'credential' or market signal – an indication of an individual's quality, but not of any value the individual has acquired through education – or it may give entry to a favoured social class, where labour markets are 'segmented', i.e. there is not free competition for jobs between members of different groups in society (as some of the results of Hunter and Leiper, 1993, suggest). All these theories, however, conceive the work/study decision as essentially a problem in intertemporal choice, with the attractions of immediate employment and income being forgone for the sake of better future prospects.

What evidence is there that the dominant human capital view is more than an ideologically powerful metaphor? Although level of education is certainly not the sole determinant of subsequent earnings, the empirical literature indeed supports the proposition that it is a major determinant, and in fact is becoming ever more important. Autor, Katz and Krueger (1998) showed by cross-industry analysis that, in the US, increasing computerisation (measured by the percentage of employees using a keyboard) is associated with higher relative demand for well-qualified employees, and thus with higher economic returns from education. It is not surprising, therefore, that during the 1980s there was a sharp rise in the 'college premium' on wages, the differential between the pay of those with university education and those who only have high-school qualifications (e.g. Grogger and Eide, 1995; Weisberg, 1995). This rise was despite the flattening effect which is to be expected from the increase in the number of graduates: van der Ploeg (1994) showed that, in the Netherlands from 1955 to 1990, average qualifications rose faster than the average occupational level, but that nonetheless the returns to tertiary education have continued to increase; returns to higher secondary education, however, are no longer rising, and those to lower secondary education are now almost zero. Van der Ploeg argues that increasing penetration of qualifications in fact increases the economic returns to them up to the point where about 60 per cent of the population have them. Even where the economic returns from education are not obvious, they turn out to be there: for example, Zhao (1997) shows that, although the apparent returns from education in rural China were very low in the late 1970s and early 1980s, while school attendance rates were very high, the actual returns from education were higher because only educated young people were permitted to migrate to the cities where higher wages were available.

It seems, therefore, that tertiary education gives the highest returns. They are also more uniform across regions, since the labour market for graduates is more national (Bennett, Glennerster and Nevison, 1995). Some have argued that, compared with direct entry to the labour market, education from 16 to 18 has a positive impact on lifetime earnings only for those who go on to higher education (e.g. Hammer and Furlong, 1996). Lindley (1996) argues that current policies encouraging higher and further education do nothing for the less able and disadvantaged groups within society, and Autor *et al.* (1998) note how the increasing college premium fits into the general increase in inequality in Western economies during the 1980s. However, Grubb (1993, 1997) showed that even sub-degree post-school education can give economic returns, though perhaps by a different, indirect mechanism; and at this level it is critical that young people should complete their courses. The question of whether non-degree training has real returns is of course confounded, since the social inheritance of privilege necessarily implies that returns from education may be lower for those of disadvantaged ethnic or social groups (see, for example, Jones, 1993; Kimmel, 1997), and people from these groups are also less likely to enter higher education; on the other hand Bennett *et al.* (1995) found that returns from vocational education were higher in disadvantaged regions, and Kysel *et al.*'s (1992) results, discussed above, imply that disadvantaged groups saw more advantage in staying on than did the majority population. For a person who has no prospect of a job at all when untrained, the returns for lower-level education look more positive, not least because little is lost by staying in study.

Mere years of education are not the only relevant factor. Quality of schooling can also be important in realising the potential gains, both in developing countries (e.g. Bedi, 1997) and developed economies (e.g. Card and Krueger, 1992), though not all studies find any effect (e.g Betts, 1995), and not much of the difference in earnings impacts between different schools can be accounted for by objective measures of school quality (Crawford, Johnson and Summers, 1997). In some cases it can be demonstrated that it is not the content of education that matters, but the contacts that an élite college makes possible: Lee and Brinton (1996) interpret this effect in terms of J. S. Coleman's (e.g. 1994) version of the social capital concept, and draw a distinction between 'institutional social capital' (mediated by the school or university) and 'personal social capital' (mediated by friends and family). In the meritocratic society of South Korea, it is institutional social capital that is more effective.

All the literature we have discussed so far has been concerned with the effects of the work/study choice. But these effects can only explain young people's choices to stay or not to stay in study if they are actually perceived by the potential students or those who advise them, and if the young people are actually able to put the choices they make into effect. There is considerable doubt about both these propositions. Bowes and Goodnow (1996) showed that most young people were at best vague about the links between school work and subsequent economic prosperity, and Morgan (1998) showed that young people tend to overestimate their chances of completing successfully any additional education. Menon (1997) showed that entrants to higher education perceived its rates of return as higher than entrants to the labour market did; of course, although those who went straight into work were wrong about the general trend, they may have been right about their own personal probable outcomes. Similarly, Morgan noted that potential students' estimates of their chances responded to the same variables as the true probabilities, so they could be considered as 'rational fantasies'.

Furthermore, the literature has focused on lifetime earnings as a measure of the returns from education, and only in a minority of studies have these been discounted to their present value. But within the framework of intertemporal choice, such discounting is crucially important, and there is no guarantee that objective discount rates will correctly predict behaviour. Bennett, Glennerster and Nevison (1995) show that using discount rates as low as 10 per cent can tip the balance between positive and negative returns to some kinds of sub-degree education, at least in some regions of the UK; and these rates are low compared with those needed to explain adult savings behaviour (see Chapter 5). Wright *et al.* (1997) suggest that the association of long hours in employment and high delinquency among schoolboys can be explained by seeing both as preferences for present gratification, rather than the long-term advantages of commitment to school.

In this context, it is well to remember that, as well as the future economic effects, there are also psychological impacts of choosing to go into work or study at any given point in one's life, and these may be more immediate. We have already seen that at least some teenagers see school as an unpleasant environment where they are accorded no respect. A well-designed longitudinal study by van der Velde, Feij and Taris (1995) looked at the impact on personal characteristics of choosing to go into employment, at three different ages: their respondents were aged 18 to 26 at the beginning of the study. Although they found that, overall, changes in traits such as attributional style and work values were surprisingly small over a four-year period, the changes were somewhat larger in those who entered employment: these young people showed lowered levels of boredom, depression and neuroticism, and raised self-esteem. Thus the immediate benefits from choosing employment rather than study do not come only in the form of income, giving an extra twist to the delay of gratification involved in continuing in study.

Looking for work

How do young people find their first job? Heaven (1995) asked young people who were not yet in regular employment how they would go about looking for work. Factor analysis of their responses showed that their approaches could be classified along two broad dimensions – using their own efforts, and seeking help from others. There were marked gender differences, with girls tending to make more effort both for themselves and in getting help from others. Girls may indeed need to put more effort into getting help: Sanders (1995) found that young women were less likely to be spontaneously offered help in finding a job through the informal networks that are still critically important in getting work, though the effect did not explain the earnings gap between them and boys of the same age, education and experience.

Methods of job search, and their actual and perceived effectiveness, vary with economic conditions: for example, in a Canadian sample Osberg (1993) found that public employment agencies were more helpful in the trough of a recession, and in the UK Thomas (1997) also found that such agencies tended only to be used by people who had exhausted other channels; he argued that they then might be quite successful. But in given economic conditions, the job search strategies of young people with poor chances of employment (for example, because they come from disadvantaged ethnic groups) are not very different from those of their more 'employable' peers (Munene, 1983). Something other than job search, therefore, must explain their different outcomes. Since in many cases so-called 'unemployables' come from minority ethnic groups, an obvious possibility is prejudice and discrimination among employers, but this is not necessarily the right explanation. An influential alternative hypothesis was put forward by Kain (1968). His spatial matching hypothesis stresses the extra difficulties that young people in disadvantaged groups face when looking for jobs, for purely geographical reasons. This theory is discussed further below. As we have already seen, social and cultural capital may also be important in job search. In their Seoul study, Lee and Brinton (1996) point to both formal and informal networks that are available to the graduates of the more prestigious universities.

Youth unemployment: introduction

Hayes and Nutman (1981) could summarise the literature on the psychology of unemployment in a 150-page book with only a couple of short summaries of special questions about young people: since then, two decades of intermittent recession have led to a mass of research. The tendency for firms to shed staff by voluntary redundancy and early retirement, with no recruitment of young people, has made youth unemployment a particular concern, with rates typically twice those for older workers (Winefield, 1997). There have been regular reviews of the literature, for example by Furnham (1985), Banks and Ullah (1988), the book edited by Petersen and Mortimer (1994), and a special issue of the *Journal of Adolescence* edited by Winefield (1997).

Unemployment does not only cover those who are counted as unemployed in government statistics. There are also the 'hidden unemployed': people who are studying when they would really rather be in employment, who are on government training schemes of various sorts which they frequently regard as poor substitutes for 'real' jobs, or who are otherwise unwillingly out of the labour force. In addition, there are those who are 'underemployed' (Clogg, 1979), which includes those who, working for as many hours per day or days per year as they would wish, are being paid poverty wages, or are not using their abilities or qualifications in any real sense. Underemployment is an increasing problem especially among young people, according to several authors; for example, Feldman and Turnley (1995) reckon that 25 per cent of college graduates are underemployed. To some extent this can be seen as an inevitable reflection of average level of qualifications in the population rising faster than the average level of occupations, as reported for example by van der Ploeg (1994) and discussed above. Goldsmith, Veum and Darity (1995) show that being formally unemployed and being out of the labour market have effectively identical impacts on young men's self-esteem, and underemployment has the same impacts as total unemployment on young people's self-esteem (Prause and Dooley, 1997) and life satisfaction (Feldman and Turnley, 1995).

In discussing the causes and effects of youth unemployment, it is essential to bear in mind that, in every country, members of disadvantaged racial or other groups figure disproportionately in the youth unemployment statistics, whether it is blacks or native Americans in the United States (Petterson, 1997; Ramasamy, 1996), Aboriginals in Australia (Jones, 1993), Turks in Germany (Faist, 1993), or Catholics in Northern Ireland (Murphy and Shuttleworth, 1997). In general, such effects cannot be accounted for by differences in education or cognitive ability, even where these exist at all (Raudenbush and Kasim, 1998). Kain (1968) put forward his 'spatial mismatch' hypothesis to explain the effect, arguing essentially that jobs tend not to be located in the districts where disadvantaged young people grow up. Much econometric effort has gone into investigating this hypothesis, and many recent studies have provided empirical support for Kain's position (e.g. Holzer, Ihlanfeldt and Sjoquist, 1994; Rogers, 1997), but it is likely that prejudice and discrimination also play a part.

Furnham (1985) commented that despite the plethora of studies on youth unemployment, it was difficult to extract clear replicated findings or coherent theories for the causes, correlates and consequences of unemployment among young people. Furnham argues that this confusion results at least partly from poor methodology, with many studies failing to control obviously important factors like individual differences, demographic variables and work experience. Hammarström (1994) complains about the lack of theoretical underpinning, and the lack of attention to direction of causality, in much of the literature. Nonetheless, we shall sift the literature in an effort to extract answers for some of the more obvious and important questions.

Causes of youth unemployment

The gross level of unemployment in an economy is determined by government policies and macro-economic forces (though these may in turn result from the behaviour of individuals: Katona, 1975; Lea, Tarpy and Webley, 1987, chapter 20). Who becomes unemployed, however, is a function of social and individual differences. In many ways the literature on unemployment risks is the mirror image of the literature on career success, which we considered earlier: those who have favourable social backgrounds, better education and higher ability are always less likely to be unemployed. But psychological factors also need to be considered.

To what extent is youth unemployment the result of unwillingness to work, or unwillingness to work at the jobs and for the wages that are in practice available? It is sometimes argued that the education system, or the mass media, gives young people unrealistic expectations about work, so that they do not take up what opportunities are available. Signorielli (1993), for example, found that among US high-school students, those who watched more TV than average tended to want jobs that were both prestigious and well paid, but would also include long holidays and be relatively easy. This is an unrealistic pattern of demands in the real world:

as Signorelli points out, TV projects an unrepresentative view of the world of work, just as it does of the world of consumption (O'Guinn and Shrum, 1997). It has been claimed that young black men in the US are particularly unrealistic, reporting high 'reservation wages' (the wage below which you would be unwilling to work). However, Petterson (1997) showed that such self-reports do not reflect the wages at which people actually take jobs, and there were no race differences in the latter, nor did those who reported high reservation wages take longer to find work; young blacks' high stated reservation wages were put forward as expressions of their aspirations and self-worth, not out of any lack of willingness to work.

A simple-minded economic analysis of unemployment would suggest that unwillingness to work would be related to the availability of other sources of income. But careful econometric analysis does not support this view, at least in times of high unemployment. For example Narendranathan (1993) and Arulampalam and Stewart (1995) found no evidence that receiving income while unemployed (usually social-security benefits) tends to prolong unemployment, at least beyond the first three months, though the impact of receiving benefits was a little higher for young people than for the population as a whole. But it is clear that the psychological disutility of unemployment, which we shall be discussing in a moment, overwhelms the presumed economic disutility of work.

Perhaps the clearest picture of what really puts young people at risk of unemployment comes from longitudinal studies. Elliott (1996), in a sample of white women in the US, found that those who had lower self-esteem in 1980 (when they were aged 15–23) were more likely to be unemployed in 1987. Caspi *et al.* (1998) studied a cohort of 21-year-old New Zealanders who had been followed since their births in 1972–73, and found that unemployment on leaving school was associated with a complex of variables to do with early social and economic disadvantage, such as low IQ, poor reading ability, weak attachment to school, and anti-social behaviour. Caspi *et al.* comment that such early personal and family characteristics affect labour-market outcomes, not only because they restrict the accumulation of human, social and personal capital, but also because they directly affect labour-market behaviours such as job search and job performance.

Effects of youth unemployment

From Eisenberg and Lazarsfeld's (1938) classic study on, the psychological impacts of unemployment have been seen as unambiguously negative. There is debate about whether unemployment has especially bad impacts on young people: Eisenberg and Lazarsfield thought that it would, but on the basis of the accumulated evidence, Winefield (1997) argued that the young are less badly affected than older people. What is certain is that the impacts of unemployment on the young are likely to be different, because they are more likely never to have had the experience of employment.

Warr (1987), among others, has made a plea that the generalisation that unemployment is bad should not be accepted uncritically – that there can be 'bad work' and 'good unemployment' as well. While this argument may hold good for some individuals, at the level of overall trends it is hard to find evidence to support it. Almost all the evidence shows deleterious effects. For example, O'Brien, Feather and Kabanoff (1994) surveyed Australian young people shortly before they left school, and then one and two years later, when they had progressed to employment, further study, or unemployment. They found that being unemployed was associated with effects such as depression and low life satisfaction, and these trends were not affected by the quality of the activities with which the unemployed young people filled their time. In the very different situation of India, Singh, Singh and Rani (1996) showed that unemployment was associated with a poorer self-concept in young men. Goldsmith, Veum and Darity (1996), with a US sample, again confirmed the damaging impact of unemployment on young people's self-esteem, and concluded that this impact was primarily due to depression rather than anxiety or alienation, though these two variables also had some correlations with past unemployment. From a comprehensive review of the literature on health impacts on unemployment, Hammarström (1994) concludes that consistent relationships are found between unemployment and minor psychological disorders. Unemployment is associated with increased consumption of both alcohol and tobacco as well as illicit drugs (especially among young men), and with a higher mortality rate, in particular from suicides and accidents.

Against this bleak picture, it should be noted that, like the risk of unemployment, its deleterious consequences may have their roots in young people's earlier lives, as was found, for example, for several psychiatric disorders in a birth cohort study undertaken in New Zealand (Fergusson, Horwood and Lynskey, 1997). Patterson (1997) argues that employment is not essential for good self-esteem in adolescence, and both she and Prause and Dooley (1997) note that higher previous levels of self-esteem protect against the damaging effects of unemployment. Furthermore, some of the supposed effects of unemployment could actually be causes instead: for example, it is frequently discussed whether the association between poor mental health and unemployment could be due to selection rather than causation (e.g. Schaufeli, 1997), though the consensus is that though both effects may operate, causation is the stronger.

The most banal correlate of youth unemployment is simply that it makes later unemployment more likely, even when structural, cultural and personal characteristics are controlled for (e.g. Hammer, 1997); this is a depressing conclusion both for the individuals affected and for society. Hammer argues that this result too may reflect a selection rather than a causation process, though the various health behavioural impacts of unemployment do seem likely to make subsequent employment harder to get. Munene (1983) reviews some of the earlier literature on such 'unemployability'. The cycle of unemployment inducing unemployability is one of the reasons why, in recent decades, governments have often responded to the problem of rising youth unemployment by instituting various kinds of training scheme, designed both to improve young people's chances of later employment, and to give them a work-like experience. Lindley (1996) describes such schemes as offering 'work without an employment contract', and he questions their effectiveness, given that the level of unemployment is largely determined by macro-economic and structural factors. Young people themselves treat such schemes as very much a second best to employment (Andrews and Bradley, 1997), though another study using the same database showed that completing a scheme does seem to be associated with better subsequent employment outcomes, even with educational level, health and race controlled (Mealli, Pudney and Thomas, 1996). Green, Hoskins and Montgomery (1996) found that young people who had been on such schemes had lower wages than their peers even three years after completion, but Green *et al.* report just this as the political aim of the schemes – to reduce young people's reservation wages to realistic levels. The assessment of such schemes is, inevitably, a complex matter; the difficulties are discussed by Bradley (1995).

Youth unemployment takes varying forms. In difficult economic times, many young people are unable to find a first job on leaving education. Others, however, find jobs but then lose them. Winefield, Tiggemann and Winefield (1992) examined the distress due to such job loss, and found, perhaps surprisingly, that it was not related to the reasons why the young person lost their job – but it was related to the causal attributions that they made, with those who made external attributions experiencing less distress. The latter result, however, is not universal: with a smaller sample, but a more intensive methodology, Heubeck, Tausch and Mayer (1995) failed to find any attributional differences in distress due to unemployment, though they did find differences related to attributions of responsibility for solving the problem. Echoing the results of Patterson (1997) and Prause and Dooley (1997) discussed above, they found that young people with more internal attributions were less damaged.

In summary, it seems that youth unemployment is associated with a range of psychological effects, including lowered self-esteem, depression, lowered well-being, and poorer health behaviours. Although these associations may be partly selective, they are at least partly causal, and they tend to increase the risk of further unemployment. However, they are at least reduced for young people who were in better psychological health before becoming unemployed.

A First Income

Whether or not young people go into the labour market, by the end of adolescence they achieve a degree of financial independence. They are managing their own money, even if its source remains their parents or the state. This section is concerned with what young people do, at a strategic level, when they first have management of a full or nearly full income. It is not a matter of what they buy, but how they go about dividing up their income. This is a subject on which there has been surprisingly little formal research, especially considering its practical importance. Many young people are taking on adult responsibilities on very low incomes; the implications of poor money management tend to be severe, not only for them but also for their employers, parents or the state, whoever is the source of their income, and possibly also for their young children. Furthermore, standard economic theories about money management, the life-cycle theory of Modigliani and Brumberg (1954) and its derivatives, make clear predictions: young people with good incomes and low expenses because they are still living at home should save large proportions of their income, while those who have left home and face the high expenses of setting up home and supporting a young family should be ready to go into debt.

Learning money management

The issue here is how people first learn to manage serious amounts of money, maybe without much in the way of a safety net. It might be expected that there would be characteristic errors that young people, but not older, more experienced consumers, would tend to make in managing their money. As we shall see in the next section, there certainly are differences in the characteristic consumption patterns of younger and older adults. Some of these, such as an interest in high fashion items, might well be considered as errors by older, more curmudgeonly consumers, but that would be a biased judgement. In fact it is not obvious that there is widespread incompetence in the financial management of the young. Indeed, everyday experience is more inclined to regard financial competence as a dispositional variable, with some people being capable and others ineffective at every stage of their lives. Several researchers have constructed taxonomies of money management styles (Kempson, Bryson and Rowlingson 1994), and these do not seem to be strongly age-related. However, the dispositional approach does not have everything its own way, in that it has proved difficult to predict who will be a successful money manager. Walker (1997) discussed some of the differences in money management style among French teenagers, but her attempts to predict relative success from a range of objective strategies led to nothing. Similarly, although it has repeatedly been shown that young women tend to be more successful with money than young men (e.g. Davies and Lea, 1995; Vicenzi, Lea and Rumiati, 1999), Hollister, Rapp and Goldsmith (1986) found no evidence of gender differences in money management style in young teenagers.

Student and non-student debt

The consequence of incompetent money management is likely to be debt. Because of the recent shift towards loan-financing of higher education, and the predictions of life-cycle theories noted above, the use of debt and credit among students has been relatively intensively investigated. Lea (1999) argued that all discussion of debt needs to recognise the difference between credit use (an arrangement between a willing lender and a willing borrower), debt (where the lender is liable to be unwilling or unknowing) and problem debt (where there is no real prospect of repayment). In the case of students, the distinction is sometimes expressed as one between planned debt, i.e. deliberately using borrowing as a means of financing a period of study, and unplanned debt, i.e. overspending of one's sources of income *including* planned borrowing. Johnes (1994) and Gayle (1996) have reviewed the use of planned borrowing by UK students, while Davies and Lea (1995) and a number of other recent studies (e.g. Boddington and Kemp, 1999; Lea, Webley and Bellamy, 1995; Vicenzi *et al.*, 1999) have looked at the psychological processes accompanying them. Such studies have consistently shown that in the UK, young people from less wealthy home backgrounds are now dependent on borrowing if they are to follow university courses, and that the experience of using loans steadily diminishes their initial hostility towards being in debt – a hostility that recovers only slowly in post-student employment (Lea, Webley and Bellamy, 1995).

A contrasting picture was offered by Lea *et al.* (1999), who talked about money management with young unemployed people in the UK. These young people were of student age but had not attended university, and were surviving on benefit payments somewhat lower than the typical levels of student financial support, though comparable with them. Unlike students, they were very wary of credit arrangements, and those who had some experience were even more averse to them. Lea *et al.* suggest that this is because they experience the full, damaging effects of debt immediately, whereas for students using government loan schemes, the need to repay is far in the future. Nonetheless, enough non-student young people get into difficulties with unplanned debt to make its dangers a standard theme of consumer advice literature and some academic discussion (e.g. Ford, 1990). Hire purchase and/or mail-order purchasing are often seen as a particular threat to young people in new households.

Degrees of independence: hypothecation of parental support

One of the characteristics of young as against mature households is that they are likely to receive subsidies from outside, typically from parents. Webley, Lea and Portalska (1983) noted a sharp asymmetry in gift relationships in UK society – it was socially quite acceptable for parents to give students money, for example as a birthday gift, whereas the reverse gift would have been a solecism of the first order. But such gifts of money to the young emphasise the fact that they are not fully independent, and there is certainly informal evidence from our studies with students that money from parents is not regarded, or spent, in the same way as money that young people have earned for themseleves. Such hypothecation is, of course, a common trick in managing on a small income (cf. Lea *et al.*, 1997), but there seems to be more involved here. We suggest that it is also a way of making the giving more acceptable as parent and offspring move to a position of greater status equality.

Among students, parental contributions are particularly important, and the position of felt dependence may be more acute. As we shall see below, family contributions can also be important well past the student stage, when young people are buying their first houses (Rosser, 1999; Pickvance and Pickvance, 1995).

First Purchases

It has commonly been remarked that one of the most striking social changes in developed countries from the end of the Second World War onwards was the emergence of a distinct teenage market, indeed of the very concept of a teenager. That was a product of a number of simultaneous social changes. Among them were the availability of relatively well-paid jobs for teenagers as a result of full employment in economies managed according to Keynesian principles, the increasingly delayed entry to the adult labour market as a result of expansions in education at every level, and the postponement of family responsibilities as a result of increasingly acceptable and available contraception.

Against this background, it is surprising that relatively little systematic research on the adolescent consumer can be found in the academic literature. No doubt a great deal more has been done in various commercial interests, but it is not publicly available. More information could be gathered by secondary analysis of data sets of basically adult consumers among whom a good many younger people will have been sampled: it is common for consumer research reports to cite samples of people aged from 16 upwards. Mining those sources is a task for the future – here we focus on the relatively sparse research that has explicitly focused on adolescents and young adults as consumers. The theoretical basis for many of these studies is provided by G. P. Moschis's well-known book *Consumer Socialization* (1987), which sets purchasing by young consumers into a life-cycle perspective of the sort adopted in the present book.

Are young consumers different?

As in other fields, much consumer research in which adolescents and young adults participate does not treat them as a distinct group. They are either treated as somewhat elderly children or as somewhat juvenile adults, and assumed to have much the same characteristics as one or the other group.

Certainly there are some themes that do seem to represent a continuation of issues we raised in Chapter 2. Concern about the impact of the advertisements and the media, especially television, are commonly expressed (e.g. Cheung and Chan, 1996; O'Guinn and Shrum, 1997). General intra-family communication patterns affect how much adolescents are involved in family purchases (Foxman, Tansuhaj and Ekstrom, 1989; Palan, 1998). Teenagers can be quite uninformed about key consumer issues like prices even if they are knowledgeable about brands (Moore and Stephens, 1975). Parents and home life continue to exert considerable influence on young people's consumer behaviour into their teens and beyond. In the consumer taxonomy of Shim and Koh (1997), discussed in the next section, the value-maximisers were more likely to be influenced by their parents. Parental influences strongly moderate the impact of TV on adolescents (Churchill and Moschis, 1979). In a US sample, Rindfleisch, Burroughs and Denton (1997) found that young adults from families that had been disrupted by divorce or separation tended to score higher on scales of materialism. Although Flouri (1999) failed to reproduce this result in the UK, she did show that if parents have more materialistic attitudes, the same tends to be true of their children; so if separation leads to (or reflects) higher materialism in parents under US conditions, Flouri's results could be reconciled with those of Rindfleisch *et al*. Different parenting styles may well be responsible for the distinct shopping consumption styles sometimes found in young people of different gender and ethnic groups (e.g. Goldsmith, Stith and White, 1987; Shim and Gehrt, 1996), and of different nations. For example, Mexican adolescents' brand preferences were more influenced by parents than those of their US peers (Keillor, Parker and Schaefer, 1996) and the same was true of Mexican-American adolescents in the US (Shim and Gehrt, 1996).

Some childhood economic behaviours decline in adolescence, however. Collecting tends to recede (Olmsted, 1991). And in some respects adolescents are genuinely beginning to behave like adult consumers – for example, in late adolescence young people, like adults, successfully base preferences between consumer items on more than one dimension of information (Capon and Kuhn, 1980).

Nonetheless, adolescent consumers are distinctive in some ways, and when we look at their distinctiveness, it is obvious why this sector is so attractive to marketers. Within the product life-cycle theory, which describes the uptake of innovative consumer goods, being young is one of the cluster of characteristics that makes it more likely that a consumer will buy an innovative product (Stoetzel, Sauerwein and Vulpian, 1954; Rogers, 1995). Consumer preferences that are formed in young adulthood seem to stay with people for the rest of their lives, particularly in relation to 'aesthetic' goods such as fashion styles (Schindler and Holbrook, 1993), music or movies (Holbrook and Schindler, 1994). And young consumers are more likely to be sensation-seekers (cf. Hirschman, 1984), and so open to what marketers may think of as exciting, new (and profitable) product lines.

One aspect of adolescents' greater preference for new products is their interest in ethical consumption. At present, they are more likely to report 'green', pro-environmental attitudes, for example. Unfortunately, when these attitudes collide with the realities of the market, they are apt to wither away; and Banks and Tanner (1997) showed that in the UK younger people are consistently less likely to make donations to charity, and when they do give, give less in real terms than currently older members of the population, and also less than now older people did when they were young.

Consumable goods and services

A stereotypical view would see adolescents as relatively high spenders on certain kinds of consumable goods, particularly clothing and fashion items. There is some evidence to support this idea: for example, Horowitz (1982) found that young consumers (15–29-year olds) were more likely to be influenced by 'excitement' than 'economy' in making clothes purchases. But such trends do not apply to all adolescents. Shim and Koh (1997) clustered the responses of 14–18-year-olds to a survey about shopping habits, and found three major clusters, which they dubbed Value-Maximizing Recreational Shoppers, Brand-Maximizing Non-Utilitarian Shoppers and Apathetic Shoppers. Only the second of these groups really fits the stereotype of the fashion-obsessed teenager. Of course, there are many other consumable goods and services where young people represent a distinct market sector, travel and tourism being an obvious example (e.g. Abdel-Ghaffar *et al.*, 1992; Loker-Murphy and Pearce, 1995). But though these youth markets are important commercially, it is not so obvious that they are important psychologically or (in a broad sense) economically. Are young people really consuming in a different way, or are they simply consuming different products?

There is one sense in which adolescents certainly are consuming in a different way. As we saw above, they are establishing 'consumer identities': nets of tastes which will stay with them for the rest of their lives. It is likely (but has yet to be proved) that this process is linked to the more general use of establishing psychological autonomy. Consumption choice, like career choice, is partly a matter of establishing that you are a person distinct from your family background.

Consumer durables and setting up home

We have already seen that young people are important to marketers as purchasers of new products. As we write this book, it is young people's high demand for mobile phones that is in the news; by the time you read it, it will probably be something else. But young people are also important as consumers of established durables.

Consumer products go through a life-cycle. They start as innovations. But those that succeed eventually achieve a stage of maturity, which means that virtually as many people in the population own that product as are ever going to. This is the situation for, for example, ovens, refrigerators, beds, television sets and washing machines – all of which are profitable items for manufacturers and retailers to sell. The market is 'saturated', and becomes a matter of replacement rather than first acquisition. That is not to say that purchases will only be made when the old item breaks down. Purchasing in replacement durables markets is still susceptible to influence from general consumer confidence; indeed, it is the element of discretion in when replacement purchases are made that gives consumer confidence its importance as a macro-economic predictor (see Katona, 1975, Chapter 2). But it does mean that the few likely new purchasers become very important to marketers.

Among these new purchasers, young people, especially those setting up an independent household for the first time, figure largely – not least because some of them at least will have high discretionary incomes and an unrealistic view of what they can afford. O'Guinn and Shrum (1997) showed that students who watched a lot of 'light' TV (specifically, soap operas) had inflated estimates of the penetration of consumer durables, so presumably they would be more likely to try to buy them than more mature consumers.

Obviously quite a lot of durables purchasing will be associated with a first house purchase, a topic we take up in the next section. However, most young people set up home on their own some years before buying a house, and even if their accommodation comes furnished, this will create a need for durable goods.

Overall, surprisingly little seems to be known, at least in the publicly available literature, about any differences between young consumers and the general population in durables goods purchasing. There are some obvious questions. What is the order in which young people tend to acquire the standard large durable goods? Are young people 'good consumers' in the sense of using information sources (impartial consumer reports, for example) to get good value for money? Do they tend to buy new or second-hand? Very probably, practical marketers have some answers, but they are not readily available in the academic literature.

Buying a house

House purchase is the largest single economic transaction of most people's lifetimes, and it is often embarked on early in adult life. Not everyone ever buys a house, and there are major differences even between otherwise similar nations in the proportion of households that own their own house. No doubt the psychological and symbolic impacts of home purchase also vary as a result, but this has been investigated little, if at all. When it does occur, however, home purchase is the key event in the consumption life-cycle, and differences in its timing within an individual's life are an excellent indication of historical or social differences in economic and social circumstances (Henretta, 1987). The main commercial interest in house purchasing does not lie with manufacturers and retailers, as it does with conventional durables, since as Kendig (1984) points out, in developed countries only about 5 per cent of the housing stock is renewed each year. The major players commercially are the banks and other financial institutions that lend money for house purchase; they are certainly very interested in first-time buyers, but this interest does not appear to have generated much public literature on first-time buyers and their financial behaviour: we know relatively little about the psychological processes underlying house purchase.

The major theories about housing consumption (e.g. Rossi, 1955; Michelson, 1977) explicitly link house purchase to family life-cycle events: Kendig (1984) puts forward the useful concept of a 'housing career', and sees first-time house purchase as the most significant advance within such a career. It is rare for people to buy a house when they first form an independent household, so much of the available literature focuses on the transition from renting to ownership (e.g. Lassarre, 1986; Burnley, Murphy and Jenner, 1997, Henretta, 1987). Lassarre found that while family events (typically a birth) frequently precipitated the move into first home ownership, the sheer desire to own a home was also a powerful influence, a result consistently found by others also (e.g. Kendig, 1984). Indeed, Kendig argued that although family events made the desire to own more urgent, the scale of the transaction meant that actual purchase was often not tightly linked to such events. Burnley et al.'s sample consisted of Australians relocating from (mostly rented) property in central Sydney to (mostly purchased) property in the suburbs; for the largest group of their respondents, the 25–34-year-olds moving because of family formation, the key factor was housing affordability. Many first-time purchasers were making sacrifices in terms of journey time to work and seeing friends and relatives in order to get into house ownership, since in Australian cities the outer suburbs are regions of relative social disadvantage.

Affordability can be affected by changes in the economic environment, and Ortalo-Magné and Rady (1999) argue that macro-economic policy changes (specifically, financial liberalisation) in the early 1980s caused very large numbers of young people in the UK to move into owner-occupancy. Rosser (1999) looked at more individual demographic and financial impacts on a group of young business graduates' propensity to buy a house, and, again, found that family factors (cohabiting, the birth of children) were important, as were some financial ones (higher income). Surprisingly, neither house prices nor outstanding student loans had much impact. On the other hand, acquiring a capital sum by gift or inheritance also had a significant positive impact. A graduate sample does, of course, include a disproportionate number of young people from financially comfortable families, who could afford to make such gifts, but Rosser does not report what proportion of the sample received such gifts, and in a broader UK sample, Pickvance and Pickvance (1995) showed that as few as 12 per cent of first-time purchases were helped by family gifts or inheritances. Sheiner (1995) showed that the down-payments required for first house purchase had a major influence on the saving behaviour of young renters, and tax incentives for such saving are popular among young renters and can increase home ownership rates (Engelhardt, 1994).

For most new home-owners, of course, the decision to buy a house is also a decision to get into a major, virtually lifelong credit arrangement. Unsurprisingly, therefore, the cost of the consequential repayments is a key factor in the decision. As with smaller loans (Ranyard and Craig, 1995), it is the size of the regular repayment rather than the total cost of the borrowing that determines people's choice between different credit deals. Tomann (1996) argued that the relatively low rates of home ownership in Germany were due to the conservative lending policies of German banks towards young house-buyers, resulting in a high front end loading of the cost of house purchase. It is this kind of effect that the tax breaks discussed by Engelhardt (1994) were designed to alleviate.

Discussion

This chapter may have given the impression that the study of adolescence is a theory-free zone. It certainly is not: the papers we have cited have used, between them, virtually every theoretical construct in modern social psychology and sociology. In the limited space available, however, we have chosen to focus on the empirical trends that have been demonstrated, so they can be related to theories that are of particular interest to economic psychologists, most especially theories of intertemporal choice. Such theories seem peculiarly appropriate for an age of transition such as adolescence.

Another curious absence from the chapter really does reflect the literature. We have said little about how the transition to economic adulthood relates to the more or less simultaneous transitions to personal, social and sexual adulthood. Homes and families have appeared – but only as 'actors' or 'influences' in, say, the choice of study rather than work, or of a career path. But we all know that adolescence is for many people a time of emotional turbulence. The choices we have discussed in this chapter undoubtedly take place against a background, often a difficult one, of emerging sexual relationships and redefinition of relationships with parents and friends. You would barely guess it from the research papers we have surveyed. Only occasionally does a human reality poke through the web of statistics – for example when young people turn out to be leaving school because they want to be treated like adults (Varlaam and Shaw, 1984), or when Bowes and Goodnow (1996) recognise that work takes place in home and school as well as in employment, and young people's understanding of it runs across all three of these theatres.

We have dealt with a mixture of areas. Some are so well researched as to be indigestible; in others research, or at least published research, is so thin on the ground that we have had to put forward a little solid information heavily laced with speculation. The major point to be reviewed is how suddenly the transition is made from economic child to economic adult. Certainly people's circumstances undergo very sudden, even violent changes. But the evidence is that economic competence is quietly maturing in between times. There is more continuity in the years from 12 to 25 at the psychological level than there is in economic status. Nonetheless, there clearly are problems of adaptation, and some pathological circumstances. Some of these are obvious: for example, where poverty and lack of employment opportunity recruit young people into crime rather than into the labour market. Others are less obvious, like the debt culture of the student years in countries such as the UK.

From a life-cycle perspective, it makes sense to see many of these situations in terms of intertemporal choices. The decision whether to stay in education or to go straight into the labour market (or into claimancy) is obviously of this form. But so is, for example, the decision of a student to live beyond his immediate means, or the decision of a young couple to take on a mortgage to buy a house. Conventional social development theory would predict that young people's choices would show a steadily increasing time-horizon, but that would be a serious oversimplification of the data we have reviewed in this chapter. Through the teenage and young adult years, people do not just learn to look further into the future. They also get a much clearer idea of what their individual future is likely to hold. That in turn enables them to make choices with a longer reach into the future. There may still remain individual, dispositional and circumstantial, differences in how well they make them.

At the start of his critique of UK youth training schemes, Lindley (1996, p. 159) argues that, 'Young people are extremely resourceful, capable of adjustment to abrupt changes in status, and manage to reconcile themselves to the reality of the labour market'. The same might equally be said of their response to consumer markets – despite the fact that they are facing many non-economic developmental challenges. At the end of this survey, we feel that researchers have often not given young people enough credit. As economic psychologists take up the study of adolescence and young adulthood, a stronger theoretical basis, particularly in relation to intertemporal choice, will undoubtedly inform much of our research. But we hope that, in the study of adolescence, the adolescents themselves, and their undoubted economic competence, may also become more visible.

4

Economic Behaviour in the Family

Introduction

Whatever the nature of their previous relationship, when two people decide to start living together as a couple, many of the decisions they face will have economic consequences. In the first place, they may decide to cohabit rather than get married, and this may have legal implications for property ownership and inheritance. They will need somewhere to live, but should they rent a house or flat, live with parents, or embark on home ownership? (See pp. 71–72.) Having set up home together, they will then have to decide how the necessary chores will get done, and by whom. How should they organise their finances? Is it better to pool their incomes or to keep them separate? Will one person take responsibility for managing the accounts and making sure that bills are paid on time, or will they share this task between them? If they do not already have a child, then other decisions will follow, such as whether to have any children, when to start their family, and when to stop. The children will need to be looked after. In practice this responsibility is typically shouldered by the woman, who either gives up work altogether or moves to part-time working. However, in some cases, couples may decide that both can continue to work with the help of a child-minder or nanny.

All such decisions have both economic and psychological aspects, which makes them a natural target for study by economic psychologists. However, given the scope for investigation, there has been surprisingly little systematic research by psychologists. Certain economists have developed micro-economic models to account for some of the choices that people make with respect to the household division of labour, the timing of childbirth, and so on (e.g. Becker, 1991; Kooreman and Wunderink, 1996), and we shall examine some of this work below. Although these models are very powerful and mathematically rigorous, some of their assumptions and implications have been heavily criticised. For example, a fellow economist (Bergmann, 1995) has described some of Becker's conclusions as 'preposterous'. Consequently, we have to look elsewhere, to some of the sociological literature (e.g. Pahl, 1989, 1995; the SCELI (Social Change and Economic Life Initiative) project, Gallie, 1994; and the British Household Panel Survey, Buck et al., 1994) if we wish to gain an insight into what people actually do.

As we shall see, we now know a great deal about *what* people do, but far less about why and how they arrive at their decisions; nor do we know the extent to which things happen by default, rather than by some sort of active planning. In other words, the *processes* that lie behind the statistics remain obscured. There are a number of possible reasons for this. One is that it has long been conventional in economics to study the 'behaviour' of money and other goods rather than that of individual people, and the study of processes *within* the household has only recently been placed on the research agenda. Thus, in much of the work before the late 1970s, the household was used as the unit of analysis, with little attention to what took place within its bounds.

The second reason is that economic behaviour within the family is notoriously difficult to observe. It may be relatively easy to carry out a survey or a small-scale interview study, but these yield only a 'snapshot' view taken at one point in time, leaving the day-to-day processes of negotiation and decision-making out of the picture. Also, families are highly variable and fluid, with gradual or abrupt changes in composition and activity. Furthermore, it is important to bear in mind that the 'rules' that govern the division of household labour and the distribution of resources within the family are shaped not just by economic factors (both within the family and in the wider economy), but by social norms of exchange as well. This sometimes means that intra-familial redistribution of resources can *contradict* the distributive rules found outside the family (Curtis, 1986, p. 169). Much intra-familial behaviour has both expressive and instrumental features. For example, producing meals for the family is a necessary task but it can also be an expression of love, which may explain why a child's refusal to eat can be so distressing to its parent. This conjunction of expressive and instrumental concerns sometimes makes it difficult to perceive the economic implications of behaviour within the family. All these problems are compounded by the fact that money within the family can be a potential source of ambiguity and ambivalence – a topic to which we will return later. Finally, economic behaviour within the family cannot be understood without considering the nature of the family as an institution, and how it fits into the wider social and economic picture.

Consequently, the rest of the chapter is organised into four sections. First, we consider the dynamic nature of the family as an economic and social system; the second section examines the pervasive effects of gender; in the third section, we try to identify the major gaps in our knowledge, and in the fourth section we touch on some of the newer economic problems that families will face as we move into the twenty-first century.

The Family as a Dynamic System

Changing families

Although at any one time, there is a large number of single-person households, most people grow up in families, and live in some kind of multi-person household or family for a major portion of their adult lives. This often involves a pooling of resources, which may be derived from a number of different sources, such as wages, the sale of products in the market, rent income, transfers (e.g. statutory benefits) or subsistence activities such as growing food. However, before we look at economic behaviour within the family, we need to step back for a moment, and consider what kind of entity we are talking about, and how it relates to the wider social and economic domain. For example, we all have an implicit notion of what a 'family' is, and what we mean by a 'household'. But we need to bear in mind that the familiar stereotype of the nuclear family – husband, wife and roughly two children – is only one of a range of possible family forms, and currently comprises only 42 per cent of households in Europe (Antonides and van Raaij, 1998, p. 314). Changing social norms and sexual mores which have made divorce and sex outside marriage more acceptable have led to a whole spectrum of new family forms, such as cohabitation, same-sex 'marriages', lone parenthood and 'reconstituted families'. The latter, in which one or both of the parents have been married before, are increasing in frequency due to the high current rate of divorce. If there are children from previous relationships, then such families can be especially complex, with children acquiring additional sets of 'siblings', 'parents', 'grandparents', and so on. Within each different kind of family there will be the usual economic issues to resolve, and perhaps some that are unique. A full discussion of all these would take us well beyond the scope of the present chapter, but we shall touch on some of them on pages 79–93.

The second point to notice is that the terms 'household' and 'family' are often used as if they were interchangeable. However, families, even members of a 'nuclear' family, will sometimes extend across a number of households, and households may be made up of people who are unrelated by blood or marriage. Of course, both terms are abstractions or simplified social constructs. Thus, Wallerstein and Smith (1991) define the household as an 'income-pooling entity' but admit that this 'pooling' may be more conceptual than real. Finally, whether one is referring to households or to families, it is important to remember that both entities have shifting and fuzzy boundaries. Not only is there great variation in family types at any one point in time, but individual families are in a more or less continuous process of evolution and reformation, with a range of transitional states in terms of composition, sources of income, and financial management. Individuals may disagree about precisely where the family boundaries are drawn, and for what purposes. Despite the ambiguities associated with the terms, we shall follow the usual practice and use either to denote a household which contains a family of one type or another: that is, a married or cohabiting couple (with or without children and/or other family members) or a lone-parent household with one or more dependent children. Let us now consider how these households fit into the larger scheme of things.

Interacting systems: 'public' and 'private'

The generally accepted image of a family is that of a stable, autonomous institution, 'private' and separated from the 'public' world of commerce etc. However, this divide is largely illusory. As Wallerstein and Smith (1991, p. 235) point out, household boundaries are part of a historical process which locates the family within 'the larger network of structures that constitute the capitalist world economy'. At a national level, the state has an impact on individual families and their members by enforcing laws that influence such matters as family composition, how children should be cared for, and the nature of parental financial and legal responsibilities, and these rules are subject to change from time to time. Looking beyond the influences of the state, the effects of expansion and contraction within the global economy filter down to the individual households which may then have to respond by changing their economic behaviour. In a time of economic recession, one possible response is to make the household boundaries more permeable, by seeking help from the extended family or from friends (cf. Finch and Mason, 1993), looking for alternative sources of income, or switching from the purchase of market goods towards household production. In this way, the household acts as a 'buffer' to compensate for ups and downs in the economic cycle.

However, not all pressures are in the same direction; individuals and households can also have an effect on the state (though any effects on the wider global economy may be more difficult to discern). We can illustrate this with the following example. In the UK, as a result of changing norms of family life, successive governments have had to cope with huge increases in the benefits bill for lone parents. Here, the highly personal choices of individuals about their own families have added up to a major headache for any government committed to cutting public spending. In the UK, this situation prompted the first major study of lone-parent families (Bradshaw and Millar, 1991) and the creation of the Child Support Agency (CSA) in 1993 to target those 'absent fathers' who were reluctant to take financial responsibility for their children. Of course, the activities of this Agency also feed back into the system and have a further impact on families in turn. Questions have been raised about the extent to which it may have shifted poverty from first families onto stepfamilies (Cockett and Tripp, 1994). Individuals may change their behaviour in response, for example, by deciding to earn less or to hide the true extent of their earnings to avoid what they might see as excessive demands for payment.

Interacting with the formation of new family patterns have been changes in family roles, particularly those of women. In the UK, the effects of recession on the one hand, and better educational and job opportunities for women on the other, have combined in recent decades to create a huge increase in the proportion of employed women, though much of this growth has been in the service industries with typically poor rates of pay and conditions. At the same time, the scaling down of the industries which traditionally employed large numbers of men has meant a rise in male unemployment. The positive aspect of these changes is that many more women now have some measure of economic independence, and this has had an impact on the choices available to both men and women in marriage (see Bergmann, 1986, for an analysis of women's changing economic status). However, as we shall see in the next section, the changes have not always resulted in *equal* economic opportunities for women, and gender is still an important predictor of economic status.

The Central Importance of Gender

Traditional micro-economic analyses of the family have tended to regard it as a kind of 'firm', in which each partner can 'hire' or 'fire' the other. However, economic behaviour within families is intimately tied to gender, and we have to 'unpack' these effects if we want to understand what it is that makes families different from firms. In this section, we begin by considering some of the limitations of the micro-economic accounts before turning to findings from empirical studies.

Micro-economic accounts of the family

In his famous, and much-criticised *Treatise on the Family* Becker (1991) considers how the tasks of earning a living and caring for the household can best be achieved. The basic idea is that utility-maximising individuals can benefit from marriage by means of gains in trade through specialisation, the sharing of 'public goods' (such as housing), and economies of scale. According to this approach, family well-being (or utility) depends upon the total production of 'commodities' produced and consumed by the household. Subject to the constraints of time and money, commodities are obtained by combining 'market purchases' with 'own time and various environmental inputs' (Becker, 1991, pp. 23–24). Here Becker is referring, not to the various material goods that can be consumed, but to broader classes of goods such as 'children, prestige and esteem, health, altruism, envy, and pleasures of the senses' (p. 24). For example, the latter can be obtained (in part) by buying comfortable furniture and designing a room to create a harmonious living space. Each household activity is represented by a household production function, one for each commodity, though economists more commonly refer to 'the' household production function which represents a range of commodities.

The traditional division of labour casts the man as the principal breadwinner and the woman as home-maker, and Becker develops a theory of human capital to argue that this is, in fact, the most efficient solution. The theory of 'comparative advantage' implies that members of a household should invest in different types of human capital according to their relative skills and resources (Becker, 1991, p. 32). Even if the starting point were two identical people, Becker shows that both can gain from a division of labour in which one of them invests in market activities (earning the money) while the other specialises in household activities. Specialisation leads to greater efficiency, and increasing returns to investment, which results in an effective increase in time and money. In other words, one partner may enhance their earnings by acquiring and improving on market-based skills, whilst the other partner will become more expert – and thus more productive – by concentrating his or her efforts on home-based tasks. Of course, men and women are not identical in all respects, but this merely adds weight to Becker's argument. Since women already have a comparative advantage in bearing and nurturing children, they can carry out these activities at the same time as looking after the domestic chores. If this is the case, it makes sense (in economic terms) for most women to invest less heavily than men in labour-market 'capital'. They may do this in a number of ways: for example, by curtailing their education at an earlier stage, by selecting work that can be arranged around the demands of a family, or by choosing part-time rather than full-time employment. Thus, differences in investment may reinforce the biological differences between men and women. Becker argues that wage rates are lower for women partly because they invest less in market capital, and that in order to protect them from the potential disadvantages of this, women have demanded long-term contracts from men, such as marriage (pp. 30–31).

One of the major contributions of this micro-economic approach to the family is that it makes explicit something that has been overlooked in much of the earlier empirical work, namely that the activities of one partner in the labour market cannot properly be understood without taking into account the work that is done by the other partner at home – the household chores and caring for the children. Each is dependent upon the other, and a wider understanding of this fact might help to dispel the myth that the breadwinner's earning capacity is solely the result of his or her own efforts! On the other hand, Becker's theory implies a freedom of choice which simply does not exist for most men and women. For example, he points to women's lower investment in the market as the cause of their lower rates of pay, yet these lower rates of pay also make it more 'rational' for women (rather than men) to remain at home and care for the children, and this constrains the choices of both – whatever their actual investments might be – or for that matter, their preferences (Sawhill, 1980). It also means that single women, who may have invested just as much as their male counterparts in the labour market, may not receive a proper return on their investment.

The theory also ignores a range of other constraints. As Belk (1995a, p. 62) points out, 'a family is not just a decision-making consumption unit', even though their relationships may in many respects be 'mediated by consumption'. The constraints include: normative pressures for women to take a nurturing role in the family and for men to be the breadwinners (Amsden, 1980); the existence of both covert and overt sex discrimination in the labour market; and the ideological pressures which make men unwilling to do housework (Bergmann, 1986). It is within this social and economic context that men 'choose' to invest in market capital and that women 'choose' to take responsibility for childcare, so that even when a woman earns more than her partner, it might be difficult for her to assume the traditional male role.

The tendency for economic models to include only one utility function for the household has also attracted criticism. For example, Sen (1984, p. 384) describes some of Becker's assumptions as 'far-fetched', since they can only be made to work by means of some highly unrealistic constructions, such as families in which there is no disagreement at all, or where there is a despotic 'head' of the household who can bend all other household members to his or her will. The assumption of a single utility function has obscured important gender differences elsewhere. For example, Wunderink (1995) identifies some of the economic aspects of family planning, such as the costs of rearing children, and the tangible and intangible benefits that children can bring. However, Altman (1994, p. 1436) states that conventional economic models on this topic tend to reflect only *male* preferences, and that this may exaggerate the number of children required to maximise the utility of the household, especially in developing countries. He argues that, given a greater measure of control over their fertility, women, especially in developing countries, tend to have fewer children.

Becker's original model would predict an increased 'consumption' of children with increased income, but one also needs to take into account the source from which any increase in 'household' income is coming. As Bergmann points out, there tends to be a drop in the birth-rate if this increased income comes from the earnings of the *woman* (Bergmann, 1986). For earning women, both the 'opportunity costs' of children (e.g. the forgone income and promotion associated with staying at home), and the desire for independence have to be taken into account. Finally, although Becker argues that having a contract protects women from the disadvantages of investing mainly in home-based capital, it is a sad fact that, in the 'real world', contracts can all too easily be broken.

Although an economic model is bound to make simplifying assumptions when trying to account for such complex behaviour, some of Becker's other analyses have been condemned as 'fatally simplistic' and 'misleading'; in particular, his thesis that women generally have more to gain from polygamous marriages (in which one man has several wives) than from monogamous ones (Bergmann, 1995). The latter argues that in many societies that allow polygamy, women typically have very low status, very little freedom to develop their talents or choose their mates, and no opportunity to escape onerous marriages, or even, in some cases, to leave the house. In her view, the use of supply and demand curves in such areas of behaviour obscures more than it illuminates. We have dwelt on Becker's approach to the household economy because it has been highly successful in highlighting the material aspects of family life which are typically overlooked in psychological studies of interpersonal relationships (e.g. Duck, 1992, 1994a, 1994b). In a useful critique of Becker's model, Berk and Berk (1983) argue that what they refer to as the 'new home economics' has a positive contribution to make, especially when considering households 'at the margin', that is, families which have achieved an optimal allocation of time and resources. For these families, an increase in real wages will lead to an increase in demand for commodities of all kinds, and there will be a substitution in consumption away from labour-intensive home-based production towards goods produced in the market. Although the effects have been small, they cite empirical work which has largely supported these predictions. However, these authors also agree that empirical tests of the model throw up 'serious difficulties' of measurement and interpretation which 'undermine compelling conclusions'. For example, whilst it is true that the sexual division of labour can be predicted by the notion of 'comparative advantage', it can also be explained by a variety of other factors, such as sex-role socialisation and male domination, and we shall examine some of these in the following section.

Gender inequalities

The economic behaviour of individual men and women in families needs to be set against a more general background of gender differences in economic power. Despite the efforts of agencies such as the Equal Opportunities Commission in the UK, economic inequalities between men and women are still widespread. A combination of structural and normative factors means that there is a greater risk of long-term poverty for women than for men. Millar and Glendinning (1989) identify a range of factors, some of which have been touched upon in the preceding sections: discrimination in the labour market, disadvantages in the welfare and benefits system, and gender-related roles and expectations within the household and family. Thus, despite their increasing participation in the labour market, women's pay on average remains below that of men (Buck *et al.*, 1994, pp. 187–190), and their in-work benefits such as pensions and sick pay are often either lower or non-existent. The benefits system is modelled on the (once typical) male pattern of uninterrupted, full-time employment, which may hold true for the working careers of some single women, but fits poorly with the way that many women have to organise their employment around the needs of other family members, both young and old. When they do not have paid work this can leave women in a position where they either cannot claim benefits at all, or else can do so at only the lowest, means-tested rates. In many cases, they can claim only as a dependent of a male partner. So, for example, in the UK, a woman who has been entitled to a Widow's Benefit whilst living alone, forfeits this right if she starts to cohabit with a man – whether or not he is actually supporting her financially.

These structural inequalities may be compounded by gender-related asymmetries within the family, in a number of spheres, such as the control of income and assets, the consumption of household resources (including food, as demonstrated by Charles and Kerr, 1987), in power and decision-making, and in the traditional division of labour both within and outside the home. Although more and more women have been spending increasing amounts of time in paid work, their domestic responsibilities have not been adjusted accordingly. For example, the British Social Attitudes Survey found that for 75 per cent of respondents, the woman remained primarily responsible for household tasks (Jowell *et al.*, 1992). Even when men have been unemployed for long periods, they still tend to see themselves as the major breadwinners and do not take on a significant amount of the household work (James, 1996). Across a range of European countries, women, on average, spend about twice as much time as men on household production (Antonides and van Raaij, 1998). Those married women who are in paid work are less likely to have a pension scheme, assuming instead that they will be able to rely upon their husbands' arrangements (James, 1996). Of course, the arrangements in some individual households may work to the woman's advantage, and thanks to the legal and benefits systems in the UK, in some cases, separating couples may initially be better off (Davis *et al.*, 1992). For the most part, however, a combination of the above factors places women *as a group* in a weaker bargaining position within marriage, and means that individual women are more likely to face poverty if there are dependent children and the marriage breaks down.

Women are often aware of their potentially vulnerable position, yet most follow the traditional pattern of investing in their husband's earning capacity and pension (James, 1996). As we shall see in the next section, this means that where there are surplus assets and income, these are more likely to be controlled by the male partner.

Financial organisation

As we said at the beginning, most couples living together have to sort out how they will deal with money matters. There will be decisions about bank accounts and payment of bills, and negotiations about personal spending. As there has been an increase in research on these topics since the 1980s, we now know a great deal more about how couples organise their money (e.g. see Pahl, 1995, for a recent review). Prior to that time, there was a general (and convenient) assumption in economic and sociological theory, as well as in social policy, that household income was equally shared and that all household members enjoyed the same standard of living (Land, 1983). This picture is also implied by the current ideal of marriage as a partnership of equals, and, as we have already seen, by a micro-economic approach to the family which typically uses only a measure of *household* rather than *individual* utility. Surveys indicate that about half of couples in the UK have some form of pooling system for household money, but how much real equality is there in practice? The answer is – less than one might think.

Pahl's study in 1980 helped to 'take the lid' off the 'black box' of the household, and exposed some of the inequalities that can take place in marriage. She found that women living on benefits in a refuge for battered wives felt 'better-off' than when they had been at home with their husbands because even though their current 'family' income was lower in absolute terms, the women had control of all the available money. This study made it plain that women and children could be living in poverty even in relatively affluent *households*. Rather than a simple sharing model, families employ a wide variety of financial arrangements. Pahl devised the following typology:

1 *The female whole-wage system*: where the husband hands over all his wages (minus his personal spending money) and the wife uses this plus any earnings of her own to cover all the household expenses.
2 *The male whole-wage system*: in which the husband manages all household finances and typically leaves the wife with no independent access to money.
3 *The housekeeping system*: where the man usually gives his wife a fixed sum for housekeeping expenses and retains the rest.
4 *The pooling system*: where all, or nearly all, of household income is shared, usually in a joint account, and both partners have access to it.
5 *The independent management system*: where (typically) both partners have a separate source of income, and neither has access to all household funds. Partners may simply divide the cost of bills between them, or each partner may take responsibility for a part of the household expenditure.

Of course, this list does not exhaust all the possible ways that money can be organised. As Pahl herself acknowledges, categorisation is not a simple matter, since systems of financial management tend to shade into each other, and some couples' arrangements are very complex. Nonetheless, this typology has served a useful function in capturing the main patterns of influence over household income.

Much of the earlier work took the form of small-scale, qualitative studies, but their results have been confirmed in recent years by a number of large-scale surveys, such as the Social Change and Economic Life Initiative (SCELI, Anderson *et al.*, 1994) and the British Household Panel Study (BHPS). The first wave of the BHPS (Laurie and Rose, 1994) showed 36 per cent of couples using the *whole-wage* system, 49 per cent *pooling*, 11 per cent using an *allowance* system, and 4 per cent using either *independent management* or some other system of financial organisation. The second wave of the BHPS showed a very similar pattern, but comparison across the two waves indicated a high degree of fluidity from one period to the other, with only 66 per cent placing themselves in the same category at both times (Pahl, 1995). These differences may be associated with changes in employment and family composition, the birth of a child, and so on.

The pooling system seems to be the most common form of organisation, but needs to be subdivided further, because, in practice, one partner is likely to 'run' the account on a day-to-day basis and to have a greater role in financial management. Thus, in the SCELI study, Vogler and Pahl (1994) divided the pooling system (used by 50 per cent of respondents) into three sub-categories and found that in just under one-third (15 per cent) women were managing the accounts, just under a third were managed by men, and just over one-third were jointly managed.

One of the important distinctions made by Pahl is between *control* and *management* of money. For example, the female whole-wage system can appear to vest a great deal of power in the hands of the wife, but in reality, her role is more likely to be that of management. There are two reasons for this. The whole-wage system is found more frequently in lower-income households where the husband is the major breadwinner and the wife has to make ends meet. Also, the husband may retain the right to demand sums of money at any time, and may also be able to dictate how the housekeeping money is spent. In this way, overall control can remain under the control of the earner.

In order to investigate the issue of control, Vogler and Pahl (1994) designed two questions to identify the relative power of husband and wife in two spheres: (i) which partner had the final say in 'big' decisions and (ii) who made the more important decisions. By combining these two measures, they showed that just over half of all couples were egalitarian, one third were characterised by male control and only 9 per cent of couples had a system where the wife was in overall control. These asymmetries were also reflected in other aspects of power. For example, the women were significantly more likely to 'go without' than the men when resources were tight, especially in the lower-income households and where men had greater levels of control. These findings of gender inequalities in economic power have been supported by an economic analysis of the BHPS data by Dobbelsteen and Kooreman (1997) in which they found that a model based on differences in economic power fit the data better than a household production (efficiency) model.

Yet another gender difference is the finding that women tend to be more 'family-focused' than men so that an increase in 'her' income is more likely to be spent on the family than a comparable increase in 'his' (Pahl, 1989). Similarly, access to money for personal spending (as opposed to money to be spent on the family as a whole) showed predictable differences along the lines of gender and control, with the greatest levels of equality reported amongst those using the pooling system and the greatest disparity (with men having more access) in allowance and whole-wage systems. In the male-managed pooling system, 70 per cent of couples reported having equal access to personal spending money, and 20 per cent agreed that the males had greater access. For those with a housekeeping allowance system, these figures were 47 per cent and 42 per cent respectively. Although much of the foregoing work was carried out in the UK, this pattern of findings is echoed in studies carried out in New Zealand amongst both the white and the Maori populations (Fleming and Easting, 1994; Taiapa, 1994) and would appear to be a general phenomenon in developing countries as well (see, for example, Blumberg, 1991, pp. 97–127). As Pahl (1995) points out, normative constraints tend to lead to under-reporting of inequalities in amounts of spending money, so these figures are likely to paint a rosier picture of sharing and equality than may actually be the case.

Typologies are useful for classifying the broad patterns of financial management, but when used in survey work they are subject to the problems associated with socially desirable responses. One of the advantages of qualitative approaches as compared with surveys is that they enable one to get beyond the 'Sunday-best' responses that are often given when people are asked direct questions about how money is organised. An in-depth interviewing technique can reveal the finer details of how the money is used on a day-to-day basis – who has access to it and for what purposes. Using such techniques, Burgoyne and her colleagues have shown that the way that a couple organise their finances can reflect the nature of the relationship between the partners (or how they would like it to be perceived) and influence the way that partners feel about their status within the family (Burgoyne 1990). For example, when asked about how money was treated within the marriage, one wife said that it was used 'to provide support of every kind in every conceivable circumstances to each other without totting up the value of the individual resources' (Burgoyne and Lewis, 1994). This is a good example of the 'rhetoric' of sharing in marriage, and was typical of the responses that were given to a direct question of this kind. However, it emerged that many couples found it difficult to avoid 'totting up' the different contributions. A key factor here is the *source* of income. For example, if a couple say that they use a 'pooling' system, it might appear that both partners have equal access to the money but in practice this may not be the case at all. In Burgoyne's (1990) study, the money in the joint account (in most cases) had come from the man's earnings, with the women making little, if any, *financial* contribution to the family. All the women were contributing economically in other ways by running the household, cooking, cleaning, caring for the family, etc., but despite this, it was extremely difficult for the non-earning wives to regard the money as being jointly owned. Having a joint account was not enough to neutralise the psychological 'labels' of ownership associated with earned income, and the women tended to feel guilty if they spent any of the money on themselves, rather than on the family as a whole. This was true even for a couple who were striving to maintain an egalitarian relationship.

So the source of the income is an important factor in how the money will be used, and in the way that a non-earning partner may feel about their status within the relationship. Despite the wish to regard all contributions to the marriage as of equal value, the way that the women actually treated the 'joint' money suggested otherwise, and there seemed to be an implicit notion of exchange, in which caring for the family was given less weight than inputs of money. This interpretation was supported by observing the changes in behaviour that followed a change in the sources of household income. For example, if a woman moved into paid employment and started contributing financially, this led to a greater level of financial autonomy and financial decision-making, and an enhanced sense of entitlement to money for personal spending. For many women (and it appears for men too – see Stamp, 1985), being financially dependent is a source of discomfort, no matter how much other contributions to the marriage may be recognised and valued in their own right. In Burgoyne's (1990) study, some couples had acknowledged this as a problem and had set up special arrangements for the wife to have access to money of her own – money that could be spent without the need to justify it either to herself or to others in the family.

This 'earmarking' of money for different purposes is a pervasive feature of household financial organisation. For example, it is not unusual to find that people have debts in one account and savings in another. Historically, housekeeping money, or 'women's money', has been viewed very differently from earnings, so much so that Zelizer (1994) argues that it has almost been treated as a separate 'special-purpose currency'. Drawing on a variety of different sources, including court transcripts, books on etiquette, household budget studies and so on, she has analysed the changing meanings, allocation systems and uses of married women's money in the USA. Zelizer shows that money is earmarked according to the social relations in which it is embedded, and that this limits 'fungibility' – the extent to which currency units in different accounts or categories are regarded as interchangeable. Even in modern households, an example of this tendency to mark out different sources of income in different ways can be seen in the way that Child Benefit in the UK (usually paid to the mother) is frequently treated in quite a different way from earned income (Wilson, 1987).

Decision-making

As we have seen, financial organisation can have an impact on family decision-making. Family life encompasses a variety of other economic decisions: the timing of children, budgeting, spending, savings, loans and asset management. There has been a great deal of research on family decision-making, but much of it tends to be fragmented and individualistic in its approach (see Lackman and Lanasa, 1993, for an overview) and has failed to appreciate that decision-making is embedded in family life and can only be understood within that overall context (Kirchler, 1999). Other shortcomings of research in this area are that it has often focused on individual constructs and the purchase of individual products. Moreover, the influence of children in economic decisions has been overlooked because of a tendency to concentrate on the husband–wife dyad (Lackman and Lanasa, 1993). Decision-making is one area of family life where conflict can be expected to occur, since people's wants and needs differ, and hence, their priorities. Much of the research on conflict resolution has assumed that this is a rational, utility-maximisation process, with a clearly defined beginning, middle and end, but, according to Buss and Schaninger (1983), it is more likely to be a process of 'muddling through' with a series of small decisions along the way.

In a useful review of this area, Kirchler (1988) notes that much of the research to date has focused upon purchase decisions, especially those involving durables, such as cars, furniture, appliances and so on. Predictably, perhaps, wives have been found to be 'dominant' in the purchase of consumables, such as food and cleaning materials, whilst husbands have tended to have more say in decisions involving 'technically complex items'. The probability of joint decision-making tends to increase with cost, though, given Pahl's (1995) findings, we might be suspicious of what is meant by 'joint' in this context. Kirchler (1988) reports that 'role specialisation' occurs at an early stage of the decision-making process, so that men are more likely to decide about the 'need' for a car or TV set, whereas women are more likely to decide when the washing machine or rug should be replaced. However, he also found that husbands had equal or greater influence at the later stages of all decisions – i.e. in 'information search' and the 'decision to buy'. Thus, his findings would seem to accord with those of Pahl that men tend to predominate in decision-making, especially when they are the principal breadwinners. The pattern of financial organisation also interacts with the extent to which partners have to reach agreement: for example, Burgoyne and Morison (1997) found that one of the reasons for keeping money separately was to avoid conflict over spending priorities.

One of the areas of greatest expenditure is on children, with around £3,000 per year (on average) spent on each child for 'regular items' such as holidays, birthdays, Christmas, food, clothing and so on. This sum does not include the cost of childcare. In the UK, about one-fifth of average spending on a child is met by Child Benefit (Middleton, Ashworth and Braithwaite, 1997). When incomes are low, parents (especially mothers) typically try to protect their children from poverty by doing without things themselves (including 'proper' food: Kempson, 1996; Burgoyne *et al.*, 1999). Even in families surviving on benefits, the source and recipient of income are highly significant for its allocation. Goode, Callender and Lister (1998, p. 101) highlight the gendered nature of consumption within such families, with couples making a distinction between individual and collective expenditure along the lines of gender roles. These distinctions tended to legitimise men's personal spending, but defined women's *collective* expenditure, including that on children, as personal.

One important feature of household decision-making is that this is a *process*, and any research that focuses upon isolated decisions is likely to present a misleading picture. Current decisions can only be understood in the light of past decisions and expectations about the future. Part of this process is the acquisition of 'debts' in utility which are entered into some implicit type of 'account book'. If one partner gets their way over a contested decision, they incur a 'debt' which has to be repaid at some future point by giving way to the other. Partners have also been observed to use a whole range of different influence tactics in order to get their way. Kirchler (1999) argues that the way these debts are handled (their precision and the time-scale for 'repayment') is influenced by the nature of the relationship and the strength of the emotional tie, with those operating on a 'love principle' less likely to keep 'exact' calculations.

The interaction of material and non-material aspects in relationships has also been explored by Livingstone (1992). She investigated families' understanding of domestic technologies, and found that goods are viewed not just as functional objects but as part of the way that individuals within the family relate to each other. Women saw 'domestic technologies' as a necessary 'life-line', and used them to keep 'chaos at bay' in their running of the home, whereas men tended to view them as a means to demonstrate mastery and expertise. For women the home is often their place of work as well, whereas for men it is more commonly viewed as a sphere of leisure. Since it is primarily women who have the responsibility for maintaining social relationships both within and outside the family, Livingstone argues that a household item like the telephone will be regarded differently, with women using it as a resource to maintain contact with family and friends, and men using it in a more instrumental way.

These sorts of factors may underpin gender differences in the importance of decisions to purchase a range of commodities, such as a car, furniture, a new washing machine, etc. According to Kirchler (1988), social norms dictate that husbands should predominate in decisions about 'typically male items' and wives for typical female ones. Thus, it might appear that roles in decision-making are allocated according to which partner is most interested and competent. But, of course, this tends to overlook the fact that perceptions of competence may also arise out of the power structure. For example, Wilson (1987) observes that at lower income levels, women are typically seen as much better than men at dealing with money, whereas at higher levels of income, it is the men who are regarded as the experts. According to her analysis, it tends to be men who control money and make financial decisions when this is a privilege, whereas women get this job when it is more of a chore. One side effect of this division is that women at higher income levels may not be acquiring the same level of skill as men in dealing with financial institutions, and since it is usually the case that only the main breadwinner has made any arrangements about pensions and long-term security, this can leave them ill-equipped to cope if the marriage ends. As James (1996) observes, the traditional division of labour may be an optimal strategy in a situation of stable marriage, but not when marriage is only a transitory state, as it appears to be for an increasing number of families.

Divorce, lone parenthood and remarriage

In 1991, there was one divorce for every two marriages in the UK (Central Statistical Office, 1994) and the rate is comparable in other Western countries, such as the USA (National Center for Health Statistics, 1986) and New Zealand (Statistics New Zealand, 1997, pp. 66–7). According to Cameron's (1993) analysis, the factors predicting divorce are increased female earnings, decreased male earnings, unemployment, early marriage and higher levels of female education. This suggests that recent increases in the divorce rate were due to women being able to leave unsatisfactory marriages because many of them had a better chance of coping financially on their own than was the case in the past. However, in a later article (Cameron, 1996) he suggests that rates between 1981 and 1991 were increasing even when economic factors were held constant.

Quite apart from the social and psychological effects of divorce, there are economic consequences. Following the breakdown of a marriage, there is typically a significant disparity in standards of living, with the disposable incomes of men usually increasing and those for women and children falling dramatically (James, 1996; Millar, 1988). This is partly because of the custody arrangements (women tend to be awarded custody of the children) but also because time out of the labour market caring for children within marriage typically means a drop in earning power for women. This, and a combination of other gender-related factors, means that women have more to lose when marriage breaks down.

In the past, even when a court order had been obtained, many lone mothers were unable to benefit from maintenance payments because they tended to be set at a very low rate and were often paid sporadically, with the woman having to go back to court whenever the man defaulted on his payments. Burgoyne and Millar (1994) found that 'absent' fathers were more likely to pay maintenance when it was rigorously enforced, but were otherwise likely to withhold it for a variety of reasons. Many were particularly reluctant to contribute to the support of their ex-wives. Some men withheld maintenance in order to exert control, to gain access to the children when this had been denied, or because of feelings of resentment over the circumstances of the marital separation. For those men who felt responsible for the break-up, paying maintenance seemed to be a kind of reparation for past injury, but where the woman was perceived as being at fault, then not paying could be seen as a form of just retribution. However, even when maintenance is properly paid, this is only beneficial if the woman is in paid work. In some countries (such as France) reliable child care is much more widely available than in the UK where few lone mothers are able to go out to work. In the UK most are on state benefits (72 per cent of lone mothers in 1989 compared with 44 per cent of lone fathers, Bradshaw and Millar, 1991), and, under the benefit rules, any money obtained from maintenance is deducted from their allowance. The Child Support Agency has done virtually nothing to change this, having focused its efforts on families claiming benefits, so the standard of living for most lone-mother households is at a very low level. Even when the women are able to obtain paid work, their living standards tend to remain low because the jobs they can get tend to be part-time and low-paid, and they face higher child-care costs in comparison to two-parent families.

As Millar (1988) points out, these inequalities on marital breakdown are not solely the result of divorce, but have their roots in the assumption that married women should be financially dependent on their husbands, which means that men may be able to depart with their human capital (i.e. their earning power, to which the woman has been contributing indirectly) intact. Some recent changes in the divorce laws have not helped this situation. As James (1996, p. 158) puts it: 'equal division of property does not necessarily mean equal division of human capital which has . . . been accumulated by the male breadwinner'. This underlying reality can have an effect even in happy relationships where both partners are striving for equality. For example, in Burgoyne's (1990) study, one man clearly articulated the potential power he had to take his earning capacity away from the family. Although he regarded this power as illegitimate, its influence on the family dynamics could not be denied.

Thus, many mothers of dependent children after divorce are poor and find it difficult to escape from poverty. One possible route out of poverty is remarriage. In the UK, more than one in three of all marriages in 1993 were remarriages for one or both of the partners (Office of Population Censuses and Surveys, 1993). What are the prospects for families of remarriage? In a comparison of 'intact' and 'reordered' families (stepfamilies) undertaken by Cockett and Tripp (1994) in the UK, the latter seemed to be generally worse off. For example, only 4 per cent of intact families had a total income under £90 per week, compared with 22 per cent of reordered families. At the upper end of the scale, 51 per cent of intact families had incomes over £150 per week compared with only 35 per cent of reordered families. There were fewer dual-income families amongst the latter group, and three times as many in receipt of benefit than in the intact families. Not surprisingly, the reordered families had experienced greater levels of financial hardship during the previous year and more disruption due to events such as moving house.

Other studies have shown that the potential for conflict over money in families of remarriage is high. For example, there may be ongoing financial links with ex-partners (because of debts or maintenance payments); family composition may fluctuate as children move from one household to another; and there are likely to be additional problems in trying to merge (perhaps incompatible) financial habits that have crystallised over time (Coleman and Ganong, 1989). Not surprisingly, remarried couples who divorce again are more likely to report money problems than those who stay together (Wilson and Clarke, 1992). If money issues with former partners remain unresolved, then these can act as a constant reminder of past marriages and problems, and men have been reported as often unwilling to change their wills, insurance policies, etc. (Messinger, 1976). How do couples resolve such issues and what sorts of financial arrangements do they make?

Work done in America suggests that, just like first-married couples, many remarried couples adopt some form of pooling system. For example, half of the 16 stepfamilies studied by Fishman (1983) had a 'one-pot' system which (she argued) encouraged family cohesion. Similarly, Coleman and Ganong (1989) found that three-quarters of the 105 couples in their study could be categorised as 'one-pot' families. However, there have been criticisms of Fishman's somewhat simplistic dichotomous model of joint versus separate accounts (Lown and Dolan, 1994; Pasley, Sandras and Edmondson, 1994). A similar criticism could be levelled against Coleman and Ganong (1989) who classified their respondents on the basis of a *single* question about whether or not they pooled their incomes and shared all expenses. Lown and Dolan (1994) and Pasley et al. (1994) used a three-category classification: one-pot, two-pot and mixed (that is, with some separate and some joint management of money). Again, the most common pattern was a one-pot or pooling system, with only a minority of couples using a totally separate management strategy (e.g. 9 per cent in Lown and Dolan).

Although these later studies represent an advance on the earlier ones, it is possible that a great deal of information still remains hidden. Even with three categories of management rather than two, it is unlikely that enough of the diversity and complexity of day-to-day management will be captured. Moreover, Pasley *et al.* used only two items to classify their respondents: the use of (i) joint or separate bank accounts, and (ii) joint or separate savings accounts. Previous experience has shown that careful questioning is required in order to uncover the extent to which resources really are pooled and shared (see Burgoyne, 1990).

For these reasons, Burgoyne and Morison (1997) used a variant of Pahl's (1995) typology and an in-depth, semi-structured method of interviewing to collect the data in their study of twenty remarried couples. They found that ten couples had an independent management system, five had shared management (four wife-managed and one male-managed), and five had an allowance system. One key finding was a degree of separateness in financial arrangements which was in sharp contrast to the earlier findings. The notion of total sharing which typifies the ideology (if not always the substance) of first marriages seemed to be noteworthy for its absence here. Half the couples had some form of *independent management* – a pattern so uncommon in the population as a whole (less than 2 per cent) that Pahl had excluded any discussion of it in her 1995 paper. In Burgoyne and Morison's study, there appeared to be much less redistribution of resources than is commonly assumed in marriage, and in some cases this was quite deliberate. For those with children from previous relationships, this was especially marked in the way they wished their assets to be treated after death. Most couples had arranged for their surviving partner to inherit in the first place, but after that, the assets were meant to be divided along biological lines. One striking exception to this pattern was a couple where the husband had made the usual arrangement, thinking that his wife had done the same. Unknown to him, however, she had cut him out of her will and arranged for her assets to go directly to her own children!

Some of the inequalities that women often experience in first marriages seemed to follow through to the new relationship: on the whole, it was the men who owned and controlled a greater level of the household's material wealth and assets. However, some women had managed to retain some measure of autonomy with respect to their own incomes, and most couples reported quite low levels of conflict and disagreement over money.

Of course, some caution needs to be applied in drawing any strong conclusions from a study such as this, which relied upon a relatively small sample of volunteers. It is highly likely that remarried couples who did encounter serious differences over money would have parted early on, or else would not be amongst those who agreed to participate. However, more recent research corroborates the findings. For example, Fleming and Atkinson (1999) in their study of 35 families of remarriage in New Zealand suggest that a similar pattern is emerging there. Very few families used an allowance system, and the women tended to have a more 'hands-on' attitude towards control of money and a more egalitarian approach to marriage. Having lived as sole parents and managed their own money, many of the women who had an income wanted to keep it separate, whereas the men were more likely to prefer a pooling system. It was hard for many of the women to give up the independence they had experienced between marriages (see also Fleming, 1997). Similar results have been found in a study in the Netherlands by Buunk and Mutsaers (1999) with a sample of 290 remarried couples. They found that remarried men and women were generally more satisfied in their current marriage, and perceived greater levels of equity compared with the past marriage, but that on the whole men felt more advantaged than women.

Fleming and Atkinson's (1999) findings go some way towards answering an important question raised by the earlier work: is the degree of independent management and control of resources simply a matter of life stage (with fewer dependent children and both partners having an income), or does it reflect a more intense desire on the part of second-marrieds to retain control of their own incomes, perhaps in response to negative experiences in the past? In first marriages, a joint account can facilitate management in the child-bearing years when wives are less likely to be contributing substantially to the household income. Although some wives start to keep their own incomes in a separate account when they return to work (cf. Burgoyne 1990), it may be that, having started off with a joint account, it is difficult to move very far in the direction of separate management because of ideology, or inertia, or both. In contrast, for remarried couples, the pattern of management has been interrupted and this makes it easier to adopt a different system in the new relationship. Perhaps the couples in the remarried study with independent management were simply practising what first-marrieds would *like* to do, but find difficult, since it might imply a lack of trust. Further research will be required to elucidate this.

Future Research Problems

As you have been reading this chapter, you may have been reflecting on how little we really know about the economic psychology of the family. What we have here is really only the sketchiest knowledge, with not much beyond the broad brush-strokes that help to locate families in the wider social context, and this is in part because much of what we know has come from sociological sources. For economic psychologists there are many unanswered questions that cry out for more research and we shall identify some of them in this final section. An obvious starting point is with the nature of the exchanges that take place within the family.

Economic and social exchange

Money in marriage has the potential to cause conflict because of the ambiguities that arise in trying to reconcile two systems which have their own 'rules' of transaction (economic and social). According to Foa's (1971) theory of resource exchange, transactions are more satisfactory when they involve similar types of resources, for example, services or goods in exchange for money, love for love, or love for status. However, these 'rules' do not always apply. In gift exchange, for example, money can serve as a vehicle for the communication of love so long as a gift of money passes down the family status hierarchy, such as from parents or grandparents to younger generations. In such transactions, the nature of the exchange is well defined and relatively unambiguous (cf. Webley and Wilson, 1989; Burgoyne and Routh, 1991).

However, this is not always the case within marriage – here some ambiguity remains, perhaps for good reason. Consider, for example, a situation where a wife is staying at home, looking after the family and doing the housework, and her husband is the sole breadwinner. Here, the non-earning partner is receiving financial support and providing 'care' in return. If this exchange is presented as an economic transaction it might seem too much like a market exchange, which does not 'sit' easily with the idea of mutual love, so the two types of activity – economic and social – are apt to be treated (overtly at least) as belonging to separate spheres. As Curtis (1986, p. 178) argues: 'All groups, from corporations to nuclear families, have to contend at the same time with economic and non-economic principles of exchange. The conflict is between types of normative system, not simply between persons or roles.'

The following anecdote may make this a little less abstract. It concerns a family where the woman had a well-paid job, and the man was earning very little and paying maintenance to his ex-wife. They had decided to divide the housework equally between them, but when it turned out that the woman was not doing her share of the cleaning, she decided that she would employ a cleaner (using her own earnings) to do her share of the work. The man, being somewhat short of money, offered to do her share of the housework if she would pay *him* to do it instead of a cleaner, but she refused, saying that *he* should do this extra work for nothing. When this situation was described to students attending a seminar, some felt that the man had a perfectly good case for regarding this as a straightforward economic exchange, but others were distinctly unhappy about the arrangement. When pressed, they found it difficult to articulate why they felt this way, but their objections seemed to be two-fold: first, it seemed too 'coldly economic' in a relationship of this kind to think about exchanging money for housework, and secondly, by deciding to employ someone else to do her share of the cleaning (regardless of whether this was a cleaner *or* her partner), the woman was converting what should have been a social exchange (her contribution to the well-being of the household) into an economic transaction, and this was seen as illegitimate.

This story adds weight to one of our earlier criticisms of Becker's account of the household: 'the "new home economics" evaluates family activities such as housework as if economic rules of exchange alone were relevant' (Curtis, 1986, p. 179). Housework is only one of the things that a wife 'owes' her husband if he is supporting her financially, even if her work exceeds the value of his income in economic terms. Within the household, economic 'debts' are translated into social debts, with the precise terms of the repayment unspecified. This gives them 'an open-ended quality that may be very useful for people whose resources are variable and uncertain' (Curtis, 1986, p. 176). However, the very fact that such debts are left 'unspecified' can facilitate exploitation, since it is almost impossible to determine when they have been discharged. Financial support imposes social obligations of a more diffuse nature than economic debts; they are less easily quantifiable than money, and the dependent partner has few external cues with which to evaluate their contribution (Chafetz, 1991). Whereas economic rules set limits on the scale of any economic debts that can be incurred (such as the bankruptcy laws), the unspecified debts involved in non-economic exchange can be 'infinite in effect' (Curtis, 1986, p. 179). In these circumstances, perhaps a dependent partner would be well advised to get a job instead!

Tracing processes within the family

Much of the earlier discussion has focused upon the way that the different systems of financial organisation can reinforce wider economic inequalities and translate into various gender-linked asymmetries within marriage. The literature on these aspects of family life continues to grow, and with successive waves of the BHPS (British Household Panel Survey), we can look forward to tracing some of the changes that take place in sources of family income and other economic behaviour. However, there is a whole host of issues concerning economic *processes* within the family that at present we know almost nothing about, and upon which the survey data can shed little light. For example, how much discussion about money management takes place before marriage, and how has a couple arrived at their current system of financial organisation? Responses to these questions in our own research have tended to be vague and uninformative – it had 'just happened', or 'just evolved'. Although it appears that some couples make pre-nuptial contracts, we do not know whether or not this is a good strategy, nor the extent to which prior discussion might forestall problems later on.

In order to begin to elucidate some of the factors that might influence choice of financial system for young people not yet married, Burgoyne and Routh (1999) carried out a study using a series of vignettes describing a couple about to get married. The income levels of the man and woman were varied so that sometimes they were equal, and sometimes one partner earned more than the other. The preliminary findings suggest that the ideology of equality and sharing in marriage is still very strong amongst young people, with many choosing a joint pooling system and allocating personal spending money equally to each partner. However, a significant minority were influenced more by economic factors and the need for autonomy and independence, and chose systems of financial organisation and an allocation of personal spending money that reflected the power of the main earner.

Of course, this was a hypothetical situation, and little is known about how real couples make their day-to-day decisions, or how they manage to resolve any disagreements about resources. (As mentioned earlier, Kirchler's diary study has shed some light on this, but, given the demands of the study, the results are likely to be somewhat biased in the direction of the more articulate members of society.) Much of the work in this area has focused on the economic behaviour of husbands and wives. We do not know whether there are systematic differences between married and cohabiting couples, nor about intergenerational economic behaviour, such as the extent to which there is a net transfer of wealth across generations. However, work done by Cheal (1988) suggests that if there is such a transfer, this is not (as might be supposed) primarily achieved through ritual gifts such as those at Christmas. Other means of intergenerational transfer, such as wedding gifts and bequests, have also begun to be investigated (see, for example, Curasi, Price and Arnould (1997; Heisley, Cours and Wallendorf, 1997; and McGrath and Englis, 1997). What of economic transfers in the opposite direction, such as when grown-up children start work and begin to make a contribution to the household income? What factors influence whether such payments take place, and how much money changes hands?

Money can be a focus for disagreement in marriage (especially remarriage), but do conflicts about money trigger other problems, or are they simply a symptom of other problems within the relationship? James's (1996) study showed that women are not unaware of the potential risks of marital breakdown and divorce, yet (with the exception of remarried couples), few seem to take account of such risks in their financial planning – what inhibits them? Is it simply an optimistic bias (Yates, 1992) – such things happen to other people who do not manage their affairs very well, or is it a fear that focusing on the risk will increase the possibility of its happening? Some people display a similar reluctance to make a will, as if the very act of doing so will bring death nearer. If one partner made plans to cover the risk of marital breakdown, it might be seen as disloyal, or as casting doubt on the stability of the relationship. But what if both partners made the plans together? Could this be reframed as something that caring parents should do in order to protect their children from economic deprivation if the worst happened? Such a reframing has worked in the past for other types of economic planning: Zelizer (1978) describes how buying life insurance in America had to be repackaged as an act of love from the deceased father to his family, in order to overcome public resistance to the idea that a price was being put on someone's death. Future research could investigate whether it is possible to reframe the act of financial planning for divorce in a similar way.

New Problems in the Future

With changes in the global economy and the reduction in welfare provision that is taking place in many Western countries, families may have to face new economic problems as we go into the twenty-first century. For example, in many Western countries, a major new anxiety is the prospect of having to provide for the care of themselves and their relatives in old age, as authorities try to cut the cost of caring for an increasingly aged population. Efforts to reduce public-sector spending commitments have also led governments in Britain to try and reform the state-provided pension scheme, shifting the burden away from the state to individuals, who will have to make their own arrangements for a retirement pension – a very costly course of action since this will mean losing the current contributions from employers and the state. Questions remain about the viability of Britain's National Health Service, and there may be a bigger shift towards private medical insurance. How will families of the future deal with all the complexities of these changes, and how will it affect patterns of employment and inheritance?

One possibility is that it will lead to a greater emphasis on kinship networks in the extended family. This is an aspect of family economic behaviour that might repay further investigation, since the resources and constraints provided by such networks can radically change the patterns and definitions of consumption typically assumed by marketing analyses. For example, the utility of a good (such as a lawnmower) can be stretched far beyond the usual levels if it is shared between a number of households within a kinship network – a process that has been dubbed the 'velocity of circulation' (Fellerman and Debevec, 1993). However, this raises another unresolved problem: how best to study all these processes within families.

The 'lid' has certainly been taken off the household, and investigators are less inclined now to treat the family as an entity, but we cannot confine ourselves to looking just at the individuals either: Nyhus, Kvitastein and Groenhaug (1995) have highlighted some of the difficulties associated with either taking individual responses to survey items, or trying to aggregate those of several individuals within a household. Nor can we avoid the problem by focusing on the different roles within the family. As Finch and Mason (1993) have shown, family responsibilities and obligations cannot simply be 'read off' from the roles of 'mother', 'sister', 'son' and so on. Within the family, economic behaviour seems to interact with the rules of social exchange in complex and subtle ways, and this is a major challenge for future research.

Recent research has barely begun to take account of less conventional families, nor the way that family transitions may impact on social and economic exchange. But Otnes, Zolner and Lowrey (1994) have explored the way that gift giving can be used as a mechanism to mark the changing boundaries of the family after divorce and remarriage. Much of the previous research on financial organisation within families has been done with well-established families, often with dependent children or where children have already grown up and left home. Given the current trends in cohabitation and the number of women who choose either not to have children or to wait until they are in their 30s, there may be a generational change in the way that money is organised. Specialist financial services, such as those catering especially for women (e.g. Fiona Price and Partners – personal communication) indicate that today's young women may be much more clued up about their economic prospects and more inclined to take control of their finances and future financial security than their older counterparts have been able or willing to do (James, 1996). Further research that focuses upon younger couples will be needed to elucidate this.

Finally, much of our current knowledge has been based upon studies carried out in relatively affluent industrialised Western countries, and much more cross-cultural work is needed. For example, Blumberg (1991, p. 21) sets out a general overview of how families operate world-wide, with a continuum in the extent to which women (i) manage to obtain and keep resources and (ii) have the obligation to act as the primary provider for their children. He shows that the internal economy of the household varies according to geographical location, social class and ethnicity, with a growing tendency towards 'separate' rather than 'joint' arrangements for managing money. This suggests that we may have taken the 'lid' off a Pandora's box of research problems.

5

Economic Behaviour in Maturity

It might seem, especially to those readers currently coping with the economic problems facing young adults, that, by comparison, the mature economic agent has it easy. With a steady income, a clear and structured future and well-honed economic and cognitive skills, what real problems do such people face? For a start, some people do not have steady incomes and may be contemplating a very uncertain future: the widespread downsizing and re-engineering of organisations in the 1980s and 1990s has meant redundancy for many – and unemployment at this stage of life can be catastrophic (Darity, Goldsmith and Veum, 1999). Many may still be bewildered participants in an economy that is changing rapidly. They may also be caught in the particular demographic situation of the 1990s to the 2030s, where, relative to previous decades, there will be a very high dependency ratio (the number of people aged over 65 or under 16 divided by those aged 16–64). Leaving these particular issues (which are relevant only to specific cohorts) on one side, it is clear that those in the 'steady state' have their own distinct problems to deal with. They must consolidate their position, plan for the future needs of themselves and their children, and deal with the everyday reality of work. Economic dreams (perhaps more easily indulged in by the young) have to be replaced by economic reality: the loss of flexibility, the need to be economically responsible (changing jobs is more difficult for both internal and external reasons) and the need to deal with one's own limitations are all important. Maturity is a period of consolidation of economic behaviour for many, and individuals can start to take a longer perspective – so it seems entirely appropriate to begin with the issue of expectations.

Expectations

Future expectations are crucial to household decisions about spending now and saving for the future. Decisions made now will be rather different depending on whether one anticipates a future increase in income (if promotion prospects are good or a change of job is in the offing), or a reduction in income (if lay-offs are likely), or if one expects a large increase in expenditure (having to pay university fees, perhaps). One could also talk about this in terms of planning. The question would then be: what determines the content of households' medium- and long-term economic plans (e.g. purchase of consumer durables, pensions, education for children, and so on)? The problem for the individual or household is to adjust the flow of income to the flow of expenditure, and not only to decide what large purchases to make but when to make them.

We'll consider three kinds of evidence that bear on this issue: studies of consumer sentiment (or optimism), rational expectations and 'real' expectations.

Consumer sentiment

Katona introduced the index of consumer sentiment (ICS) in 1946. The ICS is a rather simple and apparently crude measure of consumer optimism: there are a number of questions of the form 'do you feel that your personal financial situation has improved, got worse or stayed the same during the past year?', 'do you feel that this is a good year to buy a new car' and 'do you expect the state of the economy to improve/stay the same/get worse during the coming year?' (Katona, 1975). Some of these items are concerned with the general situation of the economy, others with the household financial situation. Katona was interested not so much in the problem faced by individuals of when to buy goods, as in predicting aggregate expenditure. And he scored economic psychology's first major success when, in 1946, he was able to predict that the USA was about to enter a consumer-led boom and not a recession, which was what conventional economic indicators were suggesting.

There is absolutely no doubt that the ICS can predict the behaviour of the economy. Carroll, Fuhrer and Wilcox (1994) showed that in the United States lagged values of the ICS explain about 14 per cent of the variation in the growth of consumption expenditure over the forty-year period since 1954; Acemoglu and Scott (1994) showed that the explanatory power of the ICS is much greater than this for the period 1974 to 1990 in the United Kingdom, and Locarno and Parigi (1997) that it does a comparable job in Italy for the same period. There is much more debate over the claim that the ICS gives us information that cannot be obtained from conventional economic indicators. Though analyses of the first decade of EEC data were rather negative (e.g. Vanden Abeele, 1983) most recent studies (e.g. Carroll *et al*. 1994; Acemoglu and Scott, 1994; Vuchelen, 1995; Locarno and Parigi, 1997; Eppright, Arguea and Huth, 1998) seem to show that it does, though Carroll *et al*. suggest that the evidence is murky.

Even if it did not add anything to economic indicators, the ICS would still be of psychological interest: if the root causes of economic behaviour were always economic it would still be useful to understand the psychological processes through which they are mediated. Carroll *et al*. suggest one possibility, which is that consumer sentiment might, in part, be a measure of general levels of certainty about the future. Pessimism would indicate uncertainty and economic theory predicts that this would cause consumption to drop as precautionary saving increases. An alternative, suggested by van Raaij and his colleagues (van Raaij and van den Brink, 1987; van Raaij and Gianotten, 1990), is that the ICS is two-dimensional: one component is concerned with the evaluation of the general economic situation, whilst the other is based on an evaluation of the household financial situation. In their studies one of the two components of the ICS (that concerned with the general economic situation) was related to the overall demand for home loans. This makes good sense as optimism about the general economic situation is probably fairly closely linked to expectations that house prices will continue to rise.

That consumer optimism predicts changes in the economy overall is interesting (and useful) but it is surprising then that the issue of where such optimism comes from (other than from real movements in the economy) has scarcely been addressed. Why would an individual feel optimistic and therefore be more inclined to buy a house or furniture? Zullow (1991) suggests that consumer optimism reflects and is influenced by 'culturally transmitted fantasies of hope and despair'. In essence, Zullow proposes that the way in which individuals explain events, and their tendencies to ruminate about bad events (both factors which are implicated in depression) are influenced by the mass media and popular culture. Thus if popular culture dwells on bad events and fosters a pessimistic explanatory style, it will encourage individuals to see the world through grey-tinted spectacles. Zullow shows that the amount of pessimistic rumination found in the lyrics of the top 40 US pop songs predicts, with a time lag, consumer pessimism and movements in the economy. Thus, if the singles charts contain many records like the 1969 Creedance Clearwater Revival song 'Bad Moon Rising' ('I see the bad moon a-rising, I see trouble on the way. I see earthquakes and lightnin', I see bad times today'), this is an early predictor of a recession. This may seem implausible (and it should be noted that this study has not been replicated) but there is other evidence that suggests that the media may play an important role in forming people's economic expectations. Mosley (1982) looked, for example, at the coverage of economic news by three popular British daily newspapers and found that information about any particular economic variable (e.g. inflation, unemployment, rate of exchange) was most frequent when the variable was deteriorating. What is especially relevant about this research was the finding that the economic information presented by the press (e.g. the *Daily Mirror*'s 'shopping clock') was a much better predictor of government popularity than official figures (e.g. the retail price index), which suggests that the media presentation of the economy had a serious impact on people. Similarly, van Veldhoven and Keder (1988) have shown that the number of news items about economic issues in a Dutch daily paper was negatively correlated with the index of consumer sentiment. This makes sense if the Dutch paper acted like the British ones and reported 'bad' economic news more often than 'good' news.

The problem for the mature economic agent is therefore more interesting and challenging than it at first appears. That houses would always go up in price was widely believed in the UK for much of the post-war period. If it is generally believed that house prices are on a rising curve, then it may be a good time to buy. On the other hand, if the expected increase in price is recognised as being, at least in part, dependent on other people's expectations, then the price rise may be a bubble that will burst (Camerer, 1989). House prices did, in fact, fall in the 1980s after many years of sustained increases in both the UK and the Netherlands, creating serious problems for some of those who had chosen to invest in housing just before the crash.

Rational and adaptive expectations

Economists generally use a different approach to expectations, which, as is to be expected, uses the concept of rationality. This is the rational expectations approach, which has revolutionised macro-economics over the past decades. The idea at the heart of rational expectations theory is very simple: it is that people use relevant information to make forecasts of the likely future value of economic variables (such as inflation and unemployment rates) and that, on average, these will be equal to the true values. In other words, people will not make systematic errors in making forecasts, which are the result of current information processed optimally. Muth (1961, p. 376) expressed this idea succinctly – 'expectations, since they are informed predictions of future events are essentially the same as predictions of the relevant economic theory'. This does not mean that people use all possible information nor that all this information is fully processed. But if someone ignores government or Central Bank announcements in forming an expectation of the rate of interest, that person will learn that this is misguided and pay attention to these announcements in the future.

To psychologists this may sound implausible and it may also not be clear why this is important. What it implies is that people will learn to anticipate economic policy changes and change their behaviour as a result. So whilst the traditional macro-economic approach treated the economic policymaker as an engineer (someone playing a game against nature), the rational expectations approach sees the policymaker as being engaged in a game against other players – the participants in the economy. This does not imply that people have a good understanding of economics and know what the consequences of government announcements are. Most people will rely on the media or experts. What it does imply is that on aggregate people will be acting as rational expectations theory predicts.

Rational expectations theory is very important in current macro-economics (for good accounts see Miller, 1994, or Sheffrin, 1996). Our interest, however, is more psychological: how do people solve the problem of forming good expectations so that they make appropriate medium- and long-term decisions? In addition to the rational expectations model, economists have proposed an adaptive expectations model. This assumes that people will use their past forecasting errors to change their current expectations. So in the case of exchange rate expectations (which would be involved in a decision to buy foreign currency for a holiday now or later) this would be expressed as:

expected exchange rate $(t + 1)$ = expected exchange rate $(t) + k$ [actual exchange rate (t) – expected exchange rate (t)]

with k taking a value between zero and one. So if one thought that a euro in 1999 was going to be worth 1.1 dollars but it was actually worth 1 dollar, with a k of 0.5 one would expect the value of a euro next year to be 1.05 dollars. If exchange rates are stable, the value of k would be low, if they are very volatile it will be high. If k is zero, expectations stay the same – if k is one, the expectation is the same as the previous actual exchange rate.

This model of expectation formation may appear reasonable but it actually has some odd features. For instance, it implies that if there are systematic trends in economic variables, expectations will have systematic errors. So, during periods of accelerating inflation, people's expectations of inflation will always lag behind real inflation.

Another model of expectation formation (proposed within psychology) is that predictions and forecasts are extrapolative. Jones (1979) suggests that people identify trends in data (for example, a linear trend from a series that appears to increase at a constant rate or a quadratic trend from one that seems to increase by an ever-increasing amount) and then, using the last data point as an anchor forecast the future based on the trend.

What does the evidence tell us about expectation formation? There is experimental evidence in both psychology and economics and some survey work on experts' expectations of real economic variables (see Wärneryd, 1997 for a good review). None of this evidence provides much support for the rational expectations approach. Anderson and Goldsmith (1994), in a neat study, compared business managers' forecasts of changes in their industry with their own subsequent perception of the situation and found that their expectations failed most tests of rationality. Hey (1994), using standard experimental economic procedures so that participants were motivated to reveal their true expectations of two time series, concluded that people tried to behave rationally but in a way that appears adaptive. Using data from a survey of currency traders and economists in New York and London, where traders had to forecast exchange rates one week, one month, three months or six months in advance, Dutt and Ghosh (1997) and Dutt (1997) show that the rational expectations model is not supported for any time period and that experts' expectations are inconsistent over the longer time-horizon. Finally, Harvey, Bolger and McClelland (1994) carried out a study where students had to forecast the number of passengers (and the number of criminals) for each week on an underground train service. They found that forecasts fit the extrapolative model best and that participants were far too optimistic that their forecasts were correct.

Whilst supporters of rational expectations theory may not be too bothered by this evidence (they will emphasise that the theory is concerned with aggregate expectations and that more knowledge and time is needed for forecasts to become rational), it does suggest that people's expectations may often be wrong and that they may be overoptimistic in their expectations (more on this in the next section).

Real expectations and saving

Expectations about real economic variables (such as one's future income) matter, so it is somewhat surprising that there is little direct data on this issue, though this almost certainly reflects economists' negative opinion of subjective data (see Chapter 1). Dominitz and Manski (1997) point out that the longstanding scepticism about such data is based on a narrow foundation and that properly and precisely worded questions about expectations can be very useful. In their study, survey participants were asked a series of detailed questions about their expected income over the next twelve months to establish their subjective probability distribution of future income. A respondent would report both the lowest and the highest net household income that were possible and then answer questions about the probability that income would be less than a set of thresholds. So, for an individual who was very certain about their household's future income there would be little difference between the highest and lower possible income conceivable. Conversely, someone who was very uncertain would specify very different highest and lowest possible incomes and their subjective probability distribution would be very flat. Dominitz and Manski (1997) report that in their American sample the median responses for the lowest possible income was $30,000 and for the highest possible income $45,000 and that the median difference between the reported highest and lowest possible income was $8,000. The best predictor of income expectations was, unsurprisingly, past income. This is also true in Holland, where income uncertainty decreases with age and is greater if one's partner is also working (Das, 1998). What is striking is that income uncertainty is far greater in the US than it is in Holland or in Italy (Das, 1998).

Das and van Soest (1997) report that Dutch households, particularly those whose income has fallen in the past, *under*estimate their future incomes. At first sight this is a surprising result as there is considerable evidence that people have a tendency to be markedly overoptimistic in a wide variety of domains, including economic matters (Weinstein and Klein, 1996). For example, students see themselves as far more likely to get a good job and salary and far less likely to experience bad events (being fired, having a heart attack) than their fellow students. Individuals have a generally realistic view of the likelihood of divorce in the general population but very idealistic expectations about the longevity of their own marriages (Baker and Emery, 1993). In the economic domain Lea, Webley and Bellamy (1995) found that UK students overestimate their post-graduation spending power and de Meza and Southey (1996) claim that most of the stylised facts about small businesses (e.g. their high failure rate and reliance on bank credit) can be explained by unrealistic optimism on the part of novice small business people. However, Shepperd, Oullette and Fernandez (1996) point out that people may well abandon their optimism when they anticipate feedback. They show that as graduation approaches, final-year students become less optimistic about their future salary and as results day gets closer their forecasts of their exam results shift from being optimistic to being pessimistic. In our view this relates to the importance of optimism (or pessimism) as a strategy. As Armor and Taylor (1998) point out, optimistic beliefs will be held to the extent that they are both believable and personally beneficial. Which is more important will depend on the situation: if predictions are public and easy to verify there will be little optimistic bias whereas if predictions are private and hard to check beliefs may be self-serving in various ways. Optimistic forecasts may, for example, act as a motivator, as with estimates of one's ability to get work done for a deadline. It is interesting that although estimates of how quickly an individual will finish a personal project are often way out, they nonetheless correlate well with actual completion times (Armor and Taylor, 1998). In the Das and van Soest (1997) case, it is clear that underestimating one's future income is also a good strategy: it leads to sensible budgeting.

Being pessimistic and/or uncertain about future household income will obviously affect the financial decisions that people make. Individuals who face greater income uncertainty will consume less. This idea is most clearly articulated in the *buffer-stock* model of saving proposed by Carroll (1992). Carroll takes as his starting point the finding that being prepared for emergencies is usually given as the most important reason for saving in surveys. Figure 5.1 presents some data based on the Dutch socio-economic panel which illustrates this, and some other interesting trends in saving motives (it is worth noting in passing that the relative unimportance of the saving-for-old-age motives probably reflects the quality of social security and pensions provision in the Netherlands). According to Carroll, consumers are at the same time both prudent and impatient (without uncertainty they would choose to consume more than their current income). Buffer-stock savers have a target

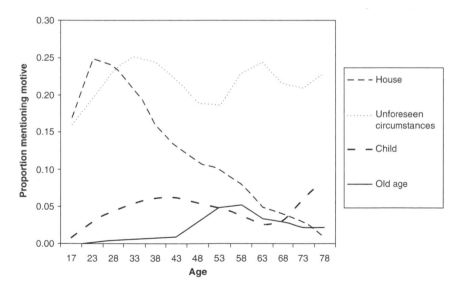

FIGURE 5.1 Motivations for saving across age in the Netherlands
(after Alessie, Lusardi and Aldershof, 1997)

wealth-to-income ratio such that if their wealth is below the target, precaution will dominate impatience and they will save. If their wealth is above the target, impatience will dominate precaution and they will dissave (that is, spend out of accumulated savings).

Saving is very important to mature households, as is evident in Figure 5.2, which gives a picture of the situation in Holland. In the US, average saving increases with age until the 50s or 60s and then drops. Tables 5.1. and 5.2 illustrate this and Table 5.1 also shows a decline in saving across the decade. What is also clear is that the median level of saving is low and many households do not save at all. A huge proportion of total saving in the American economy is due to very high-income families. Education is also important: in households where no one has a college degree saving is very low indeed. If one looks at different kinds of households, savings rates are higher for married couples with no children, lower for those with children, and lowest for single parents (Browning and Lusardi, 1996). For those households where marriages stay intact there is a big increase in assets (over 7 per cent a year) whereas for divorced households it was half this.

These data raise the question of why so many households save so little. It should be noted in passing that although the decline in saving rates shown in these data is also found in other Western countries (see Maital and Maital, 1977), there are also marked variations in saving rates across countries, and savings rates are much higher in, for example, Japan and Singapore. Though there are many possible explanations as to why households save so little in the West (for example, the existence of state or insurance-linked provision of medical care and old-age pensions), our preferred explanation is that there has been a cultural change. Whereas in the past a 'thrift

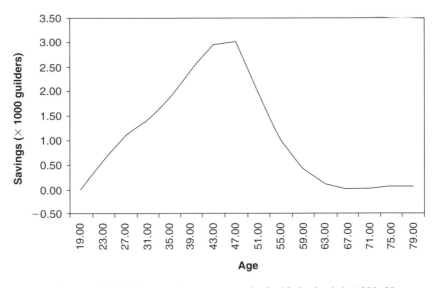

FIGURE 5.2 Median savings across age in the Netherlands in 1988–89

TABLE 5.1 *Percentage savings rates by age*

Age	25–34	35–44	45–54	55–64	65+
Savings ratio 1972/3	9.5	12.1	16.8	22.9	14.9
Savings ratio 1982/5	9.6	8.6	10.5	15.8	11.5

Source: Bosworth, Burtless and Sabelhaus, 1991
Note: saving equals income minus consumption.

TABLE 5.2 *Saving levels by age*

Age	25–34	35–44	45–54	55–64	65–69	Over 70
Mean saving	13,300	14,800	18,700	22,400	30,500	1,400
Median saving	2,400	3,200	4,200	500	500	–500

Source: Avery and Kennickell, 1991
Note: that saving equals 1986 wealth minus 1983 wealth.

ethic' was dominant and people would save up for large items, now Western society is more credit-oriented and people believe in enjoying now and paying later (Bernheim, 1991; Webley and Nyhus, 2000).

Individual Differences and Economic Behaviour

Individuals face different situations and different problems. They also develop different ways of dealing with these problems as well as having markedly different ways of approaching the economic world (though it must be acknowledged that we do not know how enduring these consumption/budgeting styles are). Individual differences matter throughout the life-span: some children are very careful with their money whilst others spend freely; some young adults are impulsive shoppers whilst others buy only after comparing all the alternatives; some 40-year-olds will make financial plans for their retirement whilst others, in similar economic circumstances, do not. But it is perhaps in economic maturity, when dispositions are well established that their influence is at its strongest.

Although it is possible to measure relevant dispositions, attitudes and styles of behaving and to explore the impact of individual differences, integrating individual differences into theoretical accounts of economic behaviour has proved to be extremely difficult. We can distinguish four different approaches to the study of individual differences within economic psychology. The first, and probably the most popular, involves devising typologies of consumers. These may be based on case studies and qualitative analysis or quantitative data and the use of techniques like cluster analysis. An example of a qualitative typology is that of Goldberg and

Lewis (1978), who take a psycho-analytic approach to people's dealing with money, and come up with a variety of types of consumer, such as the 'self-denier', the 'love-seller' and the 'godfather' (someone who buys loyalty and devotion). The second approach is to investigate individual differences in specific dimensions that fit with economic theory. So one might measure an individual's time preferences (how far they value money in the present compared to money in the future) and link this to saving behaviour (e.g. Daniel, 1997; Nyhus, 1997) or explore how differences in expectations of future income relate to indebtedness (e.g. Webley and Nyhus, 1999). The third approach is to study individual differences that may be plausibly related to economic behaviour. Thus non-materialists are more likely to give money from a windfall to a charity than materialists (Richins and Dawson, 1992) and there are links between general coping style and how people deal with reductions in household income (Walker, 1997). The final approach is to integrate the study of individual differences in economic behaviour with general personality theory (e.g. Brandstätter, 1997).

The relevance of individual differences to the theme of this book, that is, how people deal with the economic problems they face, should be clear. If we want to explain how people solve and cope with everyday economic problems we need to know what resources and dispositions they bring to the situation. If you lose your job you can cope in a variety of ways but which you choose will probably relate to dispositional differences. If you tend to be generally pessimistic about the future, regardless of the economic situation, you may consequently also tend to save more; if you are conscientious (or perhaps overly subservient) you may end up working longer hours than are good for you.

Here we will deal with an example of each approach to individual differences in turn and then make some general comments at the end.

Typologies of consumers

There are a vast number of typologies of consumers: Flouri (2000) provides a comprehensive review and Furnham and Gunter (1992) give a good summary of work in psychographics (consumer profiles). Most of these are completely atheoretical and many are designed for the sole purpose of helping firms to market their particular products more effectively. The typologies (certainly those originated by marketing firms) are themselves products – and one of the reasons for the proliferation and continued existence of such consumer typologies is that those responsible for them make money out of them. We might hope that good science would ultimately drive out the bad science but marketing firms are effectively insulated from the academic community and operate according to different rules. For example, the norm of confidentiality and providing a service to a client to give a commercial advantage conflict with scientific norms of openness and access for all. So it is possible, unfortunately, for typologies to be sustained in the commercial world whilst being of little scientific value.

So, we propose to use as an example of a typological approach to individual differences, one that is *not* commercially driven. This is what could be labelled the Stockholm school's approach to financial management, which has been developed over the last twenty years. This was initiated by the work of Lindqvist (1981), who proposed a hierarchy of saving needs based on Maslow's theory (Maslow, 1943). According to Lindqvist, there are four kinds of saving needs. The most basic is the need for cash management, which gives rise to savings that consist of money that is as yet unspent. The next need is to have a buffer against the unexpected (saving for a rainy day), then the need to have a large sum of money to pay for something expensive like a car (goal-directed saving), and finally there is the need to manage wealth. Wärneryd (1983) suggested that there may be distinct types of savers on the basis of this hierarchy of saving needs, an idea that was tested by Wahlund and Wärneryd (1988). They carried out a cluster analysis on some survey data of household economic behaviour and identified four groups of savers which roughly corresponded to the saver types proposed. Thus the cash-managers had low income and small savings that were used to settle bills, and the wealth-managers had high incomes and very large savings that were expected to grow. Though the other two groups behaved as expected as far as their saving was concerned, their other characteristics were not as expected. So the goal-directed savers were the oldest group and the buffer savers had the lowest income and were the youngest group.

This work has been developed by Gunnarson and Wahlund (1993, 1997). In their 1993 paper they also report finding four groups of savers – cash-managers (low income, few assets), buffer savers (with slightly higher incomes this time), wealth-directed savers, and a group characterised not as goal-directed savers but 'gamblers' who had chosen to invest in riskier assets. These groups differed in their time preferences and risk aversion, with cash-managers being more risk-averse and more impatient than the other groups. Gunnarson and Wahlund (1997) provide a different kind of typological analysis. They claim that Swedish households follow one of six types of financial strategies. By far the most common was the residual saving strategy, where households had few forms of saving and relied on liquid savings forms. Types of savings which involved medium- or long-term commitment were very rare. Those following the contractual saving strategy, followed by 22 per cent of households, relied on different types of loans and credit and had large amounts of debt. Security savers invested heavily in retirement-related investment schemes and avoided riskier investments. The other three strategies (risk-hedging, prudent investing, 'divergent' strategies) were each followed by less than 10 per cent of households.

This typological work is helpful ground-clearing but, in our view, is far too descriptive and too static. Though Gunnarson and Wahlund (1997) do relate their financial strategies to the life-cycle, this analysis is itself only descriptive. So we are told, for example, that a 'clear majority of both the young single households without dependants and the retired households practise a residual saving strategy' (1997, p. 231). No attempt is made to explain how and why an individual may move from using one strategy (or from meeting one saving need) to another. We believe that a good typology needs to be linked with a good theory. This would help to answer the question of how did individual or household x become type y, and, furthermore, what is the chance of household x changing into type z at a later date.

Economically relevant individual differences

Some economic theories invoke concepts and characteristics that, as psychologists, we recognise can vary greatly between individuals. Good examples are risk aversion (implicated in theories of labour supply, in theories of consumer search and at the heart of utility theory) and time preference (which is relevant to a wide range of theories dealing with choices across time). In these cases it is clear how economic theory and individual differences can be integrated: we can measure the characteristic directly (and predict certain economic behaviours as a consequence) or infer it from behaviour and again predict and generalise from this. This involves making certain assumptions, of course – that, for instance, people's preference for risk is reasonably stable and consistent across time and across different domains. Here we will consider only work on time preference to see how this approach works out in practice (for a survey of the literature on risk see Lopes, 1994).

Many of the choices we make are between outcomes that occur at different times. Students have to make a choice between regular revelry and a poor examination performance and evening studying and a better examination performance. Paul has to decide whether to spend money now on some necessary house repairs or save up for next summer's holiday (the holiday will win). And the mature economic agent is faced with the choice of spending all their money now or investing some of it in a pension that he or she may not live to enjoy. These are all *intertemporal* choices.

Economic theory assumes that people will prefer to get things of equivalent value now rather than in the future (they will *discount* the future), for a number of reasons. First, the future is inherently uncertain: goods that are promised may not arrive and one may not be around to enjoy them. So a person needs to take into account the probabilities of default or their own death in calculating the present value of something promised for the future. Second, if positive real interest rates are available, 100 euros now is worth less than 100 euros in a year's time (with a 3 per cent real interest rate 100 euros invested now is equivalent to 103 euros in a year). And, thirdly. people need to take into account the probable change in the price of the good (in the case of money this is the inflation rate). So, in inflationary periods money now is worth more than money in the future. On top of all these factors people generally show 'time preference proper' – that is, all other things being equal, they have a strong preference for things now rather than in the future.

All these things contribute to an individual's subjective discount rate, which gives a measure of the extent to which a person prefers consumption now to consumption in the future. The discount rate is given by the formula:

$$r = 100 \times (((V_f/V_p) - 1) \times 12/t)$$

where r is the discount rate, V_f is the future value, V_p is the present value and t is the time delay in months. The way this works can be shown using a study by Lea (1978), though the discount rates he obtained are atypically high. He showed people two envelopes and asked them to imagine that one contained a cheque for £5 which could be cashed immediately, whilst the other contained a cheque for £10 dated for some time in the future. The question posed was how far in the future the cheque for £10 would have to be dated for them to prefer to have £5 now. The median answer to this question was two months. This gives a discount rate of:

$$r = 100 \times (((10/5) - 1) \times 12/2) = 100 \times 6 = 600 \text{ per cent}$$

Other studies (e.g. Daniel, 1997; Nyhus, 1997) typically give much lower and more reasonable discount rates (the highest median rate that Nyhus reports is 20 per cent).

Most economic theories are based on the assumption that market interest rates reflect the aggregate time preferences of the individual members of an economy, or, to put it another way, that the subjective discount rate is the same across individuals and situations. If this assumption is relaxed, it is possible to measure subjective discount rates directly (usually by presenting people with hypothetical alternatives) and then see if they are related to behaviour in the way one would expect. The problem is that the subject discount rate does not seem to be constant across situations (Loewenstein and Thaler, 1988) and it is very difficult to devise a satisfactory measure of time preferences (Nyhus 1997). In Nyhus's study, for example, time preferences were measured using a number of paired questions in which the time period and the size of the delayed reward were varied across three situations (delayed payment, delayed receipt of money, speeding-up receipt of money). So, for example, a delayed-payment item might ask the respondent to imagine that they had to settle a tax bill and give them the option of paying in full now or paying extra for the right to settle the bill in three months' time. Nyhus found that there were distinct discount rates for delayed payment and speeding-up receipt.

Despite the measurement difficulties there have been some intriguing findings. Green and his colleagues (Green, Fry and Myerson, 1994; Green, Myerson and Ostaszewski, 1999) for example, have found that the discount rate drops with age (from childhood to older adulthood), which mirrors the finding in the delay of gratification literature that younger children find this more difficult than older children (Mischel and Metzner, 1962), and predicts that adults will show greater self-control and find behaviours that involve self-control, such as saving, easier. Those individuals with lower discount rates tend to save more (Gunnarson and Wahlund, 1994), are more likely to be regular savers (Daniel, 1997), and are less likely to be in debt (Webley and Nyhus, 1999).

This evidence is not that compelling but we feel that this approach is worth pursuing since the individual differences in subjective discount rate (SDR, not always called that, it has to be said) have been found to be important in many other areas of psychology. In health psychology, differences in SDR predict smoking and heavy drinking (Vuchinich and Simpson, 1998; Keough, Zimbardo and Boyd, 1999) and being present-oriented (and lacking self-control) is at the heart of Gottfredson and Hirschi's (1990) general theory of crime.

Individual differences that may be plausibly related to economic behaviour

Given the rather empiricist nature of economic psychology, it should come as no surprise that researchers have often tried to link a wide variety of individual differences in dispositions to particular economic behaviours. This is occasionally done on a very ad hoc basis but has sometimes been part of a sustained programme of research. So the link between need for achievement and entrepreneurship was an essential part of McClelland's overall approach (McClelland, 1961) and that between egoism (or self-servingness) and tax evasion and other economic crime has been a continuing theme of the work of Hessing and Elffers (e.g. Elffers, 1991; Hessing *et al.*, 1993; Weigel, Hessing, and Elffers, 1999). The Protestant work ethic has also been of longstanding interest (see Furnham, 1990). Here we will briefly describe recent work on materialism: the literature on need for achievement is covered in Lea, Tarpy and Webley (1987) and briefly summed up by Gilliard (1998); that on the work ethic is discussed in great detail by Furnham (1990).

Materialism is generally seen as a tendency to value and covet worldly possessions and has three important elements (Richins and Rudmin, 1994). First, materialists put possessions and the acquisition of possessions at the heart of their lives: as Csikszentmihalyi and Rochberg-Halton (1981, p. 231) wrote, 'consumption for the sake of consumption becomes a fever'. Second, possessions are seen by materialists as necessary for their well-being and are the most important sources of satisfaction in their life. And thirdly, materialists tend to judge others and themselves in terms of the number and quality of possessions owned. Belk (1985) was the first to develop a measure of materialism, which assessed the traits of envy, possessiveness and non-generosity. Recently, he has developed an improved materialism scale, which includes a fourth element, 'preservation' (the conservation of memories and events in material form). Richins (Richins and Dawson, 1992; Richins and Rudmin, 1994) has taken a rather different approach, and the scale she has developed measures the three characteristics described above (acquisition centrality, acquisition as essential for happiness, success defined by possessions) directly. Materialism has also been explored at a societal level (e.g. Inglehart, 1990) though that is not our concern here.

Many links have been found between individuals' scores on materialism scales and economic (and other) behaviours. Compared to non-materialists, materialists are less satisfied with their lives in general and particularly with their income and standard of living (Belk, 1985). They have poorer mental health and social adjustment (Kasser and Ryan, 1993). They are more likely to value possessions for appearance-related reasons – so their most important possessions are those that are expensive and publicly rather than privately consumed (Richins, 1994). Materialists report that they would be more likely to spend windfalls on things for themselves than for others (friends or charities) (Richins and Dawson, 1992). Materialists also tend to show both impulse buying (Rook, 1987) and compulsive buying (O'Guinn and Faber, 1989) and are more likely to end up in debt (Walker, 1996).

Flouri (2000) has claimed that materialism is not a unitary concept. Based on quantitative studies of the attitudes and beliefs of adolescents, she suggests that there are two types of materialists: archetypical materialists (who dream of being wealthy, are vain, are interested in style and fashion, buy on impulse, and tend to be dissatisfied with what they buy) and 'less knowledgeable' materialists, who, whilst also being very interested in possessions, buy quality items which are good value for money and are satisfied with their purchases. More importantly, she (and others) have tried to uncover the causes of a materialistic disposition and look at its development in individuals. Kasser et al. (1995), for example, have found that coming from a poorer background and having a non-nurturant mother who herself values material success were associated with the development of materialistic values. Flouri (1999) also found that a mother's materialism and the family communication style were linked to materialism in adolescents.

Though there is a long way to go we are getting closer to having a decent theoretical account of the causes and consequences of individual materialism and we feel that there is considerable merit in this approach. However, at the moment at least, it is hard to see how this can be integrated with economic theory.

Personality theory and economic behaviour

Rather than look to economic theory for appropriate individual difference dimensions (pp. 110–112), it is possible to look to personality theory. This approach has been strongly advocated by Brandstätter (1993, 1995, 1997), who has explored the relationship between personality and entrepreneurship, time spent working, saving and behaviour within experimental games. Brandstätter argues that economic psychologists should make use of well-established and comprehensive systems of personality factors and not use specific narrow-range constructs. He favours Cattell's second-order factors or the so-called big five personality dimensions (McCrae and Costa, 1987), which now represent the conventional wisdom in psychometrics. These five personality dimensions are extraversion, agreeableness, conscientiousness, emotional stability (the opposite of neuroticism) and intellect. They are supposed to subsume other more specific traits such as impulsiveness vs. self-control, so stable introverts would be high and unstable (neurotic) extraverts low on this dimension.

The evidence gathered by Brandstätter and others certainly suggests that these personality dimensions are predictors of economic behaviour, though their impact is often rather slight. He reports that those couples high on conscientiousness (especially if they are also high on introversion) have positive attitudes to saving and tend to save more. Wärneryd (1999) also found, in an analysis of the CentER panel (see Chapter 1) that conscientiousness had a significant indirect influence on both intentions to save and actual reported saving behaviour. However, Hurd and Swallen (1997), who used an American data set on saving in the elderly found no relationships whatsoever between personality factors and saving. Nonetheless, on balance, conscientiousness does seem to matter. Webley and Nyhus (1999) found that it was a good predictor of not being in debt, Routh and Burgoyne (1991) that it correlated negatively with absentmindedness with money, and Brandstätter and Güth (1998) that it correlated with saving within an experimental game.

Other personality factors are implicated in different domains. In Brandstätter's (1997) study of Austrian small businesses, for example, there were clear differences between those who were founders of a company (the original entrepreneurs) and those who had inherited companies. The former were more stable (that is, less neurotic) and more independent.

As well as the big five personality factors, there are other very well-established traits, perhaps the most relevant being 'locus of control'. Locus of control refers to generalised expectancies about one's ability to control events in life. Those who believe that most events depend upon their actions are described as having an 'internal' locus of control; those who believe that the events in their lives depend on fate, luck, chance or outside agencies have an 'external' locus of control. Not surprisingly, entrepreneurs have been found in a number of studies to have internal locus of control (see Wärneryd, 1988), as do well-educated tax-evaders (Groenland and van Veldhoven, 1983). Those in debt show evidence of having an external locus of control (Livingstone and Lunt, 1992), though this may simply relate to their general standard of living, since the poor have been shown to be 'external' (Lewis, Webley and Furnham, 1995).

This approach has the advantage of being based on well-established psychological theory but, in practice, the relationships between personality factors and economic behaviour are much less clear than one would wish. The explanations given for the relationships are in some cases rather convoluted and, for the most part, the evidence is entirely correlational. This kind of approach can be used for market segmentation but it is harder to see how personality and economic theory can be profitably fused.

Buying: The Mature Consumer

Mature consumers have thirty or more years of experience in buying a huge range of goods, from everyday necessities like food and drink, through to less-frequently purchased (and more expensive) goods such as cars, washing machines, computers and the like. They have been exposed to enormous amounts of information about goods, from advertising and marketing, from other people and from consumer organisations. They have the capacity to process this information sensibly and have developed buying strategies to help them do the best they can. So, given all of this, one might expect that the behaviour of this group of consumers would correspond most closely to that of economic man. In solving the problems of what to buy and when to buy it, their behaviour should approximate to that described by micro-economic theory.

We will look at just three areas to see if this is the case or if other kind of theories do a better job. First, we'll consider some real consumer behaviour – the purchase of consumer durables, then we'll look at economic choices made in the laboratory, and finally consider collecting.

Consumer durables – when are they acquired and when are they replaced?

Aspects of people's first purchases of consumer durables were discussed in Chapter 3 – here we deal with the order in which such goods are acquired and with replacement purchases. It is worth describing at the outset what proportion of households own certain goods (this is usually called the 'penetration' of a commodity). These figures obviously vary considerably from country to country and from one historical period to another, but are of some psychological interest as they give some indication of what consumers, in aggregate, are most interested in. For example, in Ireland, in 1998, whilst 99 per cent of households had televisions, 86 per cent had telephones, 79 per cent had a video-recorder, 68 per cent had a microwave oven, 27 per cent had a dishwasher and 10 per cent had a video camera (Medialive, 1999). The figures for Japan, in 1999, are similar but do reflect differences in the importance placed on different goods: so whilst a very similar proportion of households (78 per cent) had a video-recorder, far more had a microwave oven (93 per cent) and a video camera (36 per cent) (Statistics Bureau, 2000). This suggests that entertainment is more important than saving effort by using a dishwasher but also reflects a cultural difference in the importance of recording personal events.

Not very surprisingly, there is an underlying common order in which goods are acquired, and although this varies a little from one social group to another (e.g. those who own houses compared to those who rent), these differences are minimal (Soutar and Cornish Ward, 1997). Clarke and Soutar's (1982) results for Australia are typical: the standard order of acquisition they report is: fridge, vacuum cleaner, washing machine, first TV, toaster, first car, hi-fi, video, microwave, lawnmower, second car, deep freeze, food processor, clothes dryer. In Western Australia a deep freeze comes higher up the list for obvious climatic reasons. Dickson, Lusch and Wilkie (1983) conclude that consumers do have plans to acquire things in a specific order, though they point out that the order of acquisition can, in the main, be inferred from penetration figures.

Consumer durables do not last for ever, so at some point a household is faced with the problem of when to discard and replace them. Antonides (1988) has done some interesting work on this issue and has looked explicitly at the scrapping and replacing of washing machines. In the first of his studies, 109 people who had recently replaced a washing machine were interviewed and the machines that they had discarded were repaired and tested. This showed that about one-third of the broken-down washing machines could have been repaired at a reasonable price, which suggests that it is the perceived, rather than the actual costs of repair, that are crucial. His second study used a very large sample (over 1,000) of consumers who owned washing machines that were over five years old (machines newer than this are unlikely to break down). Respondents were interviewed and were asked to notify the researcher if their machine broke down, in which case breakdown reports were collected and they were interviewed again. Based on this data, Antonides concludes that people's decisions to scrap or repair washing machines probably are rational, but he makes a couple of important points along the way. The first is that the estimated value of the subjective discount rate from his data is 21 per cent, which is very high, and well above market interest rates. However, those who expect their income to improve over the next year (the optimists) have a higher discount rate (30 per cent) whilst those who are pessimistic have a lower rate (16 per cent), which is what one would expect (if one expects a rising income in the future one should value extra consumption in the present more). Similarly, those who are saving have a lower discount rate than non-savers (as we would expect from the work described earlier, pp. 110–112). The second point made by Antonides is that after a repair people have much more optimistic expectations of the remaining lifetime of a washing machine than before the breakdown, which he interprets as due to cognitive dissonance (in order to justify the costs of repair one has to imagine that the machine will last longer).

This study may give the impression that consumers usually replace goods when they break down or wear out. Actually, this is not the most important reason for replacing consumer durables. Wilkie and Dickson (1985, cited in Marell, Davidsson and Gärling, 1995) point out that over 60 per cent of replacement purchases of freezers, washing machines and refrigerators are made for reasons other than product failure. As far as the timing of replacement is concerned, the most important factor for colour televisions is simply the market price, though new features and styling also matter (Bayus, 1988). With car-owners, those who replace early tend to do so for styling reasons whereas those who replace later do so for cost-related reasons (e.g. that the annual cost of repairs is increasing) (Bayus, 1991).

More recently, Raymond, Beard and Gropper (1993) have looked at Americans' decisions to replace home heating systems. Their sample consisted of over 500 households in the south-eastern US. They found that the probability of replacement depended on the age of the head of household, expected system-use and the age of the system. If the head of the household was young, the expected use higher than anticipated and the system itself was old, it was much more likely to be replaced (which is exactly what economic theory would predict).

'Ownership' in the laboratory

One feature that might be relevant to the decision to replace a consumer durable (at least, one that is working well) is what has been called the *status quo bias* (Samuelson and Zeckhauser, 1988). This is simply a preference for the current state, whatever it may be. Samuelson and Zeckhauser showed that, in a variety of hypothetical choice tasks, an alternative is much more popular when it is described as the status quo, and that this effect is stronger the more alternatives there are. So, in a typical scenario, an individual has inherited a large sum of money from an uncle and must decide how to invest it: in one instance the investment options are presented in a neutral way whilst in another the scenario specifies how exactly the portfolio is currently made up. In the latter version, there is a preference to leave the portfolio as it is. This effect is also apparent with real decisions. Hartman, Doane and Woo (1991) report that when electric power consumers were asked about their preferences for different combinations of service reliability and rates (and told that their answers would help determine future company policy), the majority choose the status quo as their first choice. Those who had high reliability (but at a higher price) preferred this and those who had a cheaper but less reliable service also opted for the current state of affairs. The differences in income and electricity consumption between the two groups were minor.

Kahneman, Knetsch and Thaler (1991) consider the status quo bias to be a good demonstration of the importance of reference points in economic behaviour (as is the closely related endowment effect – see p. 11) and loss aversion (the tendency to weight losses more heavily than gains). One possible economic explanation for this bias is that when an individual owns an object, all of his or her preference functions are based, to some extent, on possessing it. If the object is lost or sold the preference functions would have to be recomputed, which is psychologically costly (Ortona and Scacciati, 1992). This would suggest that individuals should not overevaluate an object as soon as they obtain it (although most evidence suggests that they do) and an asset should increase in value the longer it is in someone's possession. The latter does seem to be the case. Strahilevitz and Loewenstein (1998) carried out a series of studies with Israeli high-school students to see to how the history of past ownership of an object (in this case a key ring) affected its value. They found that whilst simply possessing a key ring for a few minutes did increase its subjective value, owning it for hours greatly magnified the effect. Prior possession of an object which an individual no longer owned also increased its value and this effect was also greater the longer the object had been owned. They discuss two possible explanations of why duration of ownership would increase the value a person places on an asset. First, this could be the result of familiarity: the longer one has owned something the more time one has had to think about its desirable characteristics. Second, if people see objects as extensions of the self (as Belk, 1988, has argued), any possession becomes more attractive as there is a general tendency to make self-enhancing judgements.

Whilst it seems plausible that a key ring might be seen as an extension of the self, this seems unlikely, on the face of it, to be true of washing machines or heating systems (where function is much more important than display). And in these cases one is not losing or trading an object, but replacing it with something very similar and probably rather better. In a laboratory study Chapman (1998) shows that people are very willing to trade for an identical item, slightly less willing to trade for a similar item and much less willing to trade for a dissimilar item. So perhaps, after all, status quo biases are not so relevant to the decision to replace consumer durables as might be thought.

'Special' ownership: collecting in maturity

Economic factors might be expected to dominate the market for consumer durables. For a different kind of perspective on consumer behaviour in maturity we can look at collecting. Whilst it is true that this becomes less important in adolescence (see Chapter 3), for some individuals collecting is a very important part of their life. Why? What function does this behaviour serve?

Collecting in adulthood is not, despite popular stereotypes, an unusual activity confined to misfits, though it is a predominantly male activity (Olmsted, 1991). Belk (1995b) claims that one-third of Americans are collectors and that two-thirds of American households contain collectors. When asked why they collect, the four most common reasons are concerned with the self, sociability (relating to other collectors), making links with the past, and excitement (the thrill of tracking down rare items) (Formanek, 1991). Only one of Formanek's respondents referred to collecting as a strategy to counteract low spirits: most of those who gave 'self' reasons saw collecting as a challenge or as a way of maintaining self-esteem. As one antiques collector said, 'collecting serves as an extension of the collector and his creativity' (ibid., p. 281). So collections seem to provide access to a whole social world in which individuals can develop and maintain self-esteem and which give meaning to their life. What is interesting is how they enter this world. For the vast majority of stamp, car and gun collectors this is a consequence of a youthful passionate interest and attachment to the collected object rather than recruitment into the activity. The object comes first and the social world comes later. And collectors seem to begin collecting rather young or in middle age – few stamp collectors start collecting between the ages of 15 and 35 (Olmsted, 1991).

What this creates is what has been called the 'paradox of collecting' (Danet and Katriel, 1987, cited by Olmsted, 1991). This is that both collectors and others see collecting as 'crazy' but most collectors behave in a sensible and practical way. There is no paradox, of course: the objective of the collector may seen odd or even mad to the non-collector but given this objective the associated behaviour is perfectly rational. Having said that, it is the case that collecting can present problems for some individuals. Some collectors are out of control and their collecting is a form of addiction (Belk, 1995b). But, for them, a different kind of theory is probably needed.

Work and Unemployment

The changing nature of work?

In recent years there has been much public debate in the Western world about the changing nature of work. This is seen as involving a shift from lifetime employment with one company or institution to what has been called the 'boundaryless career' (Mirvis and Hall, 1994), where during their lifetime workers have many employers and several career cycles. It is seen as involving increased flexibility, where instead of working a standard 35- or 40-week on a nine-to-five basis, employees are able to work a wide range of hours and work of various degrees of part-timeness is widely available. It is claimed that work is becoming more knowledge-based and organisations becoming less hierarchical (Handy, 1984). These changes raise many issues (far more than we can possibly consider here) but we will concentrate first on what light they shed on the most basic question of all: why do people work? Specifically, we will look at why the mature worker works the hours he or she does, as this gives some idea of the constraints facing individuals as they try to solve this particular problem.

Before we do so, it is important to put our discussion on a firm empirical base. First, it is not the case that job stability has actually changed that much. After reviewing the literature on the 'boundaryless career', Smith (1997) concludes that the evidence that people are changing careers and occupations at an increasing rate is very weak. Swinnerton and Wial (1995), whose work is often cited in this regard, did find a slight and significant decrease in job stability between 1987 and 1991 in the US but point out themselves that this is not strong evidence for a trend.

Second, as far as flexibility is concerned, there is some evidence that this has increased, but not by large amounts. Rainnie (1998) reports that those categorised as flexible labour (temporary and part-time workers) accounted for 30 per cent of the total labour force in the UK in 1981, a figure that had risen to 38 per cent in 1993. But the bulk of this change took place in the 1980s and permanent full-time jobs are reappearing in the 1990s. So, to some extent, accounts of changes in work have been overdramatised. There is, however, clear evidence of the intensification of work. Many modern work practices, such as just-in-time, increase people's work rates and, as we shall see, there has been a significant squeeze on people's leisure time in recent years.

Time spent working

Classical economic theory assumes that people work in order to earn money. In deciding how many hours to work, an individual has to trade off leisure time against the money he or she can earn at work. The more hours that are worked, the more money a person has to spend but the less time they have to enjoy the fruits of their labours. So how long do people spend working? Those people in full-time jobs usually have to work, as a minimum, the number of hours in the conventional working week. They are not free to work the number of hours they like. It is clear that despite increases in flexibility, most work is still nine to five: this was true in the Netherlands in the mid-1990s for example (Breedveld, 1998).

Bell and Hart (1998) used the New Earnings Survey to provide a detailed analysis of working time in the UK over the past twenty years. They report that between 1975 and 1994 standard weekly hours for males show a slight downward trend (from 39 to 38.3 hours). The mean total hours worked is higher than this (between 41.5 and 43) and varies directly with the business cycle. About 40 per cent of men work overtime, and some do a great deal: over 4 per cent of workers in the transport industry work more than 25 hours overtime per week and between 5 and 10 per cent of workers in a wide range of industries work more than 12 hours of overtime. This overtime is more common in males in the 30s and 40s, which may reflect increased family financial commitments. In the United States, according to the official figures, there has been little change in weekly hours worked since the 1970s, though the proportion of people with a very long working week has increased. Leete and Schor (1994), however, show, using panel studies of time-use, that there is evidence of a 'time-squeeze' and that for certain groups the total annual hours worked has risen by 149. Schor (1991, p. 1) puts this more dramatically and claims that 'in the last twenty years the amount of time Americans have spent at their jobs has risen steadily. Each year the change is small, amounting to about nine hours . . . but the accumulated increase over two decades is substantial.'

Why has there been this increase in the amount worked? Is it that people simply want more money and are happy to have less time to spend it in? Does this finding indicate that work has become more enjoyable? Schor (1991) argues that there is a 'work and spend cycle' based on a growth in materialism that has a tendency to drive up people's working hours. People work more (as employers demand), earn more, spend more, luxuries become necessities, so people work more to earn more, and so on. Rhetoric aside, there is evidence that people are working more hours than they would like. Stewart and Swaffield (1997) use questions on the British Household Panel Survey to show that this is true of manual workers in the UK. Respondents are asked to say whether, assuming that they would earn the same amount per hour as at present, they would prefer to work fewer, the same or more hours than they do now. Of those male employees aged 21–64, 36 per cent would prefer to work less; for manual workers the figures were 38.8 per cent less, 52.8 per cent the same and 8.4 per cent more. Those who work overtime have an even stronger preference to work less. Stewart and Swaffield argue that employees work more hours than they would like because of job insecurity, fear of redundancy and the scarcity of suitable alternative jobs. This account implicitly emphasises the power of the employer (it is worth noting that British men work far longer hours than men in other European countries and that there has been a relative increase in the power of employers in the UK over the last two decades). However, it is at least as plausible that some of the increase in working hours is a result of the stimulation of demand by marketers and advertisers (George, 1997) and is voluntary. And for managers, some of the increase in hours is determined by positional striving to keep up with and outperform others in the organisation (Eastman, 1998).

The excessive length of the working week has led to some people 'downshifting' (Schor, 1991): that is, adjusting both household income and expenditure downwards, by moving to jobs with less pay but with more free time. But, as Etzioni (1998) says, there is not that much evidence of this phenomenon. Apparently 28 per cent of a national sample of Americans reported in 1995 that they had voluntarily made changes which resulted in a lower income, but these changes (e.g. reducing work hours, moving to lower-paid jobs) do not necessarily indicate 'downshifting'. Getting off the working treadmill is obviously not an easy problem to solve.

Unemployment in mid-life

In Chapter 3 we pointed out that although there has been a lot of research into unemployment it is quite difficult to extract clear findings from this literature. This is as true for unemployment in mid-life as it is for youth unemployment. It is important at the outset to provide some descriptive background on who is unemployed in the 1990s. In nearly all of the OECD countries males between 25 and 49 are generally less affected by unemployment than others. But the unemployment rates for other groups in society differ considerably from country to country. In the UK the typical unemployed person is young, low-skilled, lives in the North and has a background in manufacturing or construction (Clark and Layard, 1993), whereas in Spain the main body of the unemployed consists of women who have already had a job and either stopped to have children or been made redundant (Toharia, 1994). In the UK, whatever the overall unemployment rate over the past twenty years, unemployment in the 25–54 age-group has typically been about half of the rate for the 18–24-year-olds. Only 50 per cent of unemployed men are married and only 24 per cent of them have two or more children.

A distinctive feature of the European labour market over the past twenty years has been the emergence of long-term unemployment. The proportion of people who are out of work for more than a year is far higher in the European Union (between 40 and 75 per cent of the overall unemployed) than it is in other OECD countries, such as the USA, Australia, Japan or New Zealand. It is less than 10 per cent in the USA and Canada. This has been attributed to various factors, but in particular the rigidities in the European labour market compared to the relatively unregulated North American market (Benoit-Guilbot, 1994).

Unemployment – individual risk factors

Before considering the relationship between individual characteristics and unemployment it is important to make it clear that just because some people are more likely to become unemployed than others, this does not mean that they cause or are somehow responsible for their own unemployment. Most of the causes of unemployment are outside the control of individuals. But we can identify those who are most at risk of becoming and staying unemployed.

Payne *et al.* (1996) report two studies that shed some light on this issue. The first is based on the National Child Development Study (NCDS), a long-term study which follows up all the children born in a single week in 1958. The most recent survey managed to obtain data on almost three-quarters of the original cohort, over 11,000 people. This provides, among other things, information on individuals' work histories between the ages of 23 and 33. The second is the Retirement Survey run by the Department of Social Security. This gives information for a large, nationally representative sample of those over 55 on work history and other aspects.

Payne *et al.* report that a range of factors (measured prior to when unemployment began) predict whether people become unemployed between 23 and 33. Some fit human capital theory (men with better qualifications, having had formal job training and those with driving licences were less likely to become unemployed), whereas other important predictors seem likely to have an indirect effect. For instance, men who had bought a house by age 23 and those who did not have children were far less likely to become unemployed. Rather oddly, those who became unemployed had more positive attitudes towards work. Results for women were similar but there were fewer significant predictors.

Payne *et al.* also consider what distinguishes those who stay unemployed for a long time from those whose unemployment will be brief. For the 23–33-year-olds the crucial factors are again human capital factors (qualifications, training, driving licence) and personal and social capital (stable partnership, good health). For the over-50s, the older you were the more likely you were to stay unemployed. Being married increased the chances of finding a job; poor health reduced it markedly. The picture is somewhat complicated, however, as many of those who are unemployed in their 50s (especially those over 55) move into early retirement, in some cases after many months of active job search.

Other studies show that those who are unemployed tend to have friends and family who are unemployed. But this seems to be a function of structural factors (age, unemployment rate in the district, etc.) and not a consequence of shared negative attitudes towards employment (Nordenmark, 1999).

Unemployment: consequences and coping

Though some have claimed that unemployment is not necessarily bad (see Chapter 3) the evidence is overwhelming that, overall, unemployment has a serious deleterious effect on mental health. Murphy and Athanasou (1999) have looked at sixteen longitudinal studies, all of which used good quality measures of health and stress (typically the General Health Questionnaire – GHQ), and found clear evidence that unemployment was associated with poor mental health. Distress levels fell when people became re-employed, which suggests that the link is a causal one. What is particularly striking is that Murphy and Athanasou go beyond previous studies to estimate how large is the effect of unemployment on mental health. The answer is that it is substantial – those who are re-employed are estimated to be half as likely to experience depression as those who remain unemployed.

However, it is a mistake to think that being employed is always good for mental health. Certain sorts of jobs may well have a very bad effect. The most important variable is probably job insecurity, which is particularly salient for those who have lost jobs in the past. As a couple of Fineman's (1987) respondents reported 'I constantly think about the vulnerability of the job, at my age, in this recession', 'unemployment left me thinking more about security than the prospects of my job – something that never used to bother me'. Using the surveys conducted as part of the SCELI (Social Change and Economic Life Intiative) programme, Burchell (1994) shows how five different groups of employees differ in their GHQ scores. He describes the groups as:

1 'the primary segment', who were mostly male and well paid, and whose job changes had mostly been to get better jobs (40 per cent of the sample);
2 'stickers', who were predominantly female, older than the other groups (a mean of 43 compared to an overall mean of 38), and the least likely to want to change jobs (31 per cent of the sample);
3 'female descenders', who were nearly all female, low-paid and had frequently changed to same- or worse-paid jobs (13 per cent);
4 'young and mobile', who were mostly young ambitious males; and
5 'labour market descenders', who had all had a job change which involved a switch to a worse job, and many of whom had been made redundant in the past.

All these groups had GHQ scores that were better than the unemployed group but the labour market descenders were not significantly better. Those in the primary sector and the stickers had the best mental health.

If we accept that unemployment (and certain forms of employment) are bad for people's mental health, this raises two questions. Why? And, as unemployment is clearly a serious problem for the individual, what can he or she do about it? Fryer (1992) claims that the most important feature of unemployment is that it constrains people (in jargon, that it 'restricts their agency') and that the most important constraint is also the most obvious: lack of money. Unemployed people themselves say that shortage of money is the most important source of personal and family problems. Unemployment generally leads to a big drop in living standards (Davies *et al.*, 1982, report that for 50 per cent of their respondents their benefit income was less than half their previous employment income) and debt is very common (Fryer, 1992). This means that it is hard to carry out the role of the consumer (which is very important in modern Western society).

So how do those in adult employment solve this problem? It might be thought that if the major problem is lack of money, then the unemployed might try and rectify this by unorthodox and illegal means, for example by working in the black economy for cash payments or engaging in crime. Contrary to media myth, there is very little evidence that those who are unemployed are an important part of the black economy. Though good-quality evidence in this area is hard to come by, it appears that most of those who work for cash-in-hand in the UK are house-wives and those who have a main job and are working on the side (Hakim, 1992). There is some evidence that there is an overall positive relationship between male unemployment and property crime (Elliott and Ellingworth, 1998) but this effect is much stronger for youth unemployment than unemployment in adulthood (Britt, 1997).

Those who cope well with unemployment do not then turn to crime or illegal work but they do seem to share certain characteristics. Patton and Donohue (1998) identify four coping strategies of the unemployed that are associated with positive well-being: keeping busy, being optimistic, religious faith and re-evaluating expectations. Similarly, Lai and Wong (1998) show that more optimistic Hong Kong Chinese women were less psychologically affected by losing their jobs than their less optimistic peers and suggest that optimism is an important personal resource for coping with unemployment. The results of these quantitative studies fit well with the detailed case studies carried out by Fryer and Payne (1984) of eleven individuals who were well adapted to unemployment. They pointed out that what these individuals had in common was that they had identified goals they were working towards and were able to structure and fill their own lives (in other words to keep busy).

In summary, it appears as if unemployment at this stage of life can have serious deleterious effects but that it is possible, for some people at least, to cope with this. In this case, as in many others, having an optimistic outlook appears to be a good strategy.

Unemployment and self-employment

Another option for the unemployed is to become self-employed. This is not the same as being an entrepreneur or setting up one's own business since some forms of self-employment (homeworkers, labour-only subcontractors) are little different from normal employment and in others there is little concern to expand and grow. To put this in perspective, just under one-third of those in self-employment in the UK employ others (Bryson and White, 1996b).

A large proportion (roughly 40 per cent) of those entering self-employment do so from unemployment. They are different from those who enter self-employment from employment though, and tend to set up businesses that require little capital and lots of labour (e.g. services such as hairdressing). They are also different from those entering employment: the newly self-employed tend to be mature (aged 25 to 44) and mostly married whereas the newly employed tend to be younger and are more likely to be single. But the newly self-employed were less likely to have dependent children (Bryson and White, 1996b). From an economic-psychological point of view, what is interesting is that the evidence that the self-employed are less risk-averse is patchy: Taylor (1996) shows that those who value job security are less likely to be self-employed but Bryson and White (1996a), using a sample of the long-term unemployed, found no relationship between risk aversion and entering self-employment.

So, self-employment is a solution to the problem of unemployment that is used more by the mature worker, but it seems not to be a solution preferred by people with particular attitudes or beliefs. It is, however, in one respect at least, quite a good solution: this kind of job is relatively more stable than employment (seven months after getting a job from being unemployed 50 per cent of men had left it – whereas approximately 70 per cent were still self-employed).

Discussion

We have had to be highly selective in this chapter. But we hope we have provided enough evidence to give a flavour of economic life in maturity. We began by characterising this period as one of consolidation and stability, and this does seem to be true for many people. Despite large changes in society generally, worries about the increased pace of work and an increase in the fragility of families, for many mature economic agents this is probably the easiest time of their lives. They may have to work extra hours to provide for children, they may need to make plans to cope with anticipated changes in retirement, and they certainly do not have all the possessions they would like. But for the most part they have stable jobs and incomes, and have the skills and knowledge they need to solve their problems successfully. Others, however, are trapped in jobs that they don't like. They may be unemployed, or having difficulty in making ends meet, or in keeping up with the Joneses. So, whilst maturity may mean that individuals have a much wider range of skills and strategies that can be deployed, the fast-changing world may make some of these skills and approaches to the world inappropriate or obsolete.

6

The Golden Years?

Economic Behaviour in Retirement

Introduction: The Economic Nature of Old Age

In conventional social classification, the retired are included among the 'economically inactive'. That might make it seem that the economic psychology of the post-retirement years would be rather dull. The retired are, by definition, no longer in employment; their consumption needs are presumably modest, and reducing, and they have long been regarded as notoriously non-innovative consumers (Reynaud, 1981); according to economic life-cycle theory, they are living off their savings, not adding to them; and they have no need to gamble to improve a lot which is more or less fixed.

This bland picture is far from accurate. As we shall see in this chapter, the elderly, including some of the most elderly elderly, are substantially active as workers, consumers and savers; and if their gambling is, perhaps, moderate, their giving can be very substantial. Furthermore, in so far as they do withdraw from some of the more typical kinds of economic behaviour, they serve as an important comparison group, through whom we can hope to understand better the behaviour of the rest of the population. And, finally, the old are the repository of experience, in the economic sphere as in so many others, and through their memories we have the opportunity to contrast the psychological impacts of different economic conditions.

Nonetheless, economic psychology as such has largely ignored the old. The material in this chapter, therefore, has been drawn together from disparate fields: much of it from sociology, some from a variety of different branches of psychology, and some from economics. As far as economic psychology is concerned, this chapter is as much an agenda of issues as a survey of completed research. Some of these issues are to do with difference. Being old is not the same as being younger, and a proper understanding of the economic choices made by old people requires a proper understanding of the condition of being old (Posner, 1995). Some of them, however, are to do with similarity. Young or old, within a given society, we face the same economic environment. Our different responses to it may help us to understand the nature of that environment a little better.

Defining old age

Old age is not a clearly defined stage of life. When do you become old? The World Health Organization presents statistics on Ageing and Health in terms of the numbers of people over 60, or over 65, in a particular community. But if you are as old as you feel, as the saying has it, it could be at any age. For practical purposes, though, we need a sharper definition, and in this chapter we will mainly be talking about people who are past the usual retiring age for full-time employment. A definition in terms of retirement is useful for this book, because retirement is an economic fact. Of course, it is not just an economic fact: Guillemard and Rein (1993) comment that it is also a social status, and a whole set of social roles, whose contents and meanings are constantly being reworked. Furthermore, as so often in this book, this definition implies an approach dominated by conditions in modern, developed, 'Western' economies. Retirement itself is a relatively recent concept: the English words 'retire' and 'pension' did not begin to be used in their modern senses until the late eighteenth century, and the concept of retirement still has little meaning in subsistence economies. To include any material at all from other kinds of economy, therefore, we may have to project the modern Western concept of retirement onto times and places where it makes little sense. But we have little choice other than to accept this ethnocentric viewpoint, since there is virtually no research literature that we could use to construct a more universal economic psychology of old age.

Even in developed economies, however, the concept of retirement is blurred, and changing. The most striking change in recent years has been an increasing trend towards both early retirement and gradual retirement. Guillemard and Rein (1993) give a detailed account of this trend, and the complex of political, social and economic changes that underlie it and derive from it; Han and Moen (1999a) reflect on how the trend towards early retirement affects the significance of retirement within the individual's life course. Henretta (1994) predicts that the trend towards early retirement will soon reverse, because of the demographic drift towards a more elderly population; however, as Ginn and Arber (1991) comment, this prediction is not consistent with the difficulty that older people who are still below the retiring age currently have in finding jobs.

Another factor that blurs the concept of retirement is the way that couples link their decisions about retirement. It has long been common for both members of a couple to retire at the same time, even if the younger (usually the woman) has not reached the usual retiring age; or, in single-earner couples, for the non-earning partner, again usually the woman, to think of herself as 'retired' from the time when her partner retires. This pattern, too, may be changing (Han and Moen, 1999b), and women at least can choose to see themselves as 'retired', 'homemakers', or both – and these self-perceptions may have implications for psychological well-being (e.g. Adelmann, 1993).

A further blurring arises from the fact that some people who have reached the conventional retiring age for their society nonetheless continue to work, either in employment or otherwise, and this issue is taken up in later sections, pp. 136–139. In recent years some states have made it illegal to enforce retirement at a particular age, so such employment after this conventional retirement age is likely to increase.

Given these difficulties with the concept of retirement, we need a fairly inclusive definition of old age for the purposes of this chapter. We will include all those who have retired (even if they have done so early), and all those who have passed the retiring age (even if they continue to work).

The economic characteristics of older people

Given this definition of old age, what are its main characteristics that are important for economic life? The following brief summary serves as an outline of the remainder of this chapter.

As a curtain-raiser, we need to consider the act of retiring itself, and this will occupy section two of the chapter, pp. 129–132. Retirement is a distinct economic action whose psychological consequences have been studied to some extent. As we found with adolescence (Chapter 3), however, much of the best work on retirement has been done by sociologists, with their systematic interest in transitions, and we shall need to draw on their findings.

Most of this chapter, however, is concerned with life after retirement, and we can identify a number of themes within this; they will be briefly stated here, and then taken up in more detail in the rest of the chapter, after our consideration of the moment of retirement on pages 129–135.

In the post-retirement period, the simple fact of having retired is of crucial importance – this is why we have used it as part of our working definition of old age. Most fundamentally, retirement entails a transition from deriving income from employment to deriving it from pensions of one sort or another. In effect (though perhaps not in people's own perceptions) this means relying on a mixture of previous saving (either the interest from it or the capital) and transfer incomes (either from the state or from individuals). It also frequently involves a sharp drop in income, and a sharp rise in time available for leisure. Pages 132–135 will therefore deal with the incomes of older people.

Economic activity continues despite retirement. Some people will continue in work past the retiring age; others will take on new full- or part-time employment after retiring from a 'career' job; many others will engage in voluntary work, while home-based unpaid work (hobbies, gardening, do-it-yourself, housework) is pretty well inevitable. Furthermore, though we can retire from (paid) work, we cannot retire from buying. Old people remain consumers, and we need to ask in what ways their consumption patterns differ from those of the rest of the population. Other characteristic economic activities – giving, gambling, investing and, perhaps surprisingly, saving, also continue into retirement. Pages 135–143 therefore survey each of these kinds of economic behaviour.

Later sections headed Frailty and Recontructing the Past, pp. 143–146, turn to a consideration of why the economic behaviour of older people might be different. We have to be careful to distinguish age effects from cohort effects. At the time of writing this book, the people who are retired are those who were young in the years of world depression, world war and post-war recovery. Any distinctive economic behaviour they show may be the product of those particular experiences rather than of age as such.

One characteristic of the old that is unambiguously not a cohort effect is frailty, and we consider this on pages 143–145. Older people are more vulnerable to a wide range of medical problems, and are much more likely to require personal care, possibly total personal care. Both medical and social care are extremely expensive. In developed economies, insurance and state provision generally cover the costs of medical care (though there are gaps in cover), and have done so for the past fifty years or so. In contrast, it is only recently that there has been consideration of insurance against the costs of social care.

Another distinctive characteristic of the old is memory. By definition, the old have more things they can remember than the rest of us, and even if their memories are less good, they will include events beyond the reach of younger people. The implications of this fact for economic behaviour are taken up on pages 146–147. For example, distinctive attitudes may have been implanted in an earlier generation, or different experiences may give a particular perspective on the economic present.

Beyond memory and frailty, we enter a grey area. Are there other distinct psychological characteristics of older people, and do they have economic implications? Aristotle argued that, compared with young people, old people tend to be pessimistic (partly because of their dependence on memory), and self-centred, being more safety-oriented, cowardly, and careless about public opinion (Posner, 1995, Chapter 5). Posner argues that these tendencies do indeed exist, and that they have distinct economic consequences, though he admits that he is unable to produce much technical evidence. We have been equally unable to find much that would support Aristotle's conclusions, so they do not merit a separate section of the chapter, but they do turn out to be relevant at various points below.

Finally, the natural outcome of old age is death. In a modern economy, few people expect to die before retirement, and little economic behaviour (other than insurance purchase) is oriented around death in the early or middle years of life. After retirement, death is a more immediate concern, and we can identify some economic behaviours that are concerned with death or preparation for it. The section headed Economic Life After Death, pp. 147–150, therefore deals with death and the economic behaviours that surround it.

The Retirement Event

The act of retiring is recognised as a significant event in someone's life, especially the life of a full-time employee. It is one of the most significant of the 'stressful life events' studied by Holmes and Rahe (1967), and much research has been devoted to its possible deleterious effects and ways of combating them. Sociologists like Atchley (1976) and Parker (1982) have discussed the whole field of retirement, and we need to make use of their insights.

If you are in full-time employment, it is likely that your job or career is an important part of your sense of identity. This has been thought of as more of a male characteristic, with women finding their identity more through family life; however, it is likely that it is more to do with being in full-time, career work, which until recently tended to be a male preserve. To retire is to lose a large part of that identity. It is also to lose what is often your most significant social group. In other words, retirement is likely to have many of the same deleterious psychological effects as other kinds of job loss, such as redundancy or bankruptcy. Jahoda (1982) and others have argued that job loss through redundancy can give rise to a sequence of stages that mimic those following a bereavement, and in the worst case, like bereavement, can trigger off severe depression. It would be surprising if job loss through retirement did not have similar effects in at least some cases. In recent years there has been a strong emphasis on pre-retirement counselling, preparing for retirement, and gradual retirement.

Self-employed people such as farmers have always had to take their own decisions about when to retire, and such decisions can be complicated by the need or desire to hand the business on to a relative (Kimhi and Lopez, 1999). However, the relaxation of previously universal retirement ages means that, for far more employees than earlier this century, retirement involves an active decision. Feldman (1994) has provided an influential review of the growing research literature on early retirement. In many cases, the decision to retire is probably taken on the basis of inadequate information about its consequences. Unsurprisingly, where early retirement is offered, the level of financial inducement available is critical in the decision to accept it (e.g. Maule, Cliff and Taylor, 1996); beyond that, those with poor health, dangerous jobs, low job satisfaction, absorbing leisure interests, good health insurance cover outside their employers' schemes, or good pension provision are more likely to retire early. Perhaps less obviously, those whose spouses are continuing to work are less likely to retire, despite the greater household income they enjoy (e.g. Rust and Phelan, 1997; Reitzes, Mutran and Fernandez, 1998; Shultz, Morton and Weckerle, 1998). This underlines the point that married or cohabiting people usually take the decision to retire as a couple (see Henkens, 1999), though interestingly the retiring spouse tends to perceive his or her spouse's influence on the decision as greater than the spouse does (Smith and Moen, 1998), and wives seem to have more influence over their husbands' retirement than vice versa (Henkens, 1999).

Despite all these ways in which the retirement decision is more flexible than it might look, and is becoming more flexible, there remain major peaks of retirement at the conventional ages (which vary, of course, between countries, occupations and sometimes also between men and women). Rust and Phelan (1997) considered whether these peaks were due to social pressures – a feeling that 65, for example, is the 'right age to retire' – or whether they could be explained by the action of institutional factors – social security and pension fund regulations, for example – on underlying continuous preference functions. Rust and Phelan found that, at least for the US, the retirement peaks at ages 62 and 65 could be entirely explained by the rules of the Medicare scheme. In other countries, which have more advanced, comprehensive health-care systems, this particular explanation would not be relevant, but it is likely that there are comparable factors.

Hanisch and Hulin (1990) argue that there are two different and independent processes going on as someone approaches retirement, one about withdrawal from work, and the other about withdrawal from the job. Withdrawing from work while remaining in the job is one form of 'social loafing' (Latané, Williams and Harkins, 1979), while withdrawing from the job while continuing to work brings us into the realm of bridge jobs and voluntary work, discussed below (pp. 136–139). In a substantial proportion of cases early retirement, though presented as voluntary, is effectively forced on unwilling workers, so that it is really a form of disguised redundancy, with corresponding problems (Gowan, 1998). Some people are, of course, forced to retire from their lifetime jobs on reaching a certain age, though this is becoming less of a norm. Hayes and Vanden Heuvel (1994) showed that attitudes to such mandatory retirement vary with education and employment status, and strikingly between countries, with strong disapproval in the US, where enforced retirement has been illegal since 1986. 'Type A' men (those who are hard-driving, achievement oriented and have a chronic sense of time urgency) were more likely than the average to continue in employment until forced to retire (Swan, Dame and Carmelli, 1991). However, early retirement as such does not seem to make much difference to subsequent life satisfaction and psychological well-being, either in this group or more generally (Knesek, 1992): what matters far more is whether retirement was perceived as truly voluntary (e.g. Shultz et al., 1998), and what people do in their retirement, whether it occurs early or at the 'normal' time (see pp. 135–143).

As well as the decision to retire itself, the act of retirement brings other economic decisions in its train. In some pension schemes, people will receive a large lump sum on retirement, which it is their responsibility (with more or less advice from their pension scheme) to invest or use. How do people decide what mixture of capital drawings and interest to use to support themselves? Annuities are a traditional solution to this problem, but what determines someone to buy an annuity, and how do they choose between the different products on offer? Economists, and the pensions industry, have investigated such decisions from a normative perspective (e.g. Milevsky, 1998), but empirical or psychological analysis of them is poorly developed. Benartzi and Thaler (1999) take an experimental approach and then apply it to real-life decisions, showing that if people are given an insight into the longer-term consequences of their decisions, they become more likely to purchase stocks (which probably are a better long-term investment than annuities).

We started this section by comparing retirement to bereavement. The analogy makes it clear that, both sociologically and psychologically, retirement is not so much an event as a process (Atchley, 1976). Psychological well-being a year after retirement, and five or six years later, are predicted by different variables (Gall, Evans and Howard, 1997). As Gall *et al*. argue, the process nature of retirement may explain the inconsistencies in the empirical literature about the overall impact of retirement, with some authors finding it to be a positive influence on well-being and other associated variables, while others find it to be deleterious. Atchley argued for a 'honeymoon' effect early in retirement, which is subsequently undermined, not least by failing health. We turn, therefore, to look in more detail at life in retirement.

The State of Retirement

The rest of this chapter concentrates on economic life after retirement. It is important to realise that although this is a new stage of life, it is not a new life. Those who were better-off during employment will, in the great majority of cases, be better-off during retirement. Patterns of social disadvantage, by race, gender and class, inevitably continue into old age, and as Ginn and Arber (1991) and Calasanti (1993) argue, they need to be taken into account if we are to understand the experience of retirement. Age itself remains an important variable: there are marked differences between the 'young old', even if they are retired, and the 'old old'. In saving behaviour, Hamermesh (1984), found that 62–69-year-olds were running down net savings, whereas older groups were adding to them, while in income trends, Ginn and Arber found that gender differences in income were lower for the over 75-age-group than for the younger elderly.

There are two reasons why it is essential to recognise the heterogeneity of the old. First, to generalise across all elderly people will lead us into error: different subgroups will experience retirement in different ways and behave in different ways, and if we simply look for global trends we will not understand either the phenomena or their causation. From their practical perspective, marketers have recognised the need to segment the elderly market (e.g. Bone, 1991). Secondly, though, as Ginn and Arber argue, to treat all elderly people as the same is simply ageist: it is classifying people by an over-simple attribute instead of recognising their individuality. And as Calasanti argues, such stereotyped thinking will prevent us recognising the problems of particular subgroups of the elderly – problems that are often continuations of the same subgroups' problems at younger ages.

A related error is to mistake effects that exist throughout the life-cycle for retirement-specific effects: for example, in a study of retired people's views of advertising, Burnett (1991) reports that the upper-income group have more sceptical views of advertising than their middle-income counterparts – but this is a difference that is surely not confined to the retired. Thus the retired are both a heterogeneous group, and one that is not always distinctive from the rest of the population.

In relation to such demographic and socio-economic differences, however, one aspect of retired life is distinctive: women greatly outnumber men, for three obvious reasons. First, women have substantially the greater life expectancy. Secondly, employed women have traditionally had an earlier retirement age than men. Finally, husbands are typically a little (sometimes a lot) older than their wives – and as we have seen employed couples tend to retire more or less simultaneously, while non-employed women have tended to adopt a retired lifestyle when their husbands retire.

Even across such socio-demographic differences and asymmetries, however, reduced income remains a key fact about retirement. This section might equally well have been entitled 'Life on a pension'. There is extensive literature on pensions in economics, social policy and sociology. Much recent research is concerned with the mechanics of pension provision – what mixture of private and state provision will best ensure that everyone has an adequate pension, and how people can be persuaded to put a high enough proportion of income into private pension provision during their working years. This literature is not of direct interest for the economic psychology of the old, since by the time people retire, it is too late for them to change their pension plans. It is not, however, too late for them to vote for better state pension provision, or to engage in other forms of political activity: the 'Grey Panther' vote has been thought to be decisive in some US elections, and in the UK the retired trade-union leader Jack Jones built himself a new political platform as a spokesman for the interests of the elderly. However, such behaviour belongs more to political than economic psychology. For economic psychologists, three features of pensions as a form of income seem important: their source, their uncontrollability and their level. We will discuss each of these in turn.

The sources of pensioners' income

All pensions are funded either from savings or from transfer incomes. This fact has specific psychological and behavioural implications. In so far as pensions are funded from savings, there are practical problems about the management of the money concerned, but, as we saw above, there is as yet no significant psychological literature dealing with these. But there is one very striking fact about money management by the retired. If pensions are derived from saving, standard economic analysis finds it surprising that people go on adding to some forms of savings after retirement. Yet the data suggest that saving is quite prominent among the old. In terms of any kind of life-cycle theory, this looks irrational. There are a number of ways of accounting for it: among the obvious ones are liquidity preferences, a belief that expense may be concentrated in later old age (whereas the real value of pension income may fall with the years) or bequest motives. In addition, almost all old people derive some income from interest on savings (Ginn and Arber, 1991, report that 96 per cent claimed some income from this source in the 1985–86 UK General Household Survey), but the amounts are likely to be low, and saving purely for interest when your life expectancy is quite low does not fit into any rational choice model. Saving in the elderly is discussed further on pages 141–142.

The alternative source for pension income is transfer payments. For the most part, these will be intergenerational, in that younger people will be the source of the funds. The transfers can be either state-mediated or personal. Where state pensions (or social security payments to old people made on the grounds of low income) are 'unfunded', i.e. the money from them comes from current taxation rather than the interest on investments, they constitute an organised form of transfer income. The acceptability of such benefits is very variable: in the UK, the basic state pension has a very high take-up rate and is seen as an entitlement, whereas the take-up of means-tested payments available to the old is poor (Drakeford, 1998).

Most personal transfers occur within families, although charitable giving to organisations working among the old is a more generalised form. Transfers within families have excited considerable research interest.

In societies where modern social security and pensions systems have not yet developed, old people may be completely dependent on their adult offspring, and receive both financial and direct support (e.g. Lillard and Willis, 1997). In developed societies, transfers to elderly people in the form of money may not be quantitatively very significant, at least on average (Eggebeen, 1992); Ginn and Arber (1991) give a figure of less than one per cent of old people counting regular payments from friends or relatives among their income. Shi (1993, 1994) has analysed the situation of China, a society in transition from traditional to modern provision, and shown how state pension support is supplanting families' financial support for elderly relatives, while traditional reciprocity norms hold for non-financial exchanges. There are some special circumstances where payments to an elderly relative are more probable even in developed societies (for example, when a family farm has been given to a son or daughter on the owner's retirement: Kimhi and Lopez, 1999). And in general when parents get sufficiently old or frail, the taboo on making them presents of money may be relaxed to some extent; for example, Eggebeen reports that widowed (but not divorced) parents do tend to receive financial support from their adult children. There is also likely to be considerable camouflage going on as people seek to reconcile economic facts with social conventions. There may also be a need to circumvent state regulations, where old people receive means-tested benefits that would be threatened if significant transfers from younger relatives became visible. But in any case, if we consider not money but goods and services, huge transfers to the elderly take place in the form of unpaid care of elderly relatives; indeed, this is probably one of the most significant forms of non-market work in the current UK economy.

Pensions as uncontrollable income

Retired people are to a considerable extent the prisoners of the pension provision they or others have made. You cannot, as we have already said, go back after retirement and decide to save more during your working life. Nor can you have much influence over interest rates and inflation, which may radically alter the real value (or the money value) of your savings. As noted above, it is in principle possible to have some influence over state transfer payments, but it is likely to be marginal. There may be more scope for influencing interpersonal transfers of either money or services, either by previous giving (see Henretta *et al.*, 1997) or by explicit or implicit promises of future bequests: in some cases it is understood within a family that those who care for elderly relatives will be favoured in their wills (e.g. Tsuya and Martin, 1992).

Overall, however, pension income remains harder to control than employment income. Pensioners cannot seek promotion, or change their jobs, or get a better pension by undertaking training or study, or take industrial action to gain a rise. This seems likely to add to the perceived economic insecurity of the old – especially when coupled with the relatively low levels of retirement incomes (see *The levels of pensions*, below). The result is likely to be raised anxiety/stress levels, and perhaps a more cautious approach to spending than the same level of a more controllable income might justify.

The levels of pensions

Some alarmist commentators (e.g. Johnson, Conrad and Thompson, 1989) have suggested that the retired are now dangerously affluent. In reality, however, in terms of money income at least, at every level to be on a pension is to be less well off than you were in work. The basic state pension in the UK now provides only about 14 per cent of average earnings (Jupp, 1997). Most occupational pensions schemes in the UK aim to provide a pension of 50 per cent of pre-retirement earnings to people who remain in the scheme throughout their working lives; those who change jobs, or have to rely on private pension provision, will usually do worse than this. Economic psychologists' studies of debt and poverty regularly turn up a considerable number of old people among the poorest groups.

Economic Activity After Retirement

Does it make sense to describe some older people as in a general way 'more economically active' than others? To some extent, it can be expected that the levels of different kinds of economic activity will co-vary, because they are all likely to depend on the same variables: if an elderly person is active and in good health, many forms of activity are likely to be at higher levels. Furthermore, if someone is adding to their income by paid work, other forms of economic activity become more possible; for example, Midlarsky and Hannah (1989) argued that although retired people were more generous than the younger population, they gave lower amounts to a charitable cause, because of their lower incomes; it was only those who were continuing in employment who could express their higher generosity by higher levels of giving. On the other hand, there may be substitutabilities: people who continue in employment after retirement are obviously less available for unpaid work in all its forms. The available empirical literature does not yet tell us which of these tendencies is stronger.

Paid work

The major national economic and social surveys yield useful data on the extent to which people remain 'economically active', i.e. in paid work, after the retiring age. For the UK, approximately 7.5 per cent of people over the retirement age are in paid work: 7.3 per cent of over-65 men and 7.6 per cent of over-60 women (Labour Force Survey). There are two kinds of such paid work: people continuing in their previous jobs, i.e. retiring late, and people taking new jobs after retiring from what may have been a lifetime career. Late retirement is particularly associated with certain occupations, including some of relatively high pay and public visibility (the law, politics), but it is probably commoner among less well-paid people who feel they 'cannot afford to retire'. New jobs taken after retirement, or reduced but continuing roles with the career employer, are sometimes called 'bridge jobs' since they are seen as a way of easing the passage to full retirement, and they are widespread: Ruhm (cited by Rust and Phelan, 1997) shows that fewer than 40 per cent of US workers retire directly from their career jobs.

When people take up a new job after retirement, we would expect their labour market behaviour to be different from that of more typical workers. Even those who are 'early retired' are likely to have a pension of some sort. They are also likely to be free from societal pressure to work – social conventions allow pensioners not to be working. Accordingly, their behaviour should be more governed by other motivations, among which the most likely are the social situation of the workplace, the interest and enjoyment they derive from the work itself, their (or society's) sense of the value of the work being done, and the value they set on other activities they might engage in. Standard micro-economic analysis can be used to predict how they should react – chiefly by being less sensitive to rates of pay but more sensitive to non-pecuniary incentives and opportunity costs. Thus retired workers should be unlikely to take unpleasant, low-paid work, but perhaps more willing to take low-paid but 'worthwhile' or interesting jobs. Some empirical support can be found for these obvious predictions – for example, Toughill et al. (1993) found that retired people often cited their involvement in voluntary work as a reason for not taking employment.

Retired people naturally vary in the extent to which they continue with paid work. Danigelis and McIntosh (1993) found that younger, higher-income, and more physically able retired people were more likely to be employed, and among women, the same was true of the more educated and those not currently married.

The study by Danigelis and McIntosh is one of many that suggest that continuing in paid work after retirement can aid well-being. For the early retired, Maule et al. (1996) show that the fulfilment of promises of some continuing work may be the crucial factor – and that such promises are only fulfilled in a minority of cases (24 per cent in their sample, who were followed up 18–36 months after retirement). On the other hand, continued work can be a stressor, and Suurnakki, Nygard and Ilmarinen (1991) showed that this was accentuated by ageing, especially among women and those doing physical work. Even among academics, who commonly wish to continue professional work after retirement, Dorfman (1992) found that the number of hours spent doing so was negatively correlated with general life satisfaction.

Unpaid work

We predicted earlier that retired people might be more willing to accept interesting or worthwhile but low paid work. The extreme form of this is, of course, taking on unpaid work. This can either be in an organised form, which might mean doing 'voluntary work' through an organisation or doing work-like activities in clubs and societies, or in a less organised form, which would include hobbies, do-it-yourself, gardening, and child care for relatives. Clearly the opportunity costs of all these activities are less for someone who has taken retirement, so time allocation considerations alone predict a higher level of engagement in them by the old, and common observation supports this prediction. Although, as we shall see, there are certainly data to support the idea that old people engage in most of these activities to an enhanced extent, we are not in a position to say whether the extra participation reflects on enhanced level of interest over and above the effects of enhanced opportunity.

All forms of unpaid work can be more or less 'economic'. Volunteers may be paid token fees or expenses; do-it-yourself activities may be driven by the interest of the task itself, or may be an attempt to avoid expenditure; a fruit and vegetable garden can make considerable net contributions to the household budget; child-care (typically of grandchildren) may be done for the sake of seeing the children, or to enable their parents to take up paid work or economically valuable study opportunities. Analysing a survey of working mothers, Presser (1989) found that a quarter of them depended on a grandmother's childcare contribution to enable them to take employment – and the mean time commitment was 27 hours per week. Nearly a third of the grandmothers received some payment for their help; they were more likely to do so if they contributed longer hours, and were not themselves in employment. It is quite common, in both developing and developed economies, for the availability of grandparents to look after children to make the difference between women working or leaving the labour market (e.g. Doan and Popkin, 1993); grandmothers who live with their adult children are obviously particularly relevant here. Presser shows how grandmothers and their daughters often co-ordinate their working hours to make child care possible. In some situations, it seems likely that younger family members actually exploit the availability of older relatives, so that people are doing more unpaid work than they would choose.

Almost everyone engages in some unpaid work during retirement. Even in traditionally structured households, retired men do more housework than those in employment, though their wives do less (Szinovacz and Harpster, 1994). Around 40 per cent of Americans do formal voluntary work through an organisation (Okun and Eisenberg, 1992), and there has been substantial research trying to establish which elderly people are most likely to volunteer. Grandparents of pupils provide the largest body of voluntary helpers in US schools (Strom and Strom, 1994) – perhaps an extension of their traditional role in child care. The wide involvement of elderly people in voluntary work, often quite different from the work that they did in their paid careers, demonstrates that they have greater mental flexibility and learning capacity than is often supposed. Prager (1995) makes this point strongly, demonstrating that elderly volunteers can learn a whole series of new roles as assistants on a research programme.

However, not all retired people work to the same extent, and there has been a good deal of research on who engages in unpaid work during retirement. Retired women engage in more unpaid work than retired men, both inside and outside the home (Danigelis and McIntosh, 1993). Regardless of gender, the more physically able and those living in larger households were more likely to engage in unpaid work; marital status had opposite effects for men and women – married men and unmarried women were less likely to do unpaid work. Those with a history of previous voluntary work, and a high commitment to religious and other organisations, are more likely to be regular volunteers (Okun, 1993). Among women, Moen, Dempster-McClain and Williams (1992) showed that those who occupied multiple roles in society (e.g. were active in churches, clubs or community groups) in the 1950s were more likely to be active in the 1980s, when they were retired.

The impacts of post-retirement work have also been studied. Many studies have found that those who volunteer enjoy higher life-satisfaction or well-being (e.g. Dorfman and Rubenstein, 1993; Moen, Robison and Dempster-McClean, 1995). Even housework is claimed to be good for retired people's psychological adjustment, at least among women (Szinovacz, 1992). In contrast, McIntosh and Danigelis (1995) did not find any general effect of formal voluntary work on people's affect, though they did find that giving informal voluntary help to friends, family and neighbours was associated with higher positive affect (paid work, in contrast, seemed to have no impact at all). McIntosh and Danigelis showed that the impact of voluntary work depended strongly on demographic factors such as gender and race. Knesek (1992) found that even when combined with gender, volunteerism could account for only 6 per cent of the variance of a life satisfaction scale in a sample of the retired. Okun (1993) shows that it is those who have been volunteers before who are most likely to volunteer again, so the importance of voluntary work in retirement may be that for those who have done it earlier in life, perhaps on a smaller scale, it represents the continuation of a familiar quasi-work role. New volunteers might not find so much satisfaction from it.

Indeed, for unpaid work as for employment, it seems that there is 'good work' and 'bad work' (cf. Warr, 1987). Strawbridge *et al.* (1997) find evidence that child care is a source of stress for grandparents. Nonetheless, the general trend of the results, and the generally high prevalence of post-retirement work (both unpaid and paid), provide strong evidence in favour of the idea that work has 'latent functions' (Jahoda, 1982) or provides psychological 'vitamins' (Warr, 1987). The obverse side of this argument is a sad one: for many people, retirement is a time of lowered social contact and boredom, with consequential loss of well-being and life satisfaction. However, this is only likely to be true for those who have nothing but work in their lives: for example, Sagy and Antonovsky (1992) show that those whose family networks are stronger, and more strongly felt, are less likely to experience deleterious effects of retirement, while Robbins, Lee and Wan (1994) showed that those whose life goals were more continuous across the early retirement transition tended to adjust better to retirement.

Consumption and leisure

As we have already said, you cannot retire from consumption. Retirement, however, is likely to change consumption patterns in several ways. In interaction with that, it changes the messages we receive from marketers. It is not surprising that consumer science has contributed to our understanding of the elderly as consumers, for consumer scientists have made particular use of life-cycle models in seeking to segment markets. Within this framework, elderly people generally belong to the 'empty nest' or 'survivor' stages. However, two different approaches to these stages of life have been taken. On the one hand elderly consumers are seen as unadventurous, unlikely to be innovators or opinion leaders, unlikely to be attracted by new products or influenced by fashion, and altogether an unrewarding prospect for the marketer. On the other hand, they can be seen as an economically powerful group offering some characteristic marketing opportunities. There is more disposable time for shopping, and there may be more disposable income. There are certainly new consumer needs: for more comfortable travel, even to exotic parts of the world, for medical aids and prostheses of various sorts, for specialised housing, and ultimately for long-term care and for death services. It was the scale of the economic resources of the retired in developed societies such as the United States, that led to the notion of the 'Grey Panthers', a powerful but potentially profitable sector within society. So how do elderly consumers differ from other people?

First, needs for goods and services may change: needs linked to employment disappear, needs due to increasing frailty may appear. Retired people often have a good stock of durable goods, and with the light use made of them by small households, they are able to live off this capital stock to a considerable extent (see Chattoe and Gilbert, 1999). Marketers have considered the special opportunities presented by the old, because of their need for or interest in particular commodities; Schewe and Balazs (1992) point out that the list of such commodities is both longer and more variable than a naïve analysis might suggest. Gibler, Lumpkin and Moschis

(1997) discuss elderly people's need for a wide range of different housing and care services, and argue that most potential consumers do not differentiate within this range, and as a result they do not secure the best match to their individual needs.

Needs concerned with the mechanics of consumption also change in retirement: Smith (1991) found that elderly people, even the 'young old', were unlikely to shop far from home, so that those who lived in the downtown areas of American cities faced considerable restrictions on their choice of retail outlets.

Secondly, age itself (rather than retirement) has effects. If the young are relatively innovative consumers, the old are relatively conservative. Just by wanting to go on buying what they have always bought, they may become an eccentric market sector, as younger people acquire new, different tastes. Older people probably remember less of advertising material than younger people (e.g. Ensley and Pride, 1991), and this in itself may contribute to their consumer conservatism.

Third, the fall in income characteristic of retirement will impose some changes both in purchasing and in money management – especially given old people's aversion to debt (discussed below). We can see this in the results from a qualitative survey of elderly people's budgeting and money management strategies conducted by Chattoe and Gilbert (1999). Chattoe and Gilbert did not include specific comparisons with younger consumers; however, they chose to study retired people as a sample who 'would be likely to have thought consciously about their money affairs and whose circumstances were relatively uncomplicated', which already implies some assumptions about the distinctive financial habits of the old. Furthermore their data bear these assumptions out. Even though many elderly people are not well off, they show little tendency towards the 'bill juggling' by which younger poor people often balance their budgets, and a correspondingly greater use of 'routinisation'.

Finally, retirement makes more time available, and this has multiple impacts. The pattern of shopping is likely to change. Although, as we have seen, elderly people tend not to travel far to reach shops, they may spend a long time actually in or around shops. However, such 'mall-walking' does not necessarily have any commercial intent (Duncan, Travis and McAuley, 1994). The relative time-richness of the retired also makes it feasible to buy goods and services whose consumption is time-intensive. Certain kinds of travel (e.g. long-distance cruises) are an obvious example, but in general we might expect the consumption of the old to be more leisure-oriented than that of younger people – though our stereotype view of what constitutes 'leisure' may be somewhat biased towards the leisure activities of the young.

Marketers have also considered whether special approaches are needed to sell to older people, perhaps because of their different view of time (Guy, Rittenburg and Hawes, 1994), or because they have been socialised to accept 'age-appropriate' advertising (Moschis, Mathur and Smith, 1993), or simply because they are reached by different media outlets; anyone who reads certain newspapers and periodicals can spot the marketing industry's beliefs on this topic. But there is little evidence to support the view that marketing to the elderly requires a different approach.

Music in advertisements, which had been thought to be off-putting to older consumers, does not seem to have any such effect (Gorn *et al.*, 1991), nor does the use of young models (Greco and Swayne, 1992). Tepper (1994) showed that older consumers sometimes reject marketing ploys (e.g. discounts) explicitly directed at them, in part because they are seen as demeaning, though in Tepper's study this applied more strictly to rather young 'old' people – he was investigating, for example, senior citizens' discount cards that were available to anyone over 50; the over over-65s were much less shy about accepting these. The consumer conservatism of the old might seem to make them an unattractive market segment for new products, and especially technological ones. However, marketers have recognised that there is much variation among the old: the 'young elderly' may still be attracted by new products or by fashionable clothes, especially if they have the other characteristics of early adopters, such as high income and better education (Festervand and Wylde, 1988; Jackson 1992). Stephens (1991) argues that 'cognitive age' needs to be taken into account when predicting response to advertising, alongside chronological age.

Saving

One of the surprises of the early empirical literature on saving (e.g. White, 1977; Menchik and David, 1983; Hamermesh, 1984) was that, following retirement, people do not run down their savings to a point of zero wealth at death; indeed, many continue to save. According to the economic life-cycle model of saving (see Chapter 5), this should not happen: the purpose of saving is to make possible a continuing consumption stream in times of diminished income. Retirement is the most significant of such times. All pension schemes are a form of saving (though this fact may be camouflaged by the elements of insurance that are normally also involved). Once someone is living on a pension, therefore, they are dissaving, and a simple understanding of life-cycle theory would predict that all attempts at saving would now cease.

The definitions of saving (see also Chapter 5) cause problems here. Technically or in the aggregate, most retired people are dissaving, because they are running down capital assets, or living off an annuity (though the older and wealthier old often do add to their net wealth year by year). But from their own point of view, and from the point of view of what Katona (1975) calls 'discretionary saving', the great majority of old people are engaging in saving behaviour: they are adding to savings accounts of various kinds. And even if they are not saving, they typically dissave more slowly than would be expected from the life-cycle model's prediction of a target of zero wealth at death.

Part of the reason is, once again, the wide range of life-situations that we sweep under the heading 'old age'. There is a great deal of difference – and a good chunk of life – between the needs of a fit 65-year-old and those of a frail and perhaps ill 85-year-old. Retired people see that, and save partly to defray the costs of social care that might become necessary at any time, but is very likely to become necessary if they live to join the ranks of the 'elderly elderly'. Addressing this idea more formally, Palumbo (1999) has shown by economic modelling and econometric analysis that saving after retirement is partially explained by uncertainties about future medical expenses, which function as exogenous 'shocks' in his model. But he also shows that even a generous allowance for this factor does not fully explain old people's retention of assets, and argues that optimism about their own longevity, and the desire to bequeath, need to be taken into account as well. Lillard and Weiss (1997) confirm that the benefit to a surviving spouse is a strong determinant of saving by the old and frail; if there is no possibility of such benefit, consumption increases much more sharply when ill-health strikes. Less dramatic uncertainties may also be important: Chattoe and Gilbert (1999) showed how the possibility of failure of expensive consumer durables loomed large in the minds, and the budgeting strategies, of even comfortably-situated retired people.

Thus the two chief motives for saving after retirement seem to be uncertainty about future expenditures, and the desire to bequeath (see Figure 5.1, p. 105). Kuehlwein (1993) showed by econometric analysis that for elderly people the bequest motive is at least as strong as any interest in their own consumption. This leads us naturally on to a consideration of giving by the elderly.

Giving

We saw above that, in addition to the transfers organised through state pensions, there are small but significant money transfers, and much greater transfers of services, from working people to their older relatives. Transfers in the opposite direction are also important. Direct money transfers from the elderly to their adult relations, are not, on average very great (Eggebeen, 1992), though they probably often occur in disguised forms such as payments to support grandchildren's education. It is socially and psychologically acceptable for parents to give money to their children when they are young adults, but this may cease to be true as the income differentials shift around. However, able retired people often provide significant services to their working children, especially in terms of unpaid care of grandchildren, and we have seen that this constitutes a considerable portion of retired people's continuing unpaid work. Furthermore, Henretta *et al.* (1997) showed that elderly people's financial giving can lead to very direct reciprocation – adult children who have received financial help from their parents are more likely to undertake their care if they subsequently come to need it.

The wish to bequeath to children or grandchildren is very widespread, and clearly influences the economic behaviour of older people – for example, leading them to economise on consumption, and in particular to seek to avoid going into care. Bequests are discussed in more detail on pages 149–150.

Giving can be to charitable organisations as well as to individuals, and, as we saw above, Midlarsky and Hannah (1989) argued that the elderly are more generous towards charities than younger consumers, though the actual amounts they give are less because of their lower incomes. The recent survey of UK giving by Banks and Tanner (1997) leads to the same conclusion.

Frailty

The frailty of the old has several different aspects. First, as we get older, we become more susceptible to most kinds of medical problem (though not all). Secondly, in a significant proportion of cases, the collectivity of these problems are sufficient for someone to need full-time personal care. Medical and personal care are very expensive commodities, and the risk of needing them has a major influence on elderly people's economic behaviour. Finally, we may become less able or less motivated to do all sorts of things, physical or mental, and this will impact on our economic behaviour in a variety of ways.

Medical care

In most advanced societies, medical care (particularly in old age) does not have to be paid for directly by the sick. It is provided by a mixture of personal insurance and state transfer incomes. As a direct influence on people's economic behaviour, therefore, the need for medical care is more relevant to the working years than the years of retirement. The rising cost of modern medical provision, and the increasing 'revolt of the élites' (Lasch, 1995) against bearing the welfare costs of the average and poorer members of society, mean that we cannot necessarily rely on this situation continuing. We might expect an increasing tendency for the healthy old to spend considerable proportions of their income on saving or insurance against the risk of high medical costs. We have already seen that the risk of medical costs is a factor both in the choice of a retiring age and in saving by the retired.

Social care

In contrast to the position for medical care, few societies have made thorough institutional provision for 'social care' – the low-level, but high-intensity, nursing care required in incapacitating illness, often for very long periods.

In traditional societies, social care was the responsibility of relatives. As societies have modernised, responsibility for this has passed away from families to the individuals themselves, or to state agencies, despite powerful traditions laying the responsibility on adult children: Cheng (1993) discusses how the reliable social security system of Hong Kong, and the entry of women into the jobs market, have abated the traditional approach even in Chinese society, where it was particularly strong. In 1996 the Singapore government sought to legislate to force people to take care of elderly relatives, a move that, in the light of experience elsewhere, seems doomed to failure.

In the latter half of the twentieth century, the state undertook a significant role in social care in many advanced countries. Until recent years, at least short-term respite care in the UK was often provided, without charge, through the health service: hospitals would admit elderly people who were unable to care for themselves when relatives or friends acting as carers were on holiday or themselves ill. In pursuit of more commercial accounting standards, such care is now regarded as plainly the province of social services departments, who were always responsible for long-term care, and provide it without charge only on a means-tested basis. Both old people and their relatives frequently regard the standard of provision offered by social services departments as unacceptable, and this has created a market for privately provided care.

Not all social care is expensive. Gibler *et al.* (1997) point out that many individuals need a level of care that is well short, both in extent and cost, of full-scale nursing home facilities. But full-scale long-term care is an extremely expensive item, and where that cost must be met financially (rather than falling, say, on the health and social life of a daughter), it is a source of serious anxiety to the old (Parker and Clarke, 1997). Except for a minority with very high pensions, there are basically two ways in which care can be paid for: from capital, or through insurance.

If care is paid for out of capital, it can quickly absorb a lifetime's savings, including the value of a house, creating major conflict for elderly people (who frequently wish to bequeath such property), and for their relatives (who are assumed to hope to inherit it). Since state-provided care is generally means-tested, taking it up normally requires people to first use their own savings, including the value of an owned home. Doyle (1992) describes the extreme strategy of 'voluntary self-impoverishment' (essentially, passing on assets before death) by which old people and their families in the US often seek to avoid the means test on state-provided social care, and discusses the stresses this can induce.

In many Western countries, individuals have become aware of the low and decreasing standard of assistance available through the welfare state, and government has become aware of the high cost of even the meagre provision now offered. Recent years have therefore seen growing interest in an attempt to provide insurance cover against the costs of social care: Germany, for example, has adopted the solution of compulsory social insurance. However, in the UK market-testing by the insurance industry, and research by social scientists, suggests that people are unwilling to pay the very high premiums that currently seem to be required to secure adequate cover (e.g. Parker and Clarke, 1997). Most policies currently offered are for purchase at the time of retirement; the costs could be much lower if they were purchased earlier in life (because the risk of the insurer having to pay out would be lower, premiums could be invested, and the cost could be spread), but at present younger people do not seem to have either a sufficient perception of the risk involved, or a sufficient belief that the cost ought to fall on individuals, to spend what would still be a significant proportion of income. This area therefore poses a series of classic economic psychological problems, to do with choice in the face of risk, time preferences, and the motivations for saving, and the decisions involved are difficult. Meier (1999) shows that purchase late in life is rational if the costs of disability are unknown, but not if the probability of disability is unknown. He argues that the costs are much more difficult to determine, and therefore people are behaving rationally when they put off purchase of such insurance as long as possible.

The impacts of frailty

It is important not to confuse the effects of frailty, which vary greatly between people of the same age, with the effects of age as such. The effects described in this section will not apply to all old people, not even to all of the 'old old'.

Advancing age may render people incapable of some forms of economic behaviour. For example, in a study by Madeira and Goldman (1988), almost half the sample felt that food did not taste or smell as good to them as it had in the past; this could be expected to affect their food-purchasing behaviour.

It is frequently assumed that elderly consumers will be vulnerable to economic exploitation of various kinds, perhaps by wily marketers. This is not necessarily true, and probably is not true at all of large numbers of the retired. In fact, the elderly may well be more skilled at money management than younger people, by virtue of longer experience, and, in an empty-nest family situation, they are less likely to be subject to the purchase influence attempts that can destabilise family budgets at earlier life stages. Lea, Webley and Levine (1993) found that, as well as having hostile attitudes to debt, elderly people were very unlikely to have debts, suggesting that their money management is generally successful. Might the elderly, however, be vulnerable to outright economic crime? Clearly, few old people could defend themselves against mugging – but it is questionable how many younger people could do so effectively, or whether it would be advisable for most to try. Stereotypes suggest that old people might also be vulnerable to, for example, confidence tricksters, through being mentally slow; however, Mathur and Moschis (1995) showed that they were in fact more likely to see through one common fraud, the 'bait and switch' swindle. This involves advertising an item at a very low price (the 'bait') with the intention of persuading the customer to buy a more expensive substitute and with no intention of selling the low priced item.

The most extreme form of frailty is dementia, which is an increasing risk with advancing age. If dementia sets in, money management is noticeably affected, and this poses a number of care and policy problems (see, for example, Langan and Means, 1996). A particular concern is the risk that relatives, or institutions, who are delegated to look after an old person's financial affairs may in fact use the money for themselves; such 'financial abuse' is one of the recognised categories of 'elder abuse' and Langan and Means report some evidence that it is widespread and by no means confined to the dementing.

Reconstructing the Past

In modern society, the condition of being old is not generally highly valued, and this chapter so far has followed a conventional line in reporting the difficulties of life after retirement. To be old, it seems, is to be poor, possibly bored and depressed, probably ill, and perhaps completely incapacitated. We need to remember that there is also value in being old. We have already seen that retirement brings with it freedom from time constraint, and therefore the possibility of taking up more enjoyable activities, and that is potentially valuable to individuals. The old may also have value to society. By definition they have lived a long time and had experiences that younger people have not. In traditional societies, old people (or at least some old people) are valued precisely because of this accumulated experience – what we can call wisdom.

Is there such a thing as 'economic wisdom' inherent in old people in modern societies? Of course, a literate society is not dependent on old people as its repository of information about the past in the same way as an oral society. A multi-media society such as ours can even recover images and sounds as well as words without personal help. For research purposes, however, economic psychologists might well want to make use of the economic memories of the old, to understand the psychological impacts of macro-economic changes that are now past. Kemp (1991; see also Kemp and Willetts, 1996) has shown that people who lived through the substantial inflation of the 1960s to 1980s can to some extent date price levels; his technique could be extended to study longer periods and more dramatic events, for example dramatically inflationary periods. The psychological impacts of the transitions to command economies in Eastern Europe, and back to market economies in those countries and also in the former Soviet Union, could be studied through the memories of those who lived through them. Such information sources have their limitations, of course, but they are likely to yield some data that could be obtained in no other way.

What old people can uniquely do is *feel* about the past, especially in comparison with the present. For example, several studies of debt and poverty suggest that older people's attitudes towards spending, saving and debt differ from those typical in the modern population (e.g. Lea, Webley and Levine, 1993; Lea, Webley and Walker, 1995). It may be important for society, or families and communities, to make use of such feelings.

However, feelings about the past are more likely to be useful if the past can be accurately remembered. At least at the superficial level, the economic world changes fast; indeed, we often fear that the old will be especially perplexed by economic changes such as inflation or currency reform. Although Kemp has not extended his price memory studies to elderly participants, that could easily be done, and probably soon will be, given the current interest among cognitive psychologists in studying the general memory of the old (e.g. Maylor, 1996). Since some of the economic facts of past life can be checked objectively from statistical archives, but are rarely widely available, economic materials are actually rather generally useful for investigating very long-term memory, as Kemp has argued.

As economic psychologists, however, our main interest in people's economic memory is the ways in which it affects their current economic behaviour. The distinctive attitudes and behaviour of the elderly towards debt are a good example of the questions we need to ask. Do old people resist debt because of a direct effect of being old – perhaps because it involves risk, and risk avoidance rises with age, as Aristotle argued? Do they avoid debt because of a true memory effect – for example, because in their long lives they are almost bound to have had bad experiences with it? Or is it that those who are currently old lived through periods when debt was linked to personal disaster (not necessarily their own)? This would be a cohort effect, and would lead us to predict that when today's young people come to retire they will show no aversion to debt.

Of course, it is not just the memory of the past that can impact on people's economic activity in retirement. Both economic and non-economic life-events in the past can influence how elderly people behave economically, because they shaped their economic lives and habits at the time. Conversely, past economic events and behaviour may influence the non-economic behaviour of the retired. For example, Elder and Liker (1982) showed that middle-class women who had had to become self-sufficient in the depression of the 1930s enjoyed better psychological (and general) health in retirement; and Moen *et al.* (1995) showed that, though there was no universal impact of being a carer on the health of retired women, those who had been carers in the 1950s and had had high self-esteem were in good health during retirement in the 1980s (whereas past carers who had low self-esteem were in poor health). From a small-scale study that used depth interview techniques, Glass and Jolly (1997) concluded that participation in voluntary work earlier in life had a substantial impact on life satisfaction during retirement – whereas work life and leisure did not. Similarly, Dorfman (1992) found that retired academics' ratings of the importance of their past research work correlated positively with their current life satisfaction, whereas the hours they spent on such work in retirement had a negative impact.

Economic Life After Death

Finally, the inevitable consequence of old age is death. Death can, of course, come at any time, but in old age people are increasingly aware that it is relatively close, and in various ways make preparations for it; these behaviours have a distinct economic aspect. People might even seek euthanasia or commit suicide for economic reasons, perhaps in order to avoid the costs of their care eating up a planned bequest.

Death services

Death, like every other stage of life, has its characteristic modes of consumption. And like every other kind of consumption, these give an insight into human needs: what we spend on funerals, and what we buy with the money, tell us something about the psychology of death.

At one level, the consumer of death services is the dead person's executor or heir, and what is spent on, for example, a funeral comes out of the heir's pocket in the sense that it will not be available to be inherited. However, often the dead person has made explicit requests about the nature of a funeral, or their known preferences will dictate what 'must' be done. Many people, in fact, effectively purchase their own death services, either through insurance, or by setting money aside, or by provisions in their wills. In addition, elderly people are very likely to be purchasing death services as a result of the death of a spouse, so the cost will come out of what have been seen as joint assets.

As Drakeford (1998) emphasises, the funeral market is one in which people are at exceptional risk of exploitation: by their nature, death services are purchased only very few times in one's life, and people arranging the funeral of a spouse are likely to be severely distressed. These factors are in addition to any general extra vulnerability of the old to market exploitation, by virtue of frailty, as discussed earlier (pp. 143–145). Sommer (1991) has discussed how co-operatives may protect consumers against exploitation in this peculiarly sensitive market, though Drakeford notes that the Co-operative organisation is one of the oligopolists of the UK funeral market. The funeral industry has its own standards to which members are expected to conform, but the effectiveness of these self-regulatory measures has not been tested systematically.

There is little published research on the consumption of death services. The cost is considerable: Banks (1998) estimated the average cost of a US funeral at $5,000; Drakeford (1998) gave averages of around £1,000 for cremation and £1,500 for a funeral in the UK. Although there are obviously variations in expenditure according to income, this may be attenuated by a tendency among poorer families to try to give relatives a dignified funeral as a final compensation for their lifetime deprivations (Kearl, 1989). Furthermore, people are generally not well prepared for the cost of funerals: Bern-Klug, Ekerdt and Wilkinson (1999) found that half the respondents in their survey of relatives taking responsibility for funeral arrangements had no idea what to expect in the way of cost. Nor are the prices always easy to discover (Sommer, Nelson and Hoyt, 1985).

There are obvious problems for poor people in the face of bereavement. Drakeford (1998) discusses how the initial aim of the UK welfare state to ensure that everyone could have a decent funeral has been eroded, both by rising prices within the funeral industry and by social security policy and regulatory changes, so that some bereaved relatives face serious hardship and anxiety. Drakeford also shows that alternative forms of provision for funeral cost, such as insurance or pre-death purchase, are not reliable.

What is being bought at this considerable price? Obviously there is a practical necessity for burial or cremation, but it is argued that the funeral industry chiefly provides a service of personal support for the bereaved (e.g. Hyland and Morse, 1995). Funerals themselves are of course not the only kind of death service that people consume (among the others are the placing of advertisments or obituaries, which we discuss briefly below), and the additional services may or may not be bundled within the main arrangement with an undertaker.

Some other general themes of economic psychology also find a place in behaviour around funerals. For example, a significant proportion of people inter favoured possessions with bereaved relatives (Elliott, 1990), and this can be seen as the final role of possessions in self-extension (cf. Belk, 1988).

Wills and inheritance

One of the commonest clichés about death is, 'You can't take it with you'. For economic psychology, the most interesting way of preparation for death is the planning and making of wills: whether people do it at all, and if so, what forms their wills take. Economists have long recognised that the possibility of a bequest motive seriously threatens their standard way of considering saving, as a decision to defer consumption. Life-cycle models (see Chapter 5) are fundamentally incomplete if people are aiming not to consume all they earn during their lives. Keynes (1936, p. 108) included the bequest motive among the reasons for saving, on grounds of common observation; subsequent empirical work has amply confirmed his insight. We have already seen that the desire to bequeath is one of the reasons why the elderly save, accounting for at least half their saving motivation, and some people will even impoverish themselves in order to maintain the capacity to do so in the face of the costs of social care (Doyle, 1992). It is partly because of the threat to their capacity to bequeath that people perceive the costs either of social care, or of insuring against it, as an excessive burden (Parker and Clarke, 1997).

Psychologically speaking, a bequest motive is in no way problematic. The targets of bequests are typically the same as the targets for giving during the lifetime – family, friends and 'good causes' – and we have a range of ways in biological and social psychology for explaining why and how much people give to these. Death, from this perspective, is simply an opportunity for more substantial giving: it removes the major opportunity cost of giving. The problem with giving is that money or goods given away are no longer available for one's own use, either now or in a time of possibly greater future need. The dead have no further personal need of either consumption or insurance, so that the utility they can derive (we assume in anticipation before death) from others' consumption can come fully into play.

Within that framework, however, there are some interesting variations. In a sociobiologically inspired study of a California sample, Judge and Hrdy (1992) report that on average 92 per cent of the estate was bequeathed to a spouse or children. But within that pattern wives were less likely to bequeath to their husbands than husbands to their wives, a result that was explained by the husband's greater likelihood of having children by a different spouse. Sons were treated less equally than daughters. We have already seen, in Chapter 4, that remarried couples want their assets divided along biological lines. In Japan, the inequality of bequests to sons was traditionally extreme, and remains so in less modern, wealthy sectors of society; among less traditional people, there is an increasing tendency to bequeath disproportionately to the child with whom an elderly person has lived, or who has otherwise provided most support – an interesting form of post-death reciprocation (Tsuya and Martin, 1992).

Tax structures and other constraints may mean that people seek to make their bequests before they die. Self-impoverishment to avoid paying the costs of social care (Doyle, 1992), described above, is one example. Another is self-employed people passing on their businesses to relatives, rather than selling them, on retirement: Kimhi and Lopez (1999) discuss the factors influencing this decision among Maryland farmers, among them the need for the farm to provide the retired with a pension, and the perceived importance of its remaining within the family.

Obituaries

It is not only through bequests that one's economic life can have consequences after death. The dead are remembered in a variety of ways. Kirchler (1992) studied the obituaries that are, as a matter of convention, entered in newspapers in German-speaking countries by the past employers of the person who has died. He found that the gender stereotyping that has been widely reported within working life continues even after death. The kinds of words that are used in commendation of men are different from those used in commendation of women. Euster (1991) analysed the custom of publicly suggesting contributions to a charitable cause in memory of a person who has died; memorial notices were particularly likely to mention the dead person's charitable contributions, and he argued that this was a way in which the funding they had provided was continued after their death. Similarly Alali (1994) argues that obituary advertisements in Nigerian newspapers (placed by the bereaved relatives, and thus a form of death service consumption in themselves) serve to sustain the link between the deceased and the bereaved.

Concluding Remarks

This chapter has shown convincingly that retirement and old age are not a time of economic inactivity. It illustrates the advantage of the life-span approach to economic psychology taken in this book, which has forced us to look at some stages of life that economic psychologists have hitherto largely ignored. Old age is one of these.

But the simple example of obituaries, which we have just considered, brings us to a more general point. A life-span approach is incomplete if it is simply an agglomeration of material about different stages of life: the real need is to integrate the stages into a total picture. Howe (1997) has demonstrated that biographical sources can be a powerful tool for psychological investigation. Obituaries are a specialised, and compact, kind of biography: there should be many other ways in which we can assess the psychological impact of someone's economic life when it has completed its entire span.

Kirchler's results on gender-typing in obituaries illustrate a second general point that has run through this chapter. Even in death, and certainly in retirement, people remain part of their own societies. They do not become part of a homogeneous group of 'the old'; they do not become 'economically inactive'. The economic behaviour of the old (and also economic behaviour towards the old) is an essential chapter in our understanding of the economic psychology of everyday life.

7

Afterword

Concluding chapters are notoriously difficult to write. In traditional fiction the author has to identify the murderer (and all the clues that led to his or her discovery), marry off the hero and the heroine, and generally ensure that all the loose ends are tied up. The demands of modern textbook writing are fortunately less onerous: to deal with all the loose ends we have left in the previous chapters would require another book of the same length. Our aim in this chapter is rather more modest: we will try to draw together some of the threads that run through the book, consider what economic psychology has to offer with regard to some of the economic-psychological problems of the twenty-first century, and speculate a little about the future of economic psychology.

Some Conclusions

Common features of economic problems across the life-span

Throughout the book we have tried to keep to our stated aim of considering the economic problems people encounter during their lives. It is clear that Laura, whom we met in Chapter 2 being wheeled around the supermarket by her mum, faces rather different problems from those adolescents forced to take a marginal economic role or the frail elderly pondering whether they will need to go into a home. But there are, nonetheless, similarities between the problems that people face at different times of their lives.

Two of these are very obvious and are economic: the need for a reliable income source and the need to adjust the flow of income to expenditure. The particular form these problems take differs greatly. For a child, the problem is to get hold of money that he or she can spend freely on what is wanted, whereas for the elderly it is more likely to be to get sufficient money to spend on what is needed. Both are to some extent dependent on others (parents for pocket money, the state for the state pension), whilst the mature economic agent has more scope for increasing income by changing jobs or working longer hours. But the basic problem – that of getting hold of the wherewithal – is the same. What this highlights is the importance of the external economic constraints that individuals face. The rhetoric of the market, which places so much emphasis on people's freedom to choose, makes us apt to forget just how constrained people are. For many people in the UK, and for most people across the world, ensuring an adequate income is *the* main issue in their lives. The second problem, that is, the need to adjust the flow of income to expenditure, is more obviously an economic-psychological one. Again the form this takes differs considerably for children, adolescents, adults and the elderly: the scale, the time span and the type of expenditure will be dramatically different, as will the psychological resources that each brings to bear. But in each case there is a serious problem for the individual to solve: they have to anticipate their needs across a time period (whether one week, one term or five years), predict their income across the same period and, crucially, exert sufficient self-control so as not to spend money too soon. This is as true for the young child who receives his or her pocket money each Saturday and who tries to ensure that they have sufficient left to go swimming the following Friday as it is for the student faced with a loan that must last a term or the mature consumer budgeting for his or her summer holidays.

The third theme is perhaps less obvious, though we have referred to it repeatedly. This is the importance of non-economic constraints. We highlighted this in discussing young people's career choice and devoted most of a chapter to the impact of one particular constraint, that of gender. A wide range of non-economic factors impinge on people's ability to make their way in the world in the way they would like to: in addition to gender, we have mentioned normative and ideological pressures, institutional arrangements, class, race, locality and state of the local economy. It is stating the obvious, but a black adolescent (whether living in Amsterdam, Rome or London) has a different pattern of options from his or her white counterpart: similarly (though perhaps less obviously) women graduates do not have the same objective opportunities as their men friends. Over the years we have been struck by how often our undergraduates (predominantly female) have seen equal opportunity as something that has already been achieved. They are surprised by our description of the reality of sex discrimination in the workplace and elsewhere. But these constraints are real nonetheless. That some individuals from disadvantaged groups in our society are extraordinarily successful does not alter the fact of disadvantage, and it is essential to bear this in mind when thinking about the economic psychology of everyday life. These non-economic constraints can also apply quite generally across the population: for example, the existence of a standard working week means that many people work longer hours than they wish to (see Chapter 5).

Common features of solutions to problems

Identifying common features of solutions to problems across the life-span is more difficult. Nonetheless, some are apparent. For example, a piggy bank and a savings account share an important characteristic, that they both make it harder for the individual to get hold of his or her money and so help protect the individual against lapses in self-control. Similarly the child mowing the lawn for extra cash and the pensioner doing odd jobs on the side are both solving the problem of increasing income in the most obvious way.

What is perhaps more interesting is the continuity in psychological aspects of confronting problems. We tentatively suggested in Chapter 3 that financial competence was a dispositional variable and not something that was age-related. It is also clear from the evidence presented in Chapter 5 that dispositional variables such as conscientiousness (which is known to be a stable characteristic) are associated with saving. So our guess is that, to some extent, people develop characteristic ways of approaching the problems they face: those who have long time-horizons will be making appropriate long-term financial arrangements when they begin university and later in life will be planning their pensions at age 50; those who evade taxes and commit social security fraud in their 20s may be fiddling their disability payments in their 60s (Weigel, Hessing and Elffers, 1999); and those who coped well with a period of unemployment will cope well with retirement. What may be particularly important here is optimism. Though being optimistic can lead us into error (as witness the large number of small businesses that go bust) it is also an important psychological resource that helps people cope with unemployment, retirement and a range of other problems.

Another more general resource is the range of heuristics or rules-of-thumb that we develop across the life-span to help us solve the very complicated problems we encounter. So, in choosing a career we probably satisfice, that is, choose an occupation that is at least acceptable on all the dimensions that matter to us; in deciding whether we can afford to take early retirement we simply extrapolate from current trends in inflation and rates of investment return; and in deciding to replace a washing machine that has broken down we are probably guided simply by its age. These heuristics generally work quite well (Gigerenzer and Todd, 1999) so that the solutions and decisions we arrive at are approximately optimal.

The New Millennium and the Postmodern Consumer

It is very tempting, writing in the last week of the twentieth century, to follow the example of pundits and journalists and to speculate about what new economic problems will face people in the new millennium (or at least the very first bit of it). It is straightforward to identify some of the major economic problems of our time (underdevelopment, inequality both across the world and within societies, inflation, unemployment). These clearly have a psychological context, and in an earlier text (Lea, Tarpy and Webley, 1987) we considered how an economic-psychological approach might bear on these. Here our aim is a much more modest one – to consider, first, two general economic psychological problems that confront both individuals and societies and, then, two specific issues.

The economic and the social

The first is the general problem of where to set the boundary between the economic and the social, in other words how to draw the line between the 'public' world of commerce and the private world of relationships and the family. As we pointed out in Chapter 2, the notion that the family is something quite separate from the commercial world is simply wrong: the division of parental responsibilities, for example, is partly influenced by the separate earning power of each parent, the availability of child care in the area and so on. But the idea that there *should* be two separate spheres of exchange is a potent one. This suggests that it is inappropriate (or in some cases morally wrong) for some things to be subject to economic exchange. It also implies that shifting an exchange from the social to the economic sphere will change the nature of the exchange and have implications for the future relationship between the participants. That this is a problem for society as a whole is clear, hence the legislation that makes it impossible to buy babies or to sell oneself into slavery. These are collectively agreed as things that should not be part of the market economy. But it is also a problem for individuals, as in the example given in Chapter 4 of the husband offering to do his highly paid wife's share of the housework for money and the difficulties this caused.

We cannot resolve this issue – but we can analyse the nature of the problem facing individuals. Consider two concrete examples, the unacceptability of money as a gift to one's parents (discussed in Chapter 1) and the monetary payment for sexual services within marriage. Why is each of these unacceptable and, in the second case at least, frankly offensive? One could argue that money was the ideal gift as it enables the recipient to buy exactly what he or she wants. Similarly, it could be argued that since there is a well-developed (if underground) market for sexual services, it makes more sense to pay for extra, offbeat or odd sex within marriage rather than going outside it. Part of the answer lies in the fact that money puts an exact value on the service, and, more fundamentally, that any obligation is discharged by the payment. Thus a market transaction implies that there is no continuing relationship: the goods or service have been received, payment made, and there is an end to it. One can see that the concept of 'loyalty', which embodies the notion that partners in a relationship (whether in a marriage, a company, or a football club) will stick together through thick and thin, runs counter to this. Another part of the answer is that a money transaction implies that it is the goods or services being exchanged that is important, and not the relationship with the other person involved in the exchange. A money transaction also carries with it the notion of a society of 'atomised' individuals, each maximising their individual utility: thus in a marriage it implies thinking in terms of 'I' rather than 'we'.

It is clear that in a close relationship the reasons for distributing rewards are different. It is not a matter of giving in order to receive later: there is a direct concern for the other's welfare. What this suggests is that there are a number of types of relationships. Fiske (1990) believes that there are four kinds. One type is exchange: a good example would be selling a car, where people are acting as individuals to maximise individual profit. Another is communal: the distribution rule here is that you should take as much as you need. A homely example might be a Christmas dinner. A third is a relationship ordered by strict equality. In such a relationship, people receive exactly what everyone else receives. Another homely example would be dividing a cake equally between children – a more serious example would be voting, which, in our system, is arranged this way – one person, one vote. People don't get more votes because they work harder or because they need them more. Last, relationships may be ordered by authority. In authority relationships one person orders and the others follow those orders: an example might be parents in a supermarket.

Fiske argues that these four types of relationships can (and do) occur with the same people. A mother may give her daughter as much food as she needs but also order her to tidy her room, split a chocolate bar down the middle with her but pay her for baby-sitting her young brother. So these ways of organising the social allocation of rewards and costs do not characterise relationships so much as they characterise activities within relationships. In these examples eating is organised communally and baby-sitting in an exchange way.

The problem for modern society seems to be that more and more activities are being organised in an exchange way. One can instance the increasing use of dating agencies, which can be seen either as a sensible response to the problem of finding a partner or the intrusion of the commercial world into relationships, an increase in materialism (with possession mattering more than enduring values), and the monetisation of tourism. Our favourite recent example was the observation that on the West Coast of America affluent children's parties are no longer attended by either parent but are organised by paid entertainers.

Both individuals and society need to think carefully about the consequences of the forms of relationship they adopt for different activities. Blood, for example, is donated in the United Kingdom but generally purchased in the United States, and it has been argued by Titmuss (1970) and Fernandez Montoya (1997) that a voluntary system (based on communal relationships) produces more and better blood than the market system (though this has been disputed by Johnson, 1982). In a marriage, it is probable that the more activities are dealt with on a communal basis, the more stable the relationship. But shifting activities from one sphere to another is not always easy. As far as society is concerned, Frey (1997) claims that civic virtue (doing things because they are one's duty as a good citizen and not because one is paid to do so) can be maintained and fostered by direct citizen participation via popular referenda and initiatives.

A surfeit of choice?

The second problem is that of complexity. The economic world in the West today is more complex than ever before: the consumer is faced with an enormous range of products, whether he or she is buying food in the supermarket, choosing a savings account, or buying a holiday. Similarly, though talk of the boundaryless career being the norm is rather premature (see Chapter 5), it is nonetheless true that those choosing a career today are less likely to work in one job, or for just one employer, than those of previous generations.

This makes it doubly difficult for individuals. Not only do they have to make the best choice from a bewildering range of products but they also have to learn a language of product choice that is growing more complicated daily. When Paul was looking to buy his first tent it was a choice between a Black's Companion, a YHA Special or a low-cost brand-name that has been forgotten (in the event he got a long-term loan of a tent from a friend). Now there is a much wider choice, but, more importantly, it is a choice that to those in the know can be used to display expertise, build reputation and so on.

As far as the technical side is concerned, the consumer has been greatly helped by consumer associations and consumer programmes on the television, which help individuals to make the most appropriate choice for them. Keeping abreast with the language of consumer goods is more difficult, so people specialise (they understand 'mountain bike' or 'trainer') and read the appropriate magazines. Choosing a career is a much harder task; although straightforward advice is available, this is something that most people do with little knowledge and reflection on the alternatives.

But this is not just a matter of complexity. The postmodern consumer (van Raaij, 1991) faces a world that is fragmented, where there is no one dominant ideology and consumers are encouraged to have many identities. It is a paradoxical world where irony and parody are important. And instead of dealing with the real, consumers deal with the 'hyper-real', simulations of reality such as can be found at Disney World, in computer games, on the internet, and in staged 'religious' ceremonies for tourists.

This is a problem that is likely to become more challenging in the coming years. Being a self-conscious parodist who is fond of irony is quite a challenge (though Brian seems to find it very easy) and presumably the very notion of choosing a career would be foreign to such an individual. We suspect, however, that the postmodern condition is only a problem for a minority of individuals, whilst all of us have to cope with complexity.

Specific economic-psychological problems

Two issues seem especially worth discussing. The first is the advent of new technology, particularly that which impinges directly on the day-to-day economic behaviour of the consumer (this has been less true of many previous technological changes). Rao (1999) points out that the internet will radically alter two sectors, two of which the consumer interacts with directly, namely the retail sector and the banking and financial services sector. In addition to e-commerce, there are new forms of money (debit cards, Mondex cards) and direct banking, all of which have the potential to drastically change the way people manage their economic affairs.

E-commerce (purchasing goods or services electronically over the internet), for example, allows companies to use a range of negotiation models (such as auctions, state-your-price buying, and person-to-computer haggling) as well as setting conventional fixed prices. From the consumer's point of view, they can operate in a virtual global marketplace, and spending as much time seeking information and comparing prices as they wish. To date research in this area is very limited, as e-commerce, e-money and e-banking are just at the take-off stage. But it appears that most people do not keep detailed accounts of their expenditure (Burgoyne *et al.*, 1997) and want simple ways of ensuring that they do not spend too much. This suggests that cards that can be charged up (like Mondex cards) or tokens that represent a fixed sum of money (such as phone cards) will be highly successful in the future – in other words, consumers will probably adopt high-tech solutions that work in a low-tech way.

The second issue is the impact of environmentalism on our individual economic behaviour. No one now would deny that there is an environmental crisis, with concern about global warming, over-use of resources, pollution and overpopulation. This has created a high level of environmental concern throughout society, though this is only weakly related to environmentally responsible behaviour (Beckmann, 1999). Beckmann claims that this is largely because the importance of the cultural context and social values has been neglected. Whilst this may well be the case, our concern here is with the problem consumers face of how to act in an environmentally responsible way. Are products that are labelled 'green' necessarily good for the environment? Is ethical investment actually ethical? Do fair-traded goods benefit the suppliers? Should we be worried about genetically modified crops? It is very difficult for the average citizen to know the answer to these questions. If it was possible to rely on appropriate labelling of products and services, individuals would find it relatively easy to make decisions but, in the wake of crises of food quality in Britain (BSE) and elsewhere, there is now widespread cynicism about official labelling. Such labelling anyway has its limitations. Whilst EIRIS (Ethical Investment Research Service) has taken great care to ensure that very high-quality information is available to those constructing ethical investment portfolios, many of the ethical unit trusts on offer are best described as 'not-unethical' rather than ethical (Lewis *et al.*, 1998). The evidence also suggests that most people do not possess the level of environmental knowledge that is required to understand the consequences of their actions (Kempton, Boster and Hartley, 1995), which is not perhaps very surprising.

Beckmann (1999) is then perhaps right to suggest that what is needed is to alter the institutions that help support individual action. Otherwise, as she puts it (p. 174) 'individuals may well be asked to become frugal in a society that subtly demands profligacy'.

The Future of Economic Psychology

Institutionally, economic psychology has come of age, and is very healthy. The *Journal of Economic Psychology* is over twenty years old, there are now numerous textbooks, including a number of recent original texts in French (Lassarre, 1995), German (Kirchler, 1995), Spanish (Quintanilla, 1997) and Italian (Ferrari and Romano, 1999) and a Companion, a kind of encyclopaedic dictionary, has recently appeared (Earl and Kemp, 1999). There are a number of chairs in Economic Psychology throughout Europe, annual conferences have been held for 24 years and there is a firmly established triennial summer school for postgraduates. Intellectually the picture is not quite so satisfactory. Although economics is now much more sympathetic to ideas from psychology, and behavioural economics is burgeoning, there is still far too little fusion between the two disciplines, and many economic psychologists appear content to be applied social psychologists who 'just happen' to be working in the economic arena. We do not think this is satisfactory: though economic psychology draws heavily on social psychology it also draws from economics (and other social sciences) and, at its best, contributes original ideas back to both of its parent disciplines.

Using sources from a variety of disciplines we have managed to provide a reasonable, if occasionally patchy, natural history of the economic psychology of everyday life. That is to say, we have a fair idea of what people actually *do* (for example, in terms of how households manage their money or how much people save at different stages of life) and who is doing what, but know much less about why and how they do it. The processes underlying much economic behaviour are obscure. We do not feel apologetic at all about this – getting the natural history right matters, and many aspects of both psychology and economics have in the past suffered from premature attempts at formalisation. But it does suggest the obvious next step for economic psychology to take: that is, to move from what has sometimes been described as its 'mindless empiricism' (Lewis, 1989) to devising theories and models which capture something of the underlying processes and which have some predictive power. These models will need to combine the rigour and simplicity of the best economic models with the insights of social psychologists, sociologists and other social scientists.

What might such theories and models look like? A good example is the economic-psychological model of tax paying proposed by Cullis and Lewis (1997). This takes social conventions into account and is process-oriented but still deductive. Such theories and models will in the future, we hope, share a number of features. First, there will be a recognition that individuals are not isolated units but are members of families, of social groups, of organisations and of countries (this is not an exhaustive list!). The need to do this is very evident when we consider family decision-making (where it is clear that one needs to take into account the dynamics of the family including the influence of any children) but is equally necessary when providing accounts of economic behaviour that is less obviously social. Completing a tax form, for example, may be a private act and one for which there is individual responsibility but is no less social for that: a person's decisions will be influenced by the tax-paying norms of his or her social groups, as well as by his or her general predisposition to conform with the rules. Similarly one's first purchases of a video machine or CD player are likely to be guided by what is fashionable (a very social concept), as well as its functions and the price.

Second, future theories will treat individual economic decisions within the context of the relevant series of decisions. Many current models (of buying, for instance) focus on single instances of behaviour, in this case the purchase of individual products, rather than seeing them as part of a sequence of decisions. Acquiring one's first house (discussed in Chapter 3) is a good example of how a whole series of economic decisions, in some cases stretching over many years, may be inter-linked.

Third, we hope that future theories will take a more explicit life-span approach to economic behaviour. We have not taken a formal life-span approach ourselves – we have used it more as a narrative device, and as a framework to identify important and neglected topics. This is partly because current life-span approaches tend to be stage theories, rather descriptive, and not formalised in a way that aids prediction, but this is not a necessary feature of taking the life-span seriously.

And finally, we believe, as we noted above, that future economic-psychological theories must be rigorous (or aspire to rigour). We do not mean by this that theories need to incorporate rationality assumptions and be expressed with a panoply of mathematical equations. We do mean that theories need to be as clear and precise as possible. Without this characteristic economists will not take them seriously. Now it could be argued that this is not important (on the grounds that the agenda of economists is rather different and that the last thing economic psychologists need is an injection of neo-classical economics). As Lunt (1996, p. 283) puts it, 'one tempting response is to argue that there should be an economic psychology that is free of the economic agenda and is part of applied psychology, whether social or cognitive'. But, like Lunt, we believe that it would be a mistake to cut ourselves off from one of our parent disciplines.

Lunt suggests an interesting route forward for a more social economic psychology. His starting point is Deaton's (1992) identification of two approaches in macro-economics: one that is based on the expected utility model and builds upwards from micro-economic theory, the other that builds macro models bottom-up from micro-level data. The first we have already encountered. This gives rise to models like the life-cycle theory of saving, where people are presumed to be maximising utility across the life-span. Economists working in this tradition tend, according to Lunt, to incorporate a rather individualistic psychology into their models to improve them. The second approach, which is much more empirical, seems to give scope for economic psychologists to broaden the range of data considered and to engage in the development of genuinely social economic psychological theory. This might involve, for example, linking the notion of identities and the construction of the self to economic behaviour.

Whatever the merits of the particular route suggested by Lunt, he has done economic psychology a service by highlighting the need for it to have a strong social-psychological dimension. For our part, we believe that what is essential above all is that the theories and models we devise can be shown to work, and to do a better job in some respects than current theories in both economics and psychology. What 'doing a better job' means will depend on the nature of the competing theories and models: in one case it may be an improvement in predictive power, in another integrating previously separate domains, in yet another providing a more general model.

It is much easier, of course, to identify the desirable characteristics of theories and models than to devise such theories, which will require collaboration between economists and psychologists. But we are confident that in the decades to come what we have written above will simply describe the theories that are then on offer.

References

Abdel-Ghaffar, A., Handy, M., Jafari, J., Kreul, L., and Stivala, F. (1992) 'Youth tourism', *Annals of Tourism Research* 19, 792–795.

Acemoglu, D. and Scott, A. (1994) 'Consumer confidence and rational expectations: are agents' beliefs consistent with the theory?', *Economic Journal* 104, 1–19.

Adelmann, P. K. (1993) 'Psychological well-being and homemaker vs. retiree identity among older women', *Sex Roles* 29, 195–212.

Adler, R. P. and Faber, R. J. (1980) 'Background: children's television viewing patterns', in R. P. Adler, G. S. Lesser, L. K. Mesingoff, T. S. Robertson, J. R. Rossites and S. Ward (eds) *The Effects of Television Advertising on Children: Review and Recommendation*, Lexington, MA: Lexington Books.

Ainslie, G. W. (1991) 'Derivation of "rational" economic behavior from hyperbolic discount curves', *American Economic Review* 81, 334–340.

—— (1992) *Picoeconomics*, Cambridge: Cambridge University Press.

Ajzen, I. (1985) 'From intentions to actions: a theory of planned behavior', in J. Kuhl and J. Beckman (eds) *Action Control: From Cognition to Behavior* (pp. 11–39) New York: Springer Verlag.

Alali, A. O. (1994) 'Obituary and in-memoriam advertisements in Nigerian newspapers', *Omega* 28, 113–124.

Alessie, R. A., Lusardi, A., and Aldershof, T. (1997) 'Income and wealth over the life-cycle: evidence from panel data', *Review of Income and Wealth* 1, 1–32.

Altman, M. (1994) 'A theory of population growth when women really count', in G. Antonides and W. F. van Raaij (eds) *Integrating Views on Economic Behaviour* (pp. 1427–1437), Rotterdam: Erasmus University.

Amsden, A. H. (1980) *The Economics of Men and Women and Work*, Harmondsworth: Penguin.

Anderson, M. A. and Goldsmith, A. H. (1994) 'Rationality in the mind's eye – an alternative test of rational expectations using subjective forecast and evaluation data', *Journal of Economic Psychology* 15, 379–403.

Anderson, M., Bechofer, F. and Gershuny, J. (1994) (eds) *The Social and Political Economy of the Household*, Oxford: Oxford University Press.

Andrews, M. and Bradley, S. (1997) 'Modelling the transition from school and the demand for training in the United Kingdom', *Economica* 64, 387–413.

Antonides, G. (1988) *Scrapping a Durable Consumption Good*, Alblasserdam: Offsetdrukkerij Kanters B.V.

—— (1996) *Psychology in Economics and Business: An Introduction to Economic Psychology*, Dordrecht: Kluwer.

Antonides, G. and van Raaij, W. F. (1998) *Consumer Behaviour: A European Perspective*, Chichester: Wiley.

Aries, P. (1973) *Centuries of Childhood*, trans. R. Baldick, Harmondsworth: Penguin.

Armor, D. A. and Taylor, S. E. (1998) 'Situated optimism: specific outcome expectancies and self-regulation', *Advances in Experimental Social Psychology* 30, 309–379.

Arndt, J. (1979) 'Family life cycle as a determinant of size and composition of household expenditures', in W. L. Wilkie (ed.) *Advances in Consumer Research*, vol. 6 (128–132). Ann Arbor, MI: Association for Consumer Research.

Aronson, E. and Carlsmith, J. (1968) 'Experimentation in social psychology', in G. Lindzey and E. Aronson (eds) *Handbook of Social Psychology, vol. II* (1–79) Reading, MA: Addison-Wesley.

Arulampalam, W. and Stewart, M. B. (1995) 'The determinants of individual unemployment durations in an era of high unemployment', *Economic Journal* 105, 321–332.

Astin, H. S. (1984) 'The meaning of work in women's lives – a socio-psychological model of career choice and work behaviour', *Counselling Psychologist* 12, 117–126.

Atchley, R. C. (1976) *The sociology of retirement*, New York: Wiley.

Autor, D. H., Katz, L. F., and Krueger, A. B. (1998) 'Computing inequality: have computers changed the labour market?', *Quarterly Journal of Economics* 113, 1169–1213.

Avery, R. B. and Kennickell, A. B. (1991) 'Household saving in the US', *Review of Income and Wealth* 37, 409–432.

Bailey, M. and Mallier, T. (1999) 'The summer vacation: influences on the hours students work', *Applied Economics* 31, 9–15.

Baker, L. A. and Emery, R. E. (1993) 'When every relationship is above average: perceptions and expectations of divorce at the time of marriage', *Law and Human Behavior* 17, 439–450.

Banks, D. A. (1998) 'The economics of death? A descriptive study of the impact of funeral and cremation costs on US households', *Death Studies* 22, 269–285.

Banks, J. and Tanner, S. (1997) *The State of Donation: Household Gifts to Charity*, 1974–96, London: Institute for Fiscal Studies.

Banks, M. H. and Henry, P. (1993) 'Change and stability in employment commitment', *Journal of Occupational and Organisational Psychology* 66, 177–184.

Banks, M. H. and Ullah, P. (1988) *Youth Unemployment in the 1980s*, Beckenham: Croom Helm.

Barling, J., Rogers, K. A., and Kelloway, E. K. (1995) 'Some effects of teenagers' part-time employment – the quantity and quality of work make the difference', *Journal of Organizational Behavior* 16, 143–154.

Bates, E. (1979) *The Emergence of Symbols: Cognition and Communication in Infancy*, New York: Academic Press.

Bayus, B. L. (1988) 'Accelerating the durable replacement cycle with marketing mix variables', *Journal of Product Innovation Management* 5 (3), 216–226.

—— (1991) 'The consumer durable replacement buyer', *Journal of Marketing* 55, 42–51.

Becker, G. S. (1974) *Human Capital* (2nd edition), Chicago: University of Chicago Press.

—— (1976) *The Economic Approach to Human Behavior*, Chicago: University of Chicago Press.

—— (1991) *A Treatise on the Family*, Cambridge, MA: Harvard University Press.

Beckmann, S. C. (1999) 'Ecology and consumption', in P. Earl and S. Kemp (eds) *The Elgar Companion to Consumer Research and Economic Psychology* (pp. 170–175) Cheltenham: Edward Elgar.

Bedi, A. S. (1997) 'The importance of school quality as a determinant of earnings in a developing country: evidence from Honduras', *International Journal of Educational Development* 17, 427–437.

Belk, R. W. (1985) 'Materialism; trait aspect of living in the material world', *Journal of Consumer Research* 12, 265–280.

—— (1988) 'Possessions and the extended self', *Journal of Consumer Research* 15, 139–168.

—— (1995a) 'Studies in the new consumer behaviour', in D. Miller (ed.) *Acknowledging Consumption* (pp. 58–95), London: Routledge.

—— (1995b) 'Collecting as luxury consumption: effects on individuals and households', *Journal of Economic Psychology* 16, 477–490.

Bell, D. N. F. and Hart, R. A. (1998) 'Working time in Great Britain, 1975–1994: evidence from the New Earnings Survey panel data', *Journal of the Royal Statistical Society* A, 161, 327–348.

Benartzi, S. and Thaler, R. H. (1999) 'Risk aversion or myopia? Choices in repeated gambles and retirement investments', *Management Science* 45, 364–381.

Bennett, R., Glennerster, H., and Nevison, D. (1995) 'Regional rates of return to education and training in Britain', *Regional Studies* 29 (3), 279–295.

Benoit-Guilbot, O. (1994) 'Why are there so many long-term unemployed in the EU?', in O. Benoit-Guilbot and D. Gallie (eds) *Long Term Unemployment* (pp. 1–15), London: Pinter.

Berger, A. A. (1974) 'Drug advertising and the pain, pill, pleasure model', *Journal of Drug Issues* 4, 208–212.

Bergmann, B. R. (1986) *The Economic Emergence of Women*, New York: Basic Books.
—— (1995) 'Becker's theory of the family: preposterous conclusions', *Feminist Economics* 1, 141–150.
Berk, R. A. and Berk, S. F. (1983) 'Supply-side sociology of the family: the challenge of the New Home Economics', *Annual Review of Sociology* 9, 375–395.
Bernheim, D. B. (1991) *The Vanishing Nest Egg: Reflections on Saving in America*, New York: Priority Press.
Bern-Klug, M., Ekerdt, D. J., and Wilkinson, D. S. (1999) 'What families know about funeral-related costs: implications for social work practice', *Health and Social Work* 24, 128–137.
Berrington, A. and Murphy, M. (1994) 'Changes in the living arrangements of young adults in Britain during the 1980s', *European Sociological Review* 10, 235–257.
Berti, A. E. and Bombi A. S. (1988) *The Child's Construction of Economics*, Cambridge: Cambridge University Press.
Betts, J. R. (1995) 'Does school quality matter? Evidence from the national longitudinal survey of youth', *Review of Economics and Statistics* 78, 231–250.
Bills, D. B., Helms, L. B., and Ozcan, M. (1995) 'The impact of student employment on teachers' attitudes and behaviours toward working students', *Youth and Society* 27, 169–193.
Blau, P. M. and Duncan, O. D. (1967) *The American Occupational Structure*, New York: Wiley.
Blumberg, R. L. (ed.) (1991) *Gender, Family and Economy: The Triple Overlap*, Newbury Park, California: Sage.
Boddington, L. and Kemp, S. (1999) 'Student debt, attitudes towards debt, impulsive buying and financial management', *New Zealand Journal of Psychology*, 28, 89–93.
Bone, P. F. (1991) 'Identifying mature segments', *Journal of Consumer Marketing* 8 (Fall), 19–31.
Bonn, M. and Webley, P. (2000) 'South African children's understanding of money and banking', *British Journal of Developmental Psychology*, 18, 269–278.
Bonn, M., Earle, D., Lea, S., and Webley, P. (1999) 'South African children's views of wealth, poverty, inequality and unemployment', *Journal of Economic Psychology* 20, 593–612.
Bornemann, E. (1976) *The Psychoanalysis of Money*, New York: Urizen.
Bosworth, B., Burtless, G., and Sabelhaus, J. (1991) 'The decline in saving: evidence from national surveys', *Brookings Papers on Economic Activity* 1, 183–256.
Boulier, B. L. and Goldfarb, R. S. (1998) 'On the use and non-use of surveys in economics', *Journal of Economic Methodology* 5, 1–21.

Bourdieu, P. (1984) *Distinction: a social critique of the judgement of taste*, London: Routledge.
Bowes, J. M. and Goodnow, J. J. (1996) 'Work for home, school, or labour force: the nature and sources of changes in understanding', *Psychological Bulletin* 119, 300–321.
Bradley, S. (1995) 'The youth training scheme – a critical-review of the evaluation literature', *International Journal of Manpower* 16 (4), 30–56.
Bradshaw, J. and Millar, J. (1991) *Lone Parent Families in the UK*, London: HMSO.
Branch, E. R. (1994) 'The consumer expenditure survey: a comparative analysis', *Monthly Labor Review* 117, 47–55.
Brandstätter, H. (1993) 'Should economic psychology care about personality structure?', *Journal of Economic Psychology* 14, 473–494.
—— (1995) 'Saving behaviour related to personality structure', in E. Nyhus and S. V. Troye (eds) *Frontiers in Economic Psychology* (pp. 60–78), Bergen: Norwegian School of Economics and Business Administration.
—— (1997) 'Becoming an entrepreneur – a question of personality structure?', *Journal of Economic Psychology* 18, 157–177.
Brandstätter, H. and Güth, W. (1998) 'A psychological approach to individual differences in inter-temporal consumption patterns', Humboldt-Universität Berlin, Discussion paper No. 57.
Breakwell, G. M., Fife-Schaw, C., and Devereux, J. (1988) 'Parental influence and teenagers' motivation to train for technological jobs', *Journal of Occupational Psychology* 61, 79–88.
Breedveld, K. (1998) 'The double myth of flexibilization – trends in scattered work hours, and differences in time-sovereignty', *Time and Society* 7, 129–143.
Britt, C. L. (1997) 'Reconsidering the unemployment and crime relationship: variation by age group and historical period', *Journal of Quantitative Criminology* 13, 405–428.
Browning, M. and Lusardi, A. (1996) 'Household saving: micro theories and micro facts', *Journal of Economic Literature* 34 (4), 1797–1855.
Bryson, A. and White, M. (1996a) *From Unemployment to Self-employment*, London: Policy Studies Institute.
—— (1996b) *Moving In and Out of Self-employment*, London: Policy Studies Institute.
Buck, N., Gershuny, J., Rose, D., and Scott, J. (eds) (1994) *Changing Households: The British Household Panel Survey*, Colchester: University of Essex.
Buckingham, D. (1993) *Children Talking Television: The Making of Television Literacy*, London: The Falmer Press.
Burchell, B. (1994) 'The effect of labour market position, job insecurity and unemployment on psychological health', in D. Gallie, C. Marsh and C. Vogler (eds) *Social Change and the Experience of Unemployment* (pp. 188–212), Oxford: Oxford University Press.

Burgoyne, C. B. (1990) 'Money in marriage: how patterns of allocation both reflect and conceal power', *The Sociological Review* 38, 634–665.

—— (1999) 'Gifts', in P. Earl and S. Kemp (eds) *The Elgar Companion to Consumer Research and Economic Psychology* (pp. 257–262) Cheltenham: Edward Elgar.

Burgoyne, C. B. and Lewis, A. (1994) 'Distributive justice in marriage: equality or equity?', *Journal of Community and Applied Social Psychology* 4, 101–114.

Burgoyne, C. B. and Millar, J. (1994) 'Enforcing child support obligations: the attitudes of separated fathers', *Policy and Politics* 22, 95–104.

Burgoyne, C. B. and Morison, V. (1997) 'Money in remarriage: keeping things simple and separate', *The Sociological Review* 45, 363–395.

Burgoyne, C. B. and Routh, D. A. (1991) 'Constraints on the use of money as a gift at Christmas: the role of status and intimacy', *Journal of Economic Psychology* 12, 47–69.

—— (1999) 'What factors determine financial organisation in marriage? Preliminary findings from a study using vignettes', paper presented at IAREP Colloquium, Belgirate, Italy.

Burgoyne, C. B., Lea, S. E. G., Jones, S., and Mewse, A. (1999) 'Coping with constraints: poor people's perceptions of poverty', *Internal Report 98/03*.

Burgoyne, C. B., Roberts, E., Walker, C. M. and Webley, P. (1997) *Customer Use of Financial Information*, London: NCR.

Burnett, J. J. (1991) 'Examining the media habits of the affluent elderly', *Journal of Advertising Research* 31, 33–41.

Burnley, I. H., Murphy, P. A., and Jenner, A. (1997) 'Selecting suburbia: residential relocation to outer Sydney', *Urban Studies* 34, 1109–1127.

Buss, W. C. and Schaninger, C. M. (1983) 'The influence of sex role on family decision process and outcomes', in R. P. Bagozzi and A. M. Tybout (eds) *Advances in Consumer Research* 10, 439–444. Ann Arbor, MI: Association for Consumer Research.

Buunk, B. P. and Mutsaers, W. (1999) 'Equity perceptions and marital satisfaction in former and current marriage: a study among the remarried', *Journal of Social and Personal Relationships* 16, 123–132.

Calasanti, T. M. (1993) 'Bringing in diversity: toward an inclusive theory of retirement', Special Issue: Socialist–feminist perspectives, *Journal of Ageing Studies* 7, 133–150.

Camerer, C. (1989) 'Bubbles in asset prices', *Journal of Economic Surveys* 3, 3–41.

Cameron, S. (1993) 'A review of economic research on determinants of divorce', Unpublished manuscript, University of Bradford.

—— (1996) 'Shifting parameters in the economic model of divorce: evidence from the United Kingdom', *Journal of Socio-Economics* 25, 663–669.

Capon, N. and Kuhn, D. (1980) 'A developmental study of consumer information processing strategies', *Journal of Consumer Research* 7, 225–233.

Card, D. and Krueger, A. B. (1992) 'Does school quality matter? Returns to education and the characteristics of public schools in the United States', *Journal of Political Economy* 100, 1–40.

Carlson, L., Walsh, A., Laczniak, R. N., and Grossbart, S. (1994) 'Family communication patterns and marketplace motivations, attitudes, and behaviours of children and mothers', *The Journal of Consumer Affairs* 28 (1), 25–53.

Carroll, C. D. (1992) 'The buffer-stock theory of savings: some macroeconomic evidence', *Brookings Papers on Economic Activity* 2, 61–156.

Carroll, C. D., Fuhrer, J. C., and Wilcox, D. W. (1994) 'Does consumer sentiment forecast household spending? If so, why?', *American Economic Review* 84, 1397–1408.

Caspi, A., Wright, B. R. E., Moffitt, T. E., and Silva, P. A. (1998) 'Early failure in the labor market: childhood and adolescent predictors of unemployment in the transition to adulthood', *American Sociological Review* 63, 424–451.

Central Statistical Office (1994) *Social Trends*, London: HMSO.

Chafetz, J. S. (1991) 'The gender division of labor and the reproduction of female disadvantage: toward an integrated theory', Chapter 3 in R. L. Blumberg (ed.) *Gender, Family and Economy: The Triple Overlap*, Newbury Park, California: Sage.

Chapman, G. B. (1998) 'Similarity and reluctance to trade', *Journal of Behavioral Decision Making* 11, 47–58.

Charles, N. and Kerr, M (1987) *Women, Food and Families*, Manchester: Manchester University Press.

Chattoe, E. and Gilbert, N. (1999) 'Talking about budgets: time and uncertainty in household decision making', *Sociology* 33, 85–103.

Cheal, D. (1988) *The Gift Economy*, London: Routledge.

Cheng, S. T. (1993) 'The social context of Hong Kong's booming elderly home industry', *American Journal of Community Psychology* 21, 449–467.

Cheung, C. K. and Chan, C. F. (1996) 'Television viewing and mean world value in Hong Kong's adolescents', *Social Behavior and Personality* 24, 351–364.

Churchill, G. A. and Moschis, G. P. (1979) 'Television and interpersonal influences on adolescent consumer learning', *Journal of Consumer Research* 6, 23–35.

Claes, R. and Quintanilla, S. A. R. (1994) 'Initial career and work meanings in seven European countries', *Career Development Quarterly* 42, 337–352.

Clark, A. and Layard, R. (1993) *UK Unemployment*, London: Heinemann.

Clarke, Y. and Soutar, G. N. (1982) 'Consumer acquisition patterns for durable goods: Australian evidence', *Journal of Consumer Research* 8, 456–460.

Clogg, C. (1979) *Measuring Underemployment: Demographic Indicators for the US*, New York: Academic Press.

Cockett, M. and Tripp, J. (1994) *The Exeter Family Study*, Exeter: University of Exeter Press.

Cole, M. (1996) *Culture in Mind*, Cambridge, MA: Harvard University Press.

Coleman, J. S. (1994) 'Social capital, human capital, and investment in youth', in

A. C. Petersen and J. T. Mortimer (eds) *Youth, Unemployment and Society* (pp. 34–50), Cambridge: Cambridge University Press.

Coleman, M. and Ganong, L. H. (1989) 'Financial management in stepfamilies', *Lifestyles* 10: 217–232.

Connell, R. (1977) *Ruling Class, Ruling Culture: Studies of Conflict, Power and Hegemony in Australian Life*, New York, Cambridge University Press.

Cowell, F. (1991) 'Tax evasion experiments: an economist's view' in P. Webley, H. S. J. Robben, H. Elffers, and D. J. Hessing *Tax Evasion: An Experimental Approach*, Cambridge: Cambridge University Press.

Cox, J. and Isaac, R. M. (1986) 'Experimental economics and experimental psychology: ever the twain shall meet', in A. J. Macfadyen and H. Macfadyen (eds) *Economic Psychology: Intersections in Theory and Application*, Amsterdam: Elsevier.

Crawford, D. L., Johnson, A. W., and Summers, A. A. (1997) 'Schools and labour market outcomes', *Economics of Education Review* 16, 255–269.

Crites, J. O. (1965) 'Measurement of vocational maturity in adolescence', *Psychological Monographs*, no. 595.

Crites, J. O. and Savickas, M. L. (1996) 'Revision of the career maturity inventory', *Journal of Career Assessment* 4, 131–138.

Crosby, L. A. and Grossbart, S. L. (1984) 'Parental style segments and concern about children's food advertising', in J. H. Leigh and C. R. Martin (eds) *Current Issues and Research in Advertising, Vol. 1: Original Research and Theoretical Contributions*, Ann Arbor, MI: Graduate School of Business Administration.

Csikszentmihalyi, M. and Rochberg-Halton, E. (1981) *The Meanings of Things: Domestic Symbols of the Self*, Cambridge: Cambridge University Press.

Cullis, J. G. and Lewis, A. (1997) 'Why people pay taxes: from a conventional economic model to a model of social convention', *Journal of Economic Psychology* 18, 305–321.

Curasi, C. F., Price, L. L., and Arnould, E. J. (1997) 'You can't take it with you: an examination of the disposition decisions of older consumers', *Advances in Consumer Research* 24, p. 242.

Curtis, R. F. (1986) 'Household and family in theory on equality', *American Sociological Review* 51, 168–183.

Damon, W. (1978) *New Directions for Child Development*, vol. 1, San Franscisco: Jossey Bass.

Daniel, T. (1997) 'The economic psychology of saving: the role of individual differences associated with intertemporal choice', in I. Quintanilla Pardo (ed.) *The 22nd IAREP Colloquium* (pp. 127–155), Valencia: Promolibro.

Danigelis, N. L. and McIntosh, B. R. (1993) 'Resources and the productive activity of elders: race and gender as contexts', *Journal of Gerontology: Social Sciences* 48, S192–S203.

Darity, W. A., Goldsmith, A. H., and Veum, J. R. (1999) 'Unemployment and well-being', in P. E. Earl and S. Kemp (eds) *The Elgar Companion to Consumer*

Research and Economic Psychology (pp. 582–590), Cheltenham, Edward Elgar.

Das, M. (1998) *On Income Expectations and other Subjective Data: A Micro-Econometric Analysis*, Tilburg University: CentER.

Das, M. and van Soest, A. (1997) 'Expected and realized income changes: evidence from the Dutch socio-economic panel', *Journal of Economic Behavior and Organization* 32, 137–154.

Davies, E. and Lea, S. E. G. (1995) 'Student attitudes to student debt', *Journal of Economic Psychology* 16, 663–679.

Davies, R., Hamill, L., Moylan, S., and Smee, C. H. (1982) 'Incomes in and out of work', *Employment Gazette* 90, 237–243.

Davis, G., Cretney, S., Bader, K., and Collins, J. (1992) 'The relationship between public and private financial support following divorce in England and Wales', in L. J. Weitzman and M. MacLean (eds) *Economic Consequences of Divorce: The International Perspective* (pp. 311–344), Oxford: Clarendon Press.

Deaton, A. (1992) *Understanding Consumption*, Oxford: Oxford University Press.

de Meza, D. and Southey, C. (1996) 'The borrower's curse: optimism, finance and entrepreneurship', *The Economic Journal* 106, 375–386.

Denison, E. F. (1974) *Accounting for United States Economic Growth 1929–1969*, Washington DC: The Brookings Institution.

Derscheid, L. E., Kwon, Y.-H., and Fang, S.-R. (1996) 'Preschoolers' socialization as consumers of clothing and recognition of symbolism', *Perceptual and Motor Skills* 82, 1171–1181.

de Zwart, R. and Warnaar, M. F. (1997) *Nationaal Scholierenonderzoek 1996*, Utrecht: NIBUD.

Dickson, F. R., Lusch, R. F., and Wilkie, W. L. (1983) 'Consumer acquisition priorities for home appliances: a replication and re-evaluation', *Journal of Consumer Research* 9, 432–435.

Dittmar, H. (1992) *The Social Psychology of Material Possessions: To Have Is to Be*, Hemel Hempstead: Harvester Wheatsheaf.

Doan, R. M. and Popkin, B. M. (1993) 'Women's work and infant care in the Philippines', *Social Science and Medicine* 36, 297–304.

Dobbelsteen, S. and Kooreman, P. (1997) 'Financial management, bargaining and efficiency within the household: an empirical analysis', *De Economist* 145, 345–366.

Dominitz, J. and Manski, C. F. (1997) 'Using expectations data to study subjective income expectations', *Journal of the American Statistical Association* 92, 855–867.

Dorfman, L. T. (1992) 'Academics and the transition to retirement', *Educational Gerontology* 18, 343–363.

Dorfman, L. T. and Rubenstein, L. M. (1993) 'Paid and unpaid activities and retirement satisfaction among rural seniors', *Physical and Occupational Therapy in Geriatrics* 12, 45–63.

Douglas, M. and Isherwood, B. (1996) *The World of Goods*, London: Routledge, originally published 1979.

Doyle, K. O. (1992) 'Long-term health care, voluntary self-impoverishment, and family stress', *American Behavioral Scientist* 35, 803–808.

Drakeford, M. (1998) 'Last rights? Funerals, poverty and social exclusion', *Journal of Social Policy* 27, 507–524.

Duck, S. (1992) *Human Relationships*, London: Sage.

—— (ed.) (1994a) *Dynamics of Relationships*, London: Sage.

—— (1994b) *Meaningful Relationships*, London: Sage.

Duff, A. and Cotgrove, S. (1982) 'Social values and the choice of careers in industry', *Journal of Occupational Psychology* 55, 97–107.

Duncan, H. H., Travis, S. S., and McAuley, W. J. (1994) 'The meaning of and motivation for mall walking among older adults', *Activities, Adaptation and Ageing* 19, 37–52.

Dunne, F., Elliott, R., and Carlsen, W. S. (1981) 'Sex differences in the educational and occupational aspirations of rural youth', *Journal of Vocational Behavior* 18, 56–66.

Dustmann, C., Rajah, N., and Smith, S. (1997) 'Teenage truancy, part-time working and wages', *Journal of Population Economics* 10, 425–442.

Dutt, S. D. (1997) 'A microstructural analysis of the exchange rate expectation formation process', *Applied Economics Letters* 4, 537–539.

Dutt, S. D. and Ghosh, D (1997) 'Are experts' expectations rational? A multi-currency analysis', *Applied Economics* 29, 803–812.

Earl, P. E. and Kemp, S. (eds) (1999) *The Elgar Companion to Consumer Research and Economic Psychology*, Cheltenham: Edward Elgar.

Eastman, W. (1998) 'Working for position: women, men, and managerial work hours', *Industrial Relations* 37, 51–66.

Edgell, S., Hetherington, K., and Worde, A. (1996) *Consumption Matters*, Oxford: Blackwell.

Egerton, M. (1997) 'Occupational inheritance: the role of cultural capital and gender', *Work, Employment and Society* 11, 263–282.

Eggebeen, D. J. (1992) 'Family structure and intergenerational exchanges', *Research on Ageing* 14, 427–447.

Eisenberg, P. and Lazarsfeld, P. F. (1938) 'The effect of unemployment on children and youth', *Psychological Bulletin* 35, 358–390.

Elder, G. H. and Liker, J. K. (1982) 'Hard times in women's lives: historical influences across forty years', *American Journal of Sociology* 88, 241–269.

Elffers, H. (1991) *Income Tax Evasion: Theory and Measurement*, Amsterdam: Kluwer.

Elliott, C. and Ellingworth, D. (1998) 'Exploring the relationship between unemployment and property crime', *Applied Economics Letters* 5, 527–530.

Elliott, H. and Halfpenny, P. (1994) 'Extracting data on charitable giving from the family expenditure survey', *ESRC Data Archive Bulletin*, 57, 8–11.

Elliott, J. R. (1990) 'Funerary artefacts in contemporary America', *Death Studies* 14, 601–612.

Elliott, M. (1996) 'Impact of work, family, and welfare receipt on women's self-esteem in young adulthood', *Social Psychology Quarterly* 59, 80–95.

Elliott, R. and Wattanasuwan, K. (1998) 'Brands as symbolic resources for the construction of identity', *International Journal of Advertising* 17 (2), 131–144.

Emler, N. and Dickinson, J. (1985) 'Children's representations of economic inequalities: the effect of social class', *British Journal of Developmental Psychology* 3, 191–198.

Engelhardt, G. V. (1994) 'Tax subsidies to saving for home purchase – evidence from Canadian RHOSPS', *National Tax Journal* 47, 363–393.

Ensley, E. E. and Pride, W. M. (1991) 'Advertisement pacing and the learning of marketing information by the elderly', *Psychology and Marketing* 8, 1–20.

Eppright, D. R., Arguea, N. M., and Huth, W. L. (1998) 'Aggregate consumer expectation indexes as indicators of future consumer expenditures', *Journal of Economic Psychology* 19, 215–235.

Erikson, E. H. (1963) *Childhood and Society*, New York: Norton.

—— (1982) *The Life-cycle Completed*, New York: Norton.

Erikson, R. and Jonsson, J. O. (1998) 'Social origin as an interest-bearing asset: family background and labour-market rewards among employees in Sweden', *Acta Sociologica* 41, 19–36.

Etzioni, A. (1988) *The Moral Dimension: Towards a New Economics*, New York: Free Press.

—— (1992) 'Socio-economics: select policy implications' in S. E. G. Lea, P. Webley and B. M. Young (eds) *New Directions in Economic Psychology: Theory, Experiment and Application* (pp. 13–27), Cheltenham: Edward Elgar.

—— (1998) 'Voluntary simplicity: characterization, select psychological implications and societal consequences', *Journal of Economic Psychology* 19, 619–643.

European Schools Project (n.d.) Pocket money: European diversity URL. *http://www.esp.educ.uva.nl/nl/msp11.htm*

Euster, G. L. (1991) 'Memorial contributions: remembering the elderly deceased and supporting the bereaved', *Omega: Journal of Death and Dying* 23, 169–179.

Faist, T. (1993) 'From school to work – public-policy and underclass formation among young Turks in Germany during the 1980s', *International Migration Review* 27, 306–331.

Feagin, J. (1975) *Subordinating the Poor*, Englewood Cliffs, NJ: Prentice Hall.

Feather, N. (1974) 'Explanations for poverty in Australian and American samples: the person, society and fate', *Australian Journal of Psychology* 26, 199–216

Feldman, D. C. (1994) 'The decision to retire early: a review and conceptualization', *Academy of Management Review* 19, 285–311.

Feldman, D. C. and Turnley, W. H. (1995) 'Underemployment among recent business college graduates', *Journal of Organizational Behavior* 16, 691–706.

Fellerman, R. and Debevec, K. (1993) 'Kinship exchange networks and family consumption', *Advances in Consumer Research* 20, 458–462.

Ferenczi, S. (1926) *Further Contributions to the Theory and Technique of Psychoanalysis*, London: Knopf.

Fergusson, D. M., Horwood, L. J., and Lynskey, M. T. (1997) 'The effects of unemployment on psychiatric illness during young adulthood', *Psychological Medicine* 27, 371–381.

Fernandez Montoya, A. (1997) 'Altruism and payment in blood donation', *Transfusion Science* 18, 379–386.

Ferrari, L. and Romano, D. (1999) *Mente e Denaro: Introduzione alla Psciologia Economica* [Mind and money: introduction to economic psychology], Milan: Raffaello Cortina Editore

Festervand, T. A. and Wylde, M. A. (1988) 'The marketing of technology to older adults', *International Journal of Technology and Ageing* 1, 156–162.

Finch, J. and Mason, J. (1993) *Negotiating Family Responsibilities*, London: Routledge

Fine, B. and Leopold, E. (1993) *The World of Consumption*, London: Routledge.

Fineman, S. (1987) 'Back to unemployment: wounds and wisdoms', in D. Fryer and P. Ullah (eds) *Unemployed People: Social and Psychological Perspectives*, Milton Keynes: Open University Press.

Fishman, B. (1983) 'The economic behavior of stepfamilies', *Family Relations* 32: 359–366.

Fiske, A. P. (1990) *Structures of Social Life: The Four Elementary Forms of Human Relations*, New York: The Free Press.

Flavell, J. H., Flavell, E. R., Green, F. L., and Korfmacher, J. E. (1990) 'Do young children think of television images as pictures or real objects?', *Journal of Broadcasting and Electronic Media* 34, 399–419.

Fleming, R. (1997) *The Common Purse*, Auckland: Auckland University Press.

Fleming, R. and Atkinson, T. (1999) *Families of a Different Kind*, Waikanae, New Zealand: Families of Remarriage Project.

Fleming, R. and Easting, S. (1994) *Couples, Households and Money*, Palmerston North, NZ: Social Policy Research Centre: Massey University.

Flouri, E. (1999) 'Materialism in adolescents', in International Association for Research in Economic Psychology (eds), Proceedings of the XXIV Symposium, 2.

—— (2000) 'A typology of materialists', Unpublished PhD thesis, University of Exeter.

Foa, U. G. (1971) 'Interpersonal and economic resources', *Science* 171, 345–351.

Ford, J. (1990) 'Credit and default among young adults: an agenda of issues', *Journal of Consumer Policy* 13, 133–154.

Formanek, R. (1991) 'Why they collect? Collectors reveal their motivations?', in F. W. Rudmin (ed.) *To Have Possession: A Handbook on Ownership and Property* (pp. 275–286), Corte Madera, CA: Select Press.

Foxall, G. R. (1990) *Consumer Psychology in Behavioural Perspective*, London: Routledge.

Foxman, E. R., Tansuhaj, P. S., and Ekstrom, K. M. (1989) 'Adolescents' influence in family purchase decisions: a socialisation perspective', *Journal of Business Research* 18, 159–172.

Frank, R., Gilovich, T., and Regan, D. (1993) 'Does studying economics inhibit cooperation?', *Journal of Economic Perspectives* 7, 159–172.

Freud, S. (1908) *Character and Anal Eroticism*, London: Hogarth.

Frey, B. S. (1997) 'A constitution for knaves crowds out civic virtues', *Economic Journal* 107, 1043–1053.

Friedman, M. (1953) *Essays in Positive Economics*, Chicago: University of Chicago Press.

Fryer, D. (1992) 'Psychological or material deprivation: why does unemployment have mental health consequences?', in E. McLaughlin (ed.) *Understanding Unemployment* (pp. 103–125), London: Routledge.

Fryer, D. and Payne, R. L. (1984) 'Pro-activity in unemployment: findings and implications', *Leisure Studies* 3, 273–295.

Furnham, A. F. (1985) 'Youth unemployment: a review of the literature', *Journal of Adolescence* 8, 109–124.

—— (1990) *The Protestant Work Ethic*, London: Routledge.

—— (1996) 'The economic socialization of children', in P. Lunt and A. Furnham (eds) *Economic Socialization: The Economic Beliefs and Behaviours of Young People*, Cheltenham: Edward Elgar.

—— (1999) 'The saving and spending habits of young people', *Journal of Economic Psychology* 20 (6), 677–697.

Furnham A. F. and Gunter, B. (1992) *Consumer Profiles: An Introduction to Psychographics*, London: Routledge.

Furnham, A. F. and Lewis, A. (1986) *The Economic Mind*, Brighton: Wheatsheaf.

Furnham, A. F. and Thomas, P. (1984) 'Pocket money: a study of economic education', *British Journal of Developmental Psychology* 2, 205–212.

Furth, H. (1980) *The World of Grown-Ups*, New York: Elsevier.

Gaines, L. and Esserman, J. (1981) 'A quantitative study of young children's comprehension of television programs and commercials', in J. F. Esserman (ed.) *Television Advertising and Children: Issues, Research and Findings* (Chapter 5, pp. 95–105), New York: Child Research Service.

Gall, T. L., Evans, D. R., and Howard, J. (1997) 'The retirement adjustment process: changes in the well being of male retirees across time', *Journal of Gerontology: Psychological Sciences* 52B, 110–117.

Gayle, V. (1996) 'The determinants of student loan take-up in the United Kingdom: another gaze', *Applied Economics Letters* 3, 25–27.

Gentner, D. (1975) 'Evidence for the psychological reality of semantic components: the verbs of possession', in D. Norman and D. Rumelhart (eds) *Explorations in Cognition* (pp. 21–246), San Francisco: W. H. Freeman.

George, D. (1997) 'Working longer hours: pressure from the boss or pressure from the marketers?', *Review of Social Economy* 55, 33–65

Gibler, K. M., Lumpkin, J. R., and Moschis, G. P. (1997) 'Mature consumer awareness and attitudes toward retirement housing and long-term care alternatives', *Journal of Consumer Affairs* 31, 113–138.

Gigerenzer, G. and Todd, P. M. (1999) *Simple Heuristics that Make us Smart*, Oxford: Oxford University Press.

Gilleard, C. (1998) 'McClelland hypothesis', in P. E. Earl and S. Kemp (eds) *The Elgar Companion to Consumer Research and Economic Psychology* (pp. 380–382), Cheltenham: Edward Elgar.

Gilovich, T. (1991) *How We Know What Isn't So: The Fallibility of Human Reason in Everyday Life*, New York: The Free Press.

Ginn, J. and Arber, S. (1991) 'Gender, class and income inequalities in later life', *British Journal of Sociology* 42, 369–396.

Glass, J. C. and Jolly, G. R. (1997) 'Satisfaction in later life among women 60 or over', *Educational Gerontology* 23, 297–314.

Goldberg, H. and Lewis, R. (1978) *Money Madness: The Psychology of Saving, Spending, Loving and Hating Money*, London: Springwood.

Goldsmith, A. H., Veum, J. R., and Darity, W. (1995) 'Are being unemployed and being out of the labour-force distinct states? A psychological approach', *Journal of Economic Psychology* 16, 275–295.

—— (1996) 'The impact of labour force history on self-esteem and its component parts, anxiety, alienation and depression', *Journal of Economic Psychology* 17, 183–220.

Goldsmith, R. E., Stith, M. T., and White, J. D. (1987) 'Race and sex differences in self identified innovativeness and opinion leadership', *Journal of Retailing* 63, 411–425.

Goldthorpe, J. H. (1979) *Social Mobility and Class Structure in Modern Britain*, Oxford: Clarendon Press.

Gombert, J. E. (1992) *Metalinguistic Development*, Hemel Hempstead: Harvester Wheatsheaf.

Goode, J., Callender, C., and Lister, R. (1998) *Purse or Wallet?*, London: Policy Studies Institute.

Gorn, G. J., Goldberg, M. E., Chattopadhyay, A., and Litvack, D. (1991) 'Music and information in commercials: their effects with an elderly sample', *Journal of Advertising Research* 31, 23–32.

Gottfredson M. R. and Hirschi, T. (1990) *A General Theory of Crime*, Stanford, CA: Stanford University Press.

Gowan, M. A. (1998) 'A preliminary investigation of factors affecting appraisal of the decision to take early retirement', *Journal of Employment Counselling*, 35, 124–140.

Greco, A. J., and Swayne, L. E. (1992) 'Sales response of elderly consumers to point-of-purchase advertising', *Journal of Advertising Research* 32, 43–53.

Green, F., Hoskins, M., and Montgomery, S. (1996) 'The effects of company training, further education and the Youth Training Scheme on the earnings of young employees', *Oxford Bulletin of Economics and Statistics* 58 (3), 469–488.

Green, L., Fry, A. F., and Myerson, J. (1994) 'Discounting of delayed rewards – a life span comparison', *Psychological Science* 5, 33–36.

Green, L., Myerson, J., and Ostaszewski, P. (1999) 'Discounting of delayed rewards across the life span: age differences in individual discounting functions', *Behavioural Processes* 46, 89–96.

Groenland, E. A. and van Veldhoven, G. M. (1983) 'Tax evasion behaviour: a psychological framework', *Journal of Economic Psychology* 3, 12–144.

Grogger, J., and Eide, E. (1995) 'Changes in college skills and the rise in the college wage premium', *Journal of Human Resources* 30, 280–310.

Grotevant, H. D., and Durrett, M. E. (1980) 'Occupational knowledge and career development in adolescence', *Journal of Vocational Behavior* 17, 171–182.

Grotevant, H. D., Cooper, C. R., and Kramer, K. (1986) 'Exploration as a predictor of congruence in adolescents' career choices', *Journal of Vocational Behavior* 29, 201–215.

Grubb, W. N. (1993) 'The varied economic returns to post-secondary education: new evidence from the class of 1972', *Journal of Human Resources* 28, 364–382.

—— (1997) 'The returns to education in the sub-baccalaureate labour market, 1984–1990', *Economics of Education Review* 16, 231–245.

Guillemard, A. M. and Rein, M. (1993) 'Comparative patterns of retirement: recent trends in developed societies', *Annual Review of Sociology* 19, 469–503.

Gunnarson, J. and Wahlund, R. (1993) 'Household financial strategies: do they exist?', Paper given at the 18th IAREP conference, Moscow.

—— (1994) 'Saving behaviour over the life-cycle and time preference in financial strategies', in G. Antonides and W. F. van Raaij (eds) *Integrating Views on Economic Behaviour: Proceedings of the 19th Annual Colloquium of IAREP*.

—— (1997) 'Household financial strategies in Sweden: an exploratory study', *Journal of Economic Psychology* 18, 201–233.

Guy, B. S., Rittenburg, T. L., and Hawes, D. K. (1994) 'Dimensions and characteristics of time perceptions and perspectives among older consumers', *Psychology and Marketing* 11, 35–56.

Hagstrom, T. and Gamberale, F. (1995) 'Young people's work motivation and value orientation', *Journal of Adolescence* 18, 475–490.

Hakim, C. (1992) 'Unemployment, marginal work and the black economy', in E. McLaughlin (ed.) *Understanding Unemployment* (pp. 144–159), London: Routledge.

Hamermesh, D. D. (1984) 'Consumption during retirement: the missing link in the life cycle', *Review of Economics and Statistics* 66, 1–7.

Hammarström, A. (1994) 'Health consequences of youth unemployment – review from a gender perspective', *Social Science and Medicine* 38, 699–709.

Hammer, T. (1997) 'History dependence in youth unemployment', *European Sociological Review* 13, 17–33.

Hammer, T. and Furlong, A. (1996) '"Staying on": the effects of recent changes in educational participation for 17–19-year-olds in Norway and Scotland', *Sociological Review* 44, 675–691.

Han, S. K. and Moen, P. (1999a) 'Work and family over time: a life course approach', *Annals of the American Academy of Political and Social Science* 562, 98–110.

—— (1999b) 'Clocking out: temporal patterning of retirement', *American Journal of Sociology* 105, 191–236.

Handy, C. (1984) *The Future of Work: A Guide to a Changing Society*, Oxford: Blackwell.

Hanisch, K. A. and Hulin, C. L. (1990) 'Job attitudes and organizational withdrawal: an examination of retirement and other voluntary withdrawal behaviors', *Journal of Vocational Behavior* 37, 60–78.

Hansen, M. N. (1996) 'Earnings in elite groups: the impact of social class origin', *Acta Sociologica* 39, 385–408.

Harbaugh, B. and Krause, K. (1999) *The Economic Behavior of Children*, http:/harbaugh/uoregon.edu/children.

Hartman, R. S., Doane, M. J., and Woo, C. K. (1991) 'Consumer rationality and the status quo', *Quarterly Journal of Economics* 106, 141–162.

Harvey, N., Bolger, F., and McClelland, A. (1994) 'On the nature of expectations', *British Journal of Psychology* 85, 203–229.

Hayes, B. C. and Vanden Heuvel, A. (1994) 'Attitudes toward mandatory retirement: an international comparison', *International Journal of Ageing and Human Development* 39, 209–231.

Hayes, J. and Nutman, P. (1981) *Understanding the Unemployed*, London: Tavistock.

Haynes, J., Burts, D. C., Dukes, A., and Cloud, R. (1993) 'Consumer socialization of pre-schoolers and kindergarteners as related to clothing consumption', *Psychology and Marketing* 10, 151–166.

Heaven, P. C. L. (1995) 'Job-search strategies among teenagers: attributions, work beliefs, and gender', *Journal of Adolescence* 18, 217–228.

Heisley, D. D., Cours, D., and Wallendorf, M. (1997) 'The social construction of heirlooms', *Advances in Consumer Research* 24, p. 242.

Henkens, K. (1999) 'Retirement intentions and spousal support: a multi-actor approach', *Journals of Gerontology Series B – Psychological Sciences and Social Sciences* 54, S63–S73.

Henretta, J. C. (1987) 'Family transitions, housing-market context, and 1st home purchase by young married households', *Social Forces* 66, 520–536.

—— (1994) 'Recent trends in retirement', *Reviews in Clinical Gerontology* 4, 71–81.

Henretta, J. C., Hill, M. S., Li, W., Soldo, B. J., and Wolf, D. A. (1997) 'Selection of children to provide care: the effect of earlier parental transfers', *Journals of Gerontology Series B – Psychological Sciences and Social Sciences* 52, 110–119.

Henriksen, L. (1996) 'Naïve theories of buying and selling: implications for teaching critical-viewing skills', *Journal of Applied Communication Research* 24, 93–109.

Henry, B. (ed.) (1986) *British Television Advertising: The First 30 Years*, London: Century Benham.

Herrnstein, R. J. (1990) 'Rational choice theory: necessary but not sufficient', *American Psychologist* 45, 356–367.

Herrnstein, R. J. and Prelec, D. (1992) 'Melioration' in G. Loewenstein and J. Elster (eds) *Choice over Time* (pp. 235–263), New York: Russell Sage.

Hesketh, B., Watson-Brown, C., and Whiteley, S. (1998) 'Time-related discounting of value and decision-making about job options', *Journal of Vocational Behavior* 52, 89–105.

Hessing, D. J., Elffers, H., Robben, H. S. J., and Webley, P. (1993) 'Needy or greedy? The social psychology of individuals who fraudulently claim unemployment benefits', *Journal of Applied Social Psychology* 23, 226–243.

Heubeck, B. G., Tausch, B., and Mayer, B. (1995) 'Models of responsibility and depression in unemployed young males and females', *Journal of Community and Applied Social Psychology* 5, 291–309.

Hey, J. D. (1992) 'Experiments in economics – and psychology', in S. E. G. Lea, P. Webley and B. M. Young (eds) *New Directions in Economic Psychology*, Cheltenham: Edward Elgar.

—— (1994) 'Expectations formation – rational or adaptive?', *Journal of Economic Behavior and Organization* 25, 329–349.

Hirschman, E. C. (1984) 'Experience seeking: a subjectivist perspective of consumption', *Journal of Business Research* 12, 115–136.

Hite, C. F. and Hite, R. E. (1995) 'Reliance on brand by young children', *Journal of the Market Research Society* 37 (2), 185–193.

Hodkinson, P. and Sparkes, A. C. (1993) 'Young people's career choices and careers guidance action planning: a case-study of training credits in action', *British Journal of Guidance and Counselling* 21, 246–261.

Holbrook, M. B. and Schindler, R. M. (1994) 'Age, sex, and attitude toward the past as predictors of consumers' aesthetic tastes for cultural products', *Journal of Marketing Research* 31, 412–422.

Hollister, J., Rapp, D., and Goldsmith, E. (1986) 'Monetary practices of sixth-grade students', *Child Study Journal* 16, 183–190.

Holmes, T. H. and Rahe, R. H. (1967) 'The social readjustment rating scale', *Journal of Psychosomatic Research* 11, 213–218.

Holzer, H. J., Ihlanfeldt, K. R., and Sjoquist, D. L. (1994) 'Work, search, and travel among white and black youth', *Journal of Urban Economics* 35, 320–345.

Horowitz, T. (1982) 'Excitement vs. economy: fashion and youth culture in Britain', *Adolescence* 17, 627–636.

Howe, M. J. A. (1997) 'Beyond psychobiography: towards more effective syntheses of psychology and biography' *British Journal of Psychology* 88, 235–248.

Hunter, A. A. and Leiper, J. M. (1993) 'On formal education, skills and earnings – the role of educational certificates in earnings determination', *Canadian Journal of Sociology* 18, 21–42.

Hurd, M. D. and Swallen, K. (1997) 'The relationship between personality measures and family status and economic outcomes', presented at the TMR/CentER conference on savings, Tilburg, The Netherlands, July 1997 and at the Gerontological Society meetings, Cincinnati, November 1997.

Hyland, L. and Morse, J. M. (1995) 'Orchestrating comfort – the role of funeral directors', *Death Studies* 19, 453–474.

Ide-Smith, S. and Lea, S. E. G. (1988) 'Gambling in young adolescents', *Journal of Gambling Behaviour* 4, 110–119.

Inglehart, R. (1990) *Culture Shift in an Advanced Industrial Society*, Princeton, NJ: Princeton University Press.

Jackson, H. O. (1992) 'Ageing and expenditures on apparel', *Clothing and Textiles Research Journal* 10, 24–28.

Jaglom, L. M. and Gardner, H. (eds) (1981) 'The pre-school television viewer as anthropologist', in H. Kelly and H. Gardner (eds) *Viewing Children through Television*, San Francisco, CA: Jossey-Bass.

Jahoda, G. (1952) 'Job attitudes and job choice among secondary modern school leavers II', *Occupational Psychology* 26, 206–222.

—— (1981) 'The development of thinking about economic institutions: the bank', *Cahiers de Psychologie Cognitive* 1, 55–73.

—— (1983) 'European "lag" in the development of an economic concept: a study in Zimbabwe', *British Journal of Developmental Psychology* 1, 113–120.

Jahoda, M. (1982) *Employment and Unemployment*, Cambridge: Cambridge University Press.

James, S. R. (1996) 'Female household investment strategy in human and non-human capital with the risk of divorce', *Journal of Divorce and Remarriage* 25, 151–167.

Jensen, L. C., Christensen, R., and Wilson, D. J. (1985) 'Predicting young women's role preference for parenting and work', *Sex Roles* 13, 531–538.

John, D. R. (1999) 'Consumer socialization of children: a retrospective look at twenty-five years of research', *Journal of Consumer Research* 26, 183–213.

Johnes, G. (1994) 'The determinants of student loan take-up in the United Kingdom', *Applied Economics* 26, 999–1005.

Johnson, D. B. (1982) 'The free-rider principle, the charity market and the economics of blood', *British Journal of Social Psychology* 21, 93–106.

Johnson, P., Conrad, C., and Thompson, D. (1989) *Workers versus Pensioners: Intergenerational Justice in an Ageing World*, Manchester: Manchester University Press.

Jones, F. L. (1993) 'Unlucky Australians – labour-market outcomes among aboriginal Australians', *Ethnic and Racial Studies* 16, 420–458.

Jones, G. V. (1979) 'A generalized polynomial model for perception of exponential series', *Perception and Psychophysics* 25, 232–234.

Jowell, R., Brook, L., Prior, G., and Taylor, B. (eds) (1992) *British Social Attitudes: the 9th report*, Aldershot: Dartmouth.

Judge, D. S. and Hrdy, S. B. (1992) 'Allocation of accumulated resources among close kin: inheritance in Sacramento, California, 1890–1984', *Ethology and Sociobiology* 13, 495–522.

Jupp, B. (1997) *Saving Sense*, London: Demos.

Kagel, J. and Roth, A. (1995) *Handbook of Experimental Economics*, Princeton, NJ: Princeton University Press.

Kahneman, D. and Tversky, A. (1979) 'Prospect theory: an analysis of decision under risk', *Econometrica* 47, 263–291.

Kahneman, D., Knetsch, J., and Thaler, R. H. (1990) 'Experimental tests of the endowment effect and the Coase theorem', *Journal of Political Economy* 98, 1325–1348.

—— (1991) 'The endowment effect, loss aversion and status quo bias', *Journal of Economic Perspectives* 5, 193–206.

Kain, J. F. (1968) 'Housing segregation, negro employment, and metropolitan decentralization', *Quarterly Journal of Economics* 82, 175–197.

Kasser, T. and Ryan, R. M. (1993) 'A dark side of the American dream – correlates of financial success as a central life aspiration', *Journal of Personality and Social Psychology* 65, 410–422.

Kasser, T., Ryan, R. M., Zax, M., and Sameroff, A. J. (1995) 'The relations of maternal and social environments to late adolescents' materialistic and prosocial values', *Developmental Psychology* 31, 907–914.

Katona, G. (1975) *Psychological Economics*, New York: Elsevier.

Kearl, M. C. (1989) *Endings: The Sociology of Death and Dying*, Oxford: Oxford University Press.

Keillor, B. D., Parker, R. S., and Schaefer, A. (1996) 'Influences on adolescent brand preferences in the United States and Mexico', *Journal of Advertising Research* 36, 47–56.

Kemp, S. (1991) 'Remembering and dating past prices', *Journal of Economic Psychology* 12, 431–445.

Kemp, S. and Willetts, K. (1996) 'Remembering the price of wool', *Journal of Economic Psychology* 17, 115–125.

Kempson, E. (1996) 'Life on a low income' *Findings. Social Policy Research 97*, York: Joseph Rowntree Foundation.

Kempson, E., Bryson, A., and Rowlingson, K. (1994) *Hard Times? How Poor Families Make Ends Meet*, London: Policy Studies Institute.

Kempton, W., Boster, J. S., and Hartley, J. A. (1995) *Environmental Values in American Culture*, Cambridge, MA: MIT Press.

Kendig, H. L. (1984) 'Housing careers, life cycle and residential mobility: implications for the housing market', *Urban Studies* 21, 271–283.

Keough, K. A., Zimbardo, P. G., and Boyd, J. N. (1999) 'Who's smoking, drinking and using drugs? Time perspective as a predictor of substance use', *Basic and Applied Social Psychology* 21, 149–164.

Kessen, W. (1979) 'The American child and other cultural inventions', *American Psychologist* 34 (10), 815–820.

Keynes, J. M. (1936) *The General Theory of Employment, Interest and Money*, London: Macmillan.

Kids' Money (1999) Kids' Allowance stats. URL http://www.kidsmoney.org/allstats.htm

Kimhi, A. and Lopez, R. (1999) 'A note on farmers' retirement and succession considerations: evidence from a household survey', *Journal of Agricultural Economics* 50, 154–162.

Kimmel, J. (1997) 'Rural wages and returns to education: differences between whites, blacks, and American Indians', *Economics of Education Review* 16, 81–96.

Kirchler, E. (1988) 'Diary reports on daily economic decisions of happy versus unhappy couples', *Journal of Economic Psychology* 9, 327–357.

—— (1992) 'Adorable woman, expert man – changing gender images of women and men in management', *European Journal of Social Psychology* 22, 363–373.

—— (1995) *Wirtschaftspsychologie; Grundlagen und Anwendungsfelder der Ökonomischen psychologie* [Economic Psychology: Foundations and Applications], Göttingen: Hogrefe.

—— (1999) 'Household decision making', in P. E. Earl and S. Kemp (eds) *The Elgar Companion to Consumer Research and Economic Psychology* (pp. 296–304), Cheltenham: Edward Elgar.

Knesek, G. E. (1992) 'Early versus regular retirement: differences in measures of life satisfaction', *Journal of Gerontological Social Work* 19, 3–34.

Kojima, S. and Hama, Y. (1982) 'Aspects of the psychology of spending', *Japanese Psychological Research* 24, 29–38.

Kooreman, P. and Wunderink, S. (1996) *The Economics of Household Behaviour*, Basingstoke: Macmillan.

Kuehlwein, M. (1993) 'Life-cycle and altruistic theories of saving with lifetime uncertainty', *Review of Economics and Statistics* 75, 38–47.

Kysel, F., West, A., and Scott, G. (1992) 'Leaving school – attitudes, aspirations and destinations of 5th-year leavers in Tower Hamlets', *Educational Research* 34, 87–105.

Lackman, C. and Lanasa, J. M. (1993) 'Family decision-making theory: an overview and assessment', *Psychology and Marketing* 10 (2), 81–93.

Lai, J. C. L. and Wong, W. S. (1998) 'Optimism and coping with unemployment among Hong Kong Chinese women', *Journal of Research in Personality* 32, 454–479.

Land, H. (1983) 'Poverty and gender: the distribution of resources within families', in M. Brown (ed.) *The Structure of Disadvantage*, London: Heinemann.

Langan, J. and Means, R. (1996) 'Financial management and elderly people with dementia in the UK: as much a question of confusion as abuse?', *Ageing and Society* 16, 287–314.

Langbourne Rust Research (1993) 'Observations: parents and children shopping together: a new approach to the qualitative analysis of observational data', *Journal of Advertising Research* 33, July/August, 65–70.

Langer, E. J. (1975) 'The illusion of control', *Journal of Personality and Social Psychology*, 32, 311–328.

—— (1983) *The Psychology of Control*, Beverly Hills, CA: Sage.

Lasch, C. (1995) *The Revolt of the Élites*, New York: Norton.

Lassarre, D. (1986) 'Moving into home ownership', *Journal of Economic Psychology* 7, 161–178.

—— (1995) *Psychologie Social et Economie* [Social Psychology and Economics], Paris: Armand Colin.

—— (1996) 'Consumer education in French families and schools', in P. Lunt and A. Furnham (eds) *The Economic Beliefs and Behaviours of Young Children* (pp. 130–148), Cheltenham: Edward Elgar.

Latané, B., Williams, K., and Harkins, S. (1979) 'Many hands make light the work: the causes and consequences of social loafing', *Journal of Personality and Social Psychology* 37, 822–832.

Laurie, H. and Rose, D. (1994) 'Divisions and allocations within households', in N. Buck, J. Gershuny, D. Rose, and J. Scott (eds) *Changing Households: The British Household Panel Survey*, Colchester: University of Essex.

Lea, S. E. G. (1978) 'The psychology and economics of demand', *Psychological Bulletin* 85, 441–466.

—— (1994) 'Rationality: the formalist view', in H. Brandstätter and W. Güth (eds) *Essays in Economic Psychology* (pp. 71–89), Berlin: Springer Verlag.

—— (1999) 'Credit, debt and problem debt', in P. E. Earl and S. Kemp (eds) *The Elgar Companion to Consumer Research and Economic Psychology* (pp. 139–144), Cheltenham: Edward Elgar.

Lea, S. E. G., Tarpy, R. M., and Webley, P. (1987) *The Individual in the Economy*, Cambridge: Cambridge University Press.

Lea, S. E. G., Webley, P., and Bellamy, G. W. (1995) 'Student debt: a psychological analysis of the UK experience', in E. Nyhus and S. V. Troye (eds) *Frontiers in Economic Psychology* (pp. 430–444), Bergen: Norges Handelshoyskole.

Lea, S. E. G., Webley, P., and Levine, R. M. (1993) 'The economic psychology of consumer debt', *Journal of Economic Psychology* 14, 85–119.

Lea, S. E. G., Webley, P., and Walker, C. M. (1995) 'Psychological factors in consumer debt: money management, economic socialization, and credit use', *Journal of Economic Psychology* 16, 681–701.

Lea, S. E. G., Burgoyne, C. B., Jones, S. M., and Beer, A. J. (1997) 'An interview study of the psychology of poverty', in *International Association for Research in Economic Psychology* (eds) The XXII International Colloquium of Economic Psychology (pp. 955–967), Valencia: Promolibro.

Lea, S. E. G., Unrath, A. K., de Wilde, C., and Wynia, J. (1999) 'Money management in young adults', *Proceedings of the XXIV Symposium* 1, 336–344.

Leahy, R. L. (1981) 'The development of conception of economic inequality. I. Descriptions and comparisons of rich and poor people', *Child Development* 52, 523–532.

Lebo, R. B., Harrington, T. F., and Tillman, R. (1995) 'Work values similarities among students from six countries', *Career Development Quarterly* 43, 350–362.

Lee, C. C. (1984) 'Predicting the career choice attitudes of rural Black, White, and Native American high school students', *Vocational Guidance Quarterly* 32, 177–184.

Lee, S. W. and Brinton, M. C. (1996) 'Elite education and social capital: the case of South Korea', *Sociology of Education* 69, 177–192.

Leete, L. and Schor, J. B. (1994) 'Assessing the time-squeeze hypothesis: hours worked in the United States, 1969–89', *Industrial Relations* 33, 25–43.

Leiser, D., Sevón, G., and Lévy, D. (1990) 'Children's economic socialisation: summarizing the cross-cultural comparison of ten countries', *Journal of Economic Psychology* 11, 591–614.

Levinson, D. J. (1986) 'A conception of adult development', *American Psychologist* 41 (1), 3–13.

Lewis, A. (1989) 'The *Handbook of Economic Psychology* by W. F. van Raaij, G. M. Veldhoven and K.-E. Wärneryd: a review', *Journal of Economic Psychology* 10 (4), 598–601.

Lewis, A., Webley, P., and Furnham, A. F. (1995) *The New Economic Mind: the Social Psychology of Economic Behaviour*, Hemel Hempstead: Harvester Wheatsheaf.

Lewis, A., Webley, P., Winnett, A., and Mackenzie, C. (1998) 'Morals and markets: some theoretical and policy implications of ethical investing', in P. Taylor-Gooby (ed.) *Choice and Public Policy: the Limits to Welfare Markets* (pp. 164–182), London: Macmillan.

Lillard, L. A. and Weiss, Y. (1997) 'Uncertain health and survival: effects on end-of life consumption', *Journal of Business and Economic Statistics* 15, 254–268.

Lillard, L. A. and Willis, R. J. (1997) 'Motives for intergenerational transfers: evidence from Malaysia', *Demography* 34, 115–134.

Lindley, R. M. (1996) 'The school-to-work transition in the United Kingdom', *International Labour Review* 135 (2), 159–180.

Lindqvist, A. (1981) 'A note on determinants of household saving behaviour', *Journal of Economic Psychology* 1, 39–57.

Livingstone, S. (1992) 'The meaning of domestic technologies', Chapter 7 in R. Silverstone and E. Hirsch (eds) *Consuming Technologies: Media and Information in Domestic Spaces*, London: Routledge.

Livingstone, S. M. and Lunt, P. (1992) 'Predicting personal debt and debt repayment: psychological, social and economic determinants', *Journal of Economic Psychology* 13 (1), 111–134.

Locarno, A. and Parigi, G. (1997) 'Clima di fiducia e consumi della famiglie: movente economico o psicologico?', *Ricerche Quantitative per la Politica Economica*, (pp. 115–161) Rome: Banca d'Italia.

Loewenstein, G. (1999) 'Experimental economics from the vantage point of behavioural economics', *The Economic Journal* 109, F25–F34.

Loewenstein, G. F. and Thaler, R. H. (1988) 'Anomalies: intertemporal choice', *Journal of Economic Perspectives* 3, 181–193.

Loker-Murphy, L. and Pearce, P. L. (1995) 'Young budget travellers – backpackers in Australia', *Annals of Tourism Research* 22, 819–843.

Lopes, L. L. (1994) 'Psychology and economics: perspectives on risk, co-operation and the marketplace', *Annual Review of Psychology* 45, 197–227.

Lopez, F. G. and Andrews, S. (1987) 'Career indecision: a family systems perspective', *Journal of Counselling and Development* 65, 304–307.

Lown, J. M. and Dolan, E. M. (1994) 'Remarried families' economic behavior: Fishman's model revisited', *Journal of Divorce and Remarriage* 22, 103–119.

Lunt, P. K. (1996) 'Rethinking the relationship between economics and psychology', *Journal of Economic Psychology* 17, 275–287.

Lunt, P. K. and Livingstone, S. M. (1992) *Mass Consumption and Personal Identity: Everyday Economic Experience*, Buckingham: Open University Press.

Lynch, L. M. (1993) 'Entry-level jobs – 1st rung on the employment ladder or economic dead end', *Journal of Labor Research* 14, 249–263.

McClelland, D. C. (1961) *The Achieving Society*, New York: Free Press

McCloskey, D. (1983) 'The rhetoric of economics', *Journal of Economic Literature* 21, 481–517.

McCracken, G. (1990) *Culture and Consumption*, Indianopolis: Indiana University Press.

McCrae, R. R. and Costa, P. T. (1987) 'Validation of the 5-factor model of personality across instruments and observers', *Journal of Personality and Social Psychology* 52, 81–90.

MacFadyen, A. J. and MacFadyen, H. (eds) (1986) *Economic Psychology: Intersections in Theory and Application*, Amsterdam: Elsevier.

McGrath, M. A. and Englis, B.G. (1997) 'An intergenerational analysis of ethnic traditions in wedding-gift giving', *Advances in Consumer Research* 24, 242–243.

McIntosh, B. R. and Danigelis, N. L. (1995) 'Race, gender and the relevance of productive activity for elders' effort', *Journal of Gerontology* 50B, S229–S239.

McKechnie, J. and Hobbs, S. (1999) 'Child labour: the view from the North', *Childhood* 6 (1), 89–100.

McKenna, A. E. and Ferrero, G. W. (1991) 'Ninth-grade students' attitudes toward nontraditional occupations', *Career Development Quarterly* 40, 168–181.

McNeal, J. U. (1992) *Kids as Customers: A Handbook of Marketing to Children*, New York: Lexington Books.

Madeira, K. and Goldman, A. (1988) 'Some aspects of sensory properties of food that relate to food habits and associated problems of elderly consumers', *Journal of Nutrition for the Elderly* 8, 3–24.

Maital, S. and Maital, S. L. (1977) 'Time preference, delay and gratification and the intergenerational transmission of economic inequality: a behavioral theory of income distribution', in O. C. Ashenfelter and W. E. Oates, *Essays in Labor Market Analysis in Memory of Yochanan Peter Comay*, New York: Wiley.

Marell, A., Davidsson, P., and Gärling, T. (1995) 'Environmentally friendly replacement of automobiles', *Journal of Economic Psychology* 16, 513–529.

Marini, M. M., Fan, P. L., Finley, E., and Beutel, A. M. (1996) 'Gender and job values', *Sociology of Education* 69, 49–65.

Markova, I. (1987) *Human Awareness*, London: Hutchinson.

Maslow, A. H. (1943) 'A theory of motivation', *Psychological Review* 50, 370–396.

Mathur, A. and Moschis, G. R. (1995) 'Older consumers' vulnerability to bait-and-switch', *Advances in Consumer Research* 22, 674–679.

Matsui, T. and Onglatco, M. L. (1992) 'Career orientedness of motivation to enter the university among Japanese high school girls: a path analysis', *Journal of Vocational Behavior* 40, 351–363.

Maule, A. J., Cliff, D. R., and Taylor, R. (1996) 'Early retirement decisions and how they affect later quality of life', *Ageing and Society* 16, 177–204.

Maylor, E. A. (1996) 'Older people's memory for the past and the future', *The Psychologist* 9, 456–459.

Mealli, F., Pudney, S., and Thomas, J. (1996) 'Training duration and post-training outcomes: a duration-limited competing risks model', *Economic Journal* 106, 422–433.

Medialive (1999) http:/www.medialive.ie/

Meier, V. (1999) 'Why the young do not buy long-term care insurance', *Journal of Risk and Uncertainty* 18, 83–98.

Meltzoff, A. N. (1988) 'Imitation of televised models by infants', *Child Development* 59 (5), 1221–1229.

Menchik, P. L. and David, M. (1983) 'Income distribution, lifetime savings, and bequests', *American Economic Review* 73, 672–690.

Menon, M. E. (1997) 'Perceived rates of return to higher education in Cyprus', *Economics of Education Review* 16, 425–430.

Messinger, L. (1976) 'Remarriage between divorced people with children from previous marriages: a proposal for preparation for remarriage', *Journal of Marriage and Family Counselling* 2, 193–200.

Michelson, W. (1977) *Environmental Choice, Human Behavior and Residential Satisfaction*, New York: Oxford University Press.

Micromegas (1993) 'Money', Micromegas synthesis paper, Paris: Micromegas.

Middleton, S., Ashworth, K., and Braithwaite, I. (1997) *Small Fortunes: Spending on Children, Childhood Poverty and Parental Sacrifice*, York: Joseph Rowntree Foundation.

Midlarsky, E. and Hannah, M. E. (1989) 'The generous elderly: naturalistic studies of donations across the life span', *Psychology and Ageing* 4, 346–351.

Milevsky, M. A. (1998) 'Optimal asset allocation towards the end of the life cycle: to annuitize or not to annuitize?', *Journal of Risk and Insurance* 65, 401–426.

Millar, J. (1988) 'The costs of marital breakdown', chapter 7 in R. Walker and G. Parker (eds) *Money Matters*, London: Sage.

Millar, J. and Glendinning, C. (1989) 'Gender and poverty', *Journal of Social Policy* 18, 363–381.

Miller, D., Jackson, P., Thrift, N., Holbrook, B., and Rowlands, M. (1998) *Shopping, Place and Identity*, London: Routledge.

Miller, J. and Yung, S. (1990) 'The role of allowances in adolescent socialization', *Youth and Society* 22, 137–159.

Miller, P. J. (1994) *The Rational Expectations Revolution: Readings from the Front Line*, Cambridge, MA: MIT Press.

Mirvis P. H. and Hall D. T. (1994) 'Psychological success and the boundaryless career', *Journal of Organizational Behavior* 15, 365–380.

Mischel H. and Mischel, W. (1962) 'The development of children's knowledge of self control strategies', *Child Development* 54, 603–619.

Mischel, W. and Metzner, R. (1962) 'Preference for delayed reward as a function of age, intelligence and length of delay interval', *Journal of Abnormal and Social Psychology* 64, 425–431.

Mitchell, P. (1996) *Acquiring a Conception of Mind: A Review of Psychological Research and Theory*, Hove: Psychology Press.

Modigliani, F. and Brumberg, R. (1954) 'Utility analysis and the consumption function: an interpretation of cross-sectional data', in K. Kurihara (ed.) *Post-Keynesian Economics*, New Brunswick, NJ: Rutgers University Press.

Moen, P., Dempster-McClain, D., and Williams, R. M. (1992) 'Successful ageing – a life course perspective on women's multiple roles and health', *American Journal of Sociology* 97, 1612–1638.

Moen, P., Robison, J., and Dempster-McClain, D. (1995) 'Caregiving and women's well-being – a life-course approach', *Journal of Health and Social Behavior* 36, 259–273.

Moore, R. L. and Stephens, L. F. (1975) 'Some communication and demographic determinants of adolescent consumer learning', *Journal of Consumer Research* 2, 80–92.

Moore-Shay, E. S. and Wilkie, W. L. (1988) 'Recent developments in research on family decisions', *Advances in Consumer Research* 15, 454–460.

Morgan, S. L. (1998) 'Adolescent educational expectations – rationalized, fantasized, or both?', *Rationality and Society* 10, 131–162.

Mortimer, J. T., Dennehy, K., Lee, C., and Finch, M. D. (1994) 'Economic socialization in the American family: the prevalence, distribution and consequences of allowance arrangements', *Family Relations* 43 (1), 23–29.

Moschis, G. P. (1995) 'Older consumers' vulnerability to bait-and-switch', *Advances in Consumer Research* 22, 674–679.

Moschis, G. P., Mathur, A., and Smith, R. B. (1993) 'Older consumers' orientations toward age-based marketing stimuli', *Journal of the Academy of Marketing Science* 21, 195–205.

Mosley, P. (1982) 'The economy as presented in the popular press', paper presented at the eighth IAREP colloquium, Edinburgh.

Müller-Peters, A., Pepermans, R., and Burgoyne, C. B. (1998) Special issue on 'A single currency in Europe: cross-national perspectives from economic psychology', *Journal of Economic Psychology* 19 (6).

Munene, J. C. (1983) 'Understanding juvenile unemployability: an exploratory study', *Journal of Adolescence* 6, 247–261.

Murphy, A. and Shuttleworth, I. (1997) 'Education, religion and the "first desti-nations" of recent school-leavers in Northern Ireland', *Economic and Social Review* 28, 23–41.

Murphy, G. C. and Athanasou, J. A. (1999) 'The effect of unemployment on mental health', *Journal of Occupational and Organisational Psychology* 72, 83–100.

Murphy, P. E. and Staples, W. A. (1979) 'A modernized family life cycle', *Journal of Consumer Research* 6, 12–22.

Muth, J. F. (1961) 'Rational expectations and the theory of price movements', *Econometrica* 29, 315–335.

Narendranathan, W. (1993) 'Job search in a dynamic environment – an empirical-analysis', *Oxford Economic Papers*, new series 45, 1–22.

National Center for Health Statistics (1986) 'Births, marriages, divorces, and deaths for July 1986', *Monthly Vital Statistics Report* 35.

Newman, B. M. and Newman, P. R. (1991) *Development through Life: A Psycho-social Approach*, Pacific Grove, CA: Brooks Cole.

Newson, J. and Newson, E. (1976) *Seven Years Old in the Home Environment*, London: Allen & Unwin.

Ng, S. K. (1983) 'Children's ideas about the bank and shop profit: development, stages and the influence of cognitive contrasts and conflicts', *Journal of Economic Psychology* 4, 209–221.

Nordenmark, M. (1999) 'The concentration of unemployment within families and social networks – a question of attitudes or structural factors?', *European Sociological Review* 15, 49–59.

Nyhus, E. K. (1997) 'On the measurement of time preference and subjective discount rates', in I. Quintanilla (ed.) *The XXII International Colloquium of Economic Psychology* pp. 1095–1111, Valencia: Promolibro.

—— (1998) 'Wealth and portfolio profiles across life-cycle categories', paper presented at the 24th International Congress of Applied Psychology, San Francisco, August.

Nyhus, E. K., Kvitastein, O. A., and Groenhaug, K. (1995) 'Constructing collective psychological variables at the household level: some challenges and tentative findings', paper presented at 20th IAREP Colloquium, Bergen, Norway.

O'Brien, G. E., Feather, N. T., and Kabanoff, B. (1994) 'Quality of activities and the adjustment of unemployed youth', *Australian Journal of Psychology* 46, 29–34.

O'Brien, K. M. (1996) 'The influence of psychological separation and parental attachment on the career development of adolescent women', *Journal of Vocational Behavior* 48, 257–274.

O'Brien, K. M. and Fassinger, R. E. (1993) 'A causal model of the career orientation and career choice of adolescent women', *Journal of Counselling Psychology* 40, 456–469.

O'Donohoe, S. (1994) 'Advertising uses and gratifications', *European Journal of Marketing* 28 (8/9), 52–75.

Office of Population Censuses and Surveys (1980) *Labour Force Survey*, London: HMSO.

Office of Population Censuses and Surveys (OPCS) (1993) *Marriage and Divorce Statistics* 21, London: HMSO.

O'Guinn T. C. and Faber R. J. (1989) 'Compulsive buying – a phenomenological exploration', *Journal of Consumer Research* 16, 147–157.

O'Guinn T. C. and Shrum, L. J. (1997) 'The role of television in the construction of consumer reality', *Journal of Consumer Research* 23, 278–294.

Okun, M. A. (1993) 'Predictors of volunteer status in a retirement community', *International Journal of Ageing and Human Development* 36, 57–74.

Okun, M. A. and Eisenberg, N. (1992) 'Motives and intent to continue organisational volunteering among residents of a retirement community area', *Journal of Community Psychology* 20, 183–187.

Olmsted, A. D. (1991) 'Collecting: leisure, investment or obsession?', *Journal of Social Behavior and Personality* 6, 287–306.

Orne, M. T. (1962) 'On the social psychology of the psychological experiment: with particular reference to demand characteristics', *American Psychologist* 17, 776–783.

Ortalo-Magné, F. and Rady, S. (1999) 'Boom in, bust out: young households and the housing price cycle', *European Economic Review* 43, 755–766.

Ortona, G. and Scacciati, F. (1992) 'New experiments on the endowment effect', *Journal of Economic Psychology* 13, 277–296.

Osberg, L. (1993) 'Fishing in different pools: job-search strategies and job-finding success in Canada in the early 1980s', *Journal of Labor Economics* 11, 348–386.

Otnes, C., Zolner, K., and Lowrey, T. M. (1994) 'In-laws and out-laws: the impact of divorce and remarriage upon Christmas gift exchange', *Advances in Consumer Research* 21, 25–34.

Packard, V. (1957) *The Hidden Persuaders*, London: Longman.

Pahl, J. (1980) 'Patterns of money management within marriage', *Journal of Social Policy* 9, 313–335.

—— (1989) *Money and Marriage*, London: Macmillan.

—— (1995) 'His money, her money: recent research on financial organisation in marriage', *Journal of Economic Psychology* 16, 361–376.

Palan, K. M. (1998) 'Relationships between family communication and consumer activities of adolescents: an exploratory study', *Journal of the Academy of Marketing Science* 26, 338–349.

Palumbo, M. G. (1999) 'Uncertain medical expenses and precautionary saving near the end of the life cycle', *Review of Economic Studies* 66, 395–421.

Parker, G. and Clarke, H. (1997) 'Will you still need me, will you still feed me? Paying for care in old age', *Social Policy and Administration* 31, 119–135.

Parker, S. (1982) *Work and Retirement*, London: Allen & Unwin.

Parsons, T., (1960) *The Social System*, Glencoe, IL: Free Press.

Pasley, K., Sandras, E., and Edmondson, M. E. (1994) 'The effects of financial management strategies on quality of family life in remarriage', *Journal of Family and Economic Issues* 15: 53–70.

Paterson, L. and Raffe, D. (1995) 'Staying-on in full-time education in Scotland, 1985–1991', *Oxford Review of Education* 21, 3–23.

Patterson, L. J. M. (1997) 'Long term unemployment amongst adolescents: a longitudinal study', *Journal of Adolescence* 20, 261–280.

Patton, W. and Donohue, R. (1998) 'Coping with long-term unemployment', *Journal of Community and Applied Social Psychology* 8, 331–343.

Paulsen, M. B. (1998) 'Recent research on the economics of attending college: returns on investment and responsiveness to price', *Research in Higher Education* 39, 471–489.

Payne, J., Casey, B., Payne, C., and Connolly, S. (1996) *Long-term Unemployment: Individual Risk Factors and Outcomes*, London: Policy Studies Institute.

Petersen, A. C. and Mortimer, J. T. (eds) (1994) *Youth Unemployment and Society*, Cambridge: Cambridge University Press.

Petterson, S. M. (1997) 'Are young Black men really less willing to work?', *American Sociological Review* 62, 605–613.

Piaget, J. (1970) 'Piaget's theory', in P. Mussen (ed.) *Carmichael's Manual of Child Psychology* (volume 1, pp. 703–732), New York: Wiley.

Pickvance, C. G. and Pickvance, K. (1995) 'The role of family help in the housing decisions of young-people', *Sociological Review* 43, 123–149.

Pirog, M. A. and Magee, C. (1997) 'High school completion: the influence of schools, families, and adolescent parenting', *Social Science Quarterly* 78, 710–724.

Pissarides, C. A. (1981) 'Staying-on at school in England and Wales', *Economica* 48, 345–363.

Plous, S. (1993) *The Psychology of Judgment and Decision Making*, New York: McGraw-Hill.

Pollock, L. A. (1983) *Forgotten Children: Parent–Child Relations from 1500 to 1900*, Cambridge: Cambridge University Press.

Poole, M. E. and Cooney, G. H. (1985) 'Careers: adolescent awareness and exploration of possibilities for self', *Journal of Vocational Behavior* 26, 251–263.

Poole, M. E., Langan-Fox, J., Ciavarella, M., and Omodei, M. (1991) 'A contextual model of professional attainment: results of a longitudinal study of career paths of men and women', *Counselling Psychologist* 19, 603–624.

Posner, R. A. (1995) *Aging and Old Age*, Chicago: University of Chicago Press.

Prager, E. (1995) 'The older volunteer as research colleague – toward generative participation for older adults', *Educational Gerontology* 21, 209–218.

Prause, J. and Dooley, D. (1997) 'Effect of underemployment on school-leavers' self-esteem', *Journal of Adolescence* 20, 243–260.

Presser, H. B. (1989) 'Some economic complexities of child-care provided by grandmothers', *Journal of Marriage and the Family* 51, 581–591.

Pugh, P. and Webley, P. (2000) 'Adolescent participation in the UK National Lottery Games', *Journal of Adolescence* 23, 1–11.

Quintanilla, I. (1997) *Psicología Económica*, Madrid: McGraw-Hill.

Rabin, M. (1998) 'Psychology and economics', *Journal of Economic Literature* 36 (1), 11–46.

Rachlin, H. (1980) 'Economics and behavioral psychology', in J. E. R. Staddon (ed.) *Limits to Action* (pp. 205–236), New York: Academic Press.

Rainnie, A. (1998) 'Flexible employment: the future of Britain's jobs', by S. Dex and A. McCulloch *Work, Employment and Society* 12, 161–167.

Ramasamy, R. (1996) 'Post-high school employment: a follow-up of Apache Native American youth', *Journal of Learning Disabilities* 29, 174–179.

Ranyard, R. and Craig, G. (1995) 'Evaluating and budgeting with instalment credit: an interview study', *Journal of Economic Psychology* 16, 449–467.

Rao, B. (1999) 'The Internet and the revolution in distribution: a cross-industry examination', *Technology in Society* 21, 287–306.

Raudenbush, S. W. and Kasim, R. M. (1998) 'Cognitive skill and economic inequality: findings from the national adult literacy survey', *Harvard Educational Review* 68, 33–79.

Raymond, J. E., Beard, T. R., and Gropper, D. M. (1993) 'Modelling the consumer's decision to replace durable goods – a hazard function approach', *Applied Economics* 25, 1287–1292.

Rees, D. I. and Mocan, H. N. (1997) 'Labor market conditions and the high school dropout rate: evidence from New York State', *Economics of Education Review* 16, 103–109.

Reilly, K. T. (1994) 'Annual hours and weeks in a life cycle labor supply model – Canadian evidence on male behavior', *Journal of Labor Economics* 12, 460–477.

Reitzes, D. C., Mutran, E. J., and Fernandez, M. E. (1998) 'The decision to retire: a career perspective', *Social Science Quarterly* 79, 607–619.

Reynaud, P. L. (1981) *Economic Psychology*, New York: Praeger.

Richins, M. L. (1994) 'Special possessions and the expression of material values', *Journal of Consumer Research* 21, 522–533.

Richins, M. L. and Dawson, S. (1992) 'A consumer values orientation for materialism and its development: scale development and validation', *Journal of Consumer Research* 19, 303–316.

Richins, M. L. and Rudmin, F. M. (1994) 'Materialism and economic psychology *Journal of Economic Psychology* 15, 217–231.

Rindfleisch, A., Burroughs, J. E., and Denton, F. (1997) 'Family structure, materialism, and compulsive consumption', *Journal of Consumer Research* 23, 312–325.

Ritson, M. and Elliott, R. (1995) 'A model of advertising literacy: the praxiology and co-creation of advertising meaning', in M. Bergadaa *et al.* (eds) *Marketing Today and for the 21st Century: Proceedings of the 24th Annual Conference of the European Marketing Academy*, ESSEC, Cergy-Pontoise, France: Imprimerie Basuyau.

Ritson, M., Elliott, R., and Eccles, S. (1996) 'Reframing IKEA: commodity-signs, consumer relativity and the social/self dialectic', *Advances in Consumer Research* 23, 127–131.

Robbins, L. (1932) *An Essay on the Nature and Significance of Economic Science*, London: Macmillan.

Robbins, S. B., Lee, R. M., and Wan, T. T. H. (1994) 'Goal continuity as a mediator of early retirement adjustment – testing a multidimensional model', *Journal of Counselling Psychology* 41, 18–26.

Roberts, D. F. (1982) 'Children and commercials: issues, evidence, interventions', *Prevention in Human Services* 2 (1–2), 19–35.

Robertson, T. S. and Rossiter, J. (1974) 'Children and commercial persuasion: an attributional theory analysis', *Journal of Consumer Research* 1, 13–20.

Rogers, C. L. (1997) 'Job search and unemployment duration: implications for the spatial mismatch hypothesis', *Journal of Urban Economics* 42, 109–132.

Rogers, E. M. (1995) *Diffusion of Innovations*, 4th edn, New York: Free Press.

Roland-Lévy, C. (1990) 'A cross-national comparison of Algerian and French children's economic socialization', *Journal of Economic Psychology* 11, 567–581.

Rook, D. W. (1987) 'The buying impulse', *Journal of Consumer Research* 14 (2), 189–199.

Rosser, M. (1999) 'Determinants of graduates' demand for housing', *Applied Economics Letters* 6, 139–142.

Rossi, P. H. (1955) *Why Families Move: A Study in the Social Psychology of Urban Residential Mobility*, Glencoe, IL: Free Press.

Routh, D. A. and Burgoyne, C. B. (1991) 'Money and the five-factor model of personality structure', IAREP/SASE Conference, Stockholm, June 1991.

Rust, J. and Phelan, C. (1997) 'How social security and medicare affect retirement behavior in a world of incomplete markets', *Econometrica* 65, 781–831.

Sagy, S. and Antonovsky, A. (1992) 'The family sense of coherence and the retirement transition', *Journal of Marriage and the Family* 54, 983–993.

Samuelson, W. and Zeckhauser, R. (1988) 'Status quo bias in decision making', *Journal of Risk and Uncertainty* 1, 7–59.

Sanders, K. (1995) 'The gift and request network – differences between women and men in the receipt and the effect of information concerning the labour-market', European *Journal of Women's Studies* 2, 205–218.

Sawhill, I. V. (1980) 'Economic perspectives on the family', Chapter 5 in A. H.

Amsden (ed.) *The Economics of Men and Women and Work*, Harmondsworth: Penguin.

Schaufeli, W. B. (1997) 'Youth unemployment and mental health: some Dutch findings', *Journal of Adolescence* 20, 281–292.

Schewe, C. D. and Balazs, A. L. (1992) 'Role transitions in older adults: a marketing opportunity', *Psychology and Marketing* 9, 85–99.

Schindler, R. M. and Holbrook, H. B. (1993) 'Critical periods in the development of men's and women's taste in personal appearance', *Psychology and Marketing* 10, 549–564.

Schor, J. B. (1991) *The Overworked American: The Unexpected Decline of Leisure*, New York: Basic Books.

Sen, A. (1984) *Resources, Values and Development*, Oxford: Basil Blackwell.

Shanahan, M. J., Miech, R. A., and Elder, G. H. (1998) 'Changing pathways to attainment in men's lives: historical patterns of school, work, and social class', *Social Forces* 77, 231–256.

Sheffrin, S. M. (1996) *Rational Expectations*, 2nd edn, Cambridge: Cambridge University Press.

Shefrin, H. M. and Thaler, R. H. (1988) 'The behavioral life-cycle hypothesis', *Economic Inquiry* 26, 609–643.

Sheiner, L. (1995) 'Housing prices and the savings of renters', *Journal of Urban Economics* 38, 94–125.

Shepperd, J. A., Oullette, J. A., and Fernandez, J. K. (1996) 'Abandoning unrealistic optimism: performance estimates and the temporal proximity of self-relevant feedback', *Journal of Personality and Social Psychology* 70, 844–855.

Shi, L. Y. (1993) 'Family financial and household support exchange between generations – a survey of Chinese rural elderly', *Gerontologist* 33, 468–480.

—— (1994) 'Elderly support in rural and suburban villages – implications for future support system in China', *Social Science and Medicine* 39, 265–277.

Shim, S. and Gehrt, K. C. (1996) 'Hispanic and Native American adolescents: an exploratory study of their approach to shopping', *Journal of Retailing* 72, 307–324.

Shim, S. and Koh, A. (1997) 'Profiling adolescent consumer decision-making styles: effects of socialization agents and social-structural variables', *Clothing and Textiles Research Journal* 15, 50–59.

Shultz, K. S., Morton, K. R., and Weckerle, J. R. (1998) 'The influence of push and pull factors on voluntary and involuntary early retirees' retirement decision and adjustment', *Journal of Vocational Behavior* 53, 45–57.

Signorielli, N. (1993) 'Television and adolescents' perceptions about work', *Youth and Society* 24, 314–341.

Simon, H. A. (1956) 'Rational choice and the structure of the environment', *Psychological Review*, 63, 129–138.

—— (1982) *Models of Bounded Rationality*, Cambridge, MA: MIT Press.

Singh, L. B., Singh, A. K., and Rani, A. (1996) 'Level of self-concepts in educated unemployed young men in India: an empirical analysis', *Journal of Economic Psychology* 17, 629–643.

Smith, D. B. and Moen, P. (1998) 'Spousal influence on retirement: his, her, and their perceptions', *Journal of Marriage and the Family* 60, 734–744.

Smith, G. C. (1991) 'Grocery shopping patterns of the ambulatory urban elderly', *Environment and Behavior* 23, 86–114.

Smith, P. B. and Bond, M. H. (1998) *Social Psychology across Cultures*, 2nd edn, London: Harvester Wheatsheaf.

Smith, V. (1997) 'New forms of work organization', *Annual Review of Sociology* 23, 315–339.

Sommer, R. (1991) 'Consciences in the marketplace – the role of cooperatives in consumer-protection', *Journal of Social Issues* 47, 135–148.

Sommer, R., Nelson, S., and Hoyt, K. (1985) 'Funeral price disclosure in an urban market', *Journal of Consumer Affairs* 19, 241–254.

Sonuga-Barke, E. J. S. and Webley, P. (1993) *Children's Saving*, Hove: Erlbaum.

Soutar, G. N. and Cornish Ward, S. P. (1997) 'Ownership patterns for durable goods and financial assets: a Rasch analysis', *Applied Economics* 29, 903–911.

Stamp, P. (1985) 'Research note: Balance of financial power in marriage: an exploratory study of breadwinning wives', *The Sociological Review* 33, 546–557.

Statistics Bureau (1998) *Japan Statistical Yearbook 2000*, Tokyo: Statistics Bureau, Management and Coordination Agency, Government of Japan.

Statistics New Zealand (1997) *Demographic Trends*, Wellington: Statistics New Zealand.

Steinberg, L. and Dornbusch, S. M. (1991) 'Negative correlates of part-time employment during adolescence – replication and elaboration', *Developmental Psychology* 27, 304–313.

Stephens, N. (1991) 'Cognitive age: a useful concept for advertising?', *Journal of Advertising* 20, 37–48.

Stewart, M. B. and Swaffield, J. K. (1997) 'Constraints on the desired hours of work of British men', *Economic Journal* 107, 520–535.

Stoetzel, J., Sauerwein, J., and Vulpian, A. de (1954) 'Sondages français: études sur la consommation', in P. L. Reynaud (ed.) *La Psychologie Economique* (pp. 161–209), Paris: Rivière.

Strahilevitz, M. A. and Loewenstein, G. (1998) 'The effect of ownership history on the valuation of objects', *Journal of Consumer Research* 25, 276–289.

Strauss, A. (1952) 'The development and transformation of monetary meanings in the child', *American Sociological Review* 17, 275–286.

Strawbridge, W. J., Wallhagen, M. I., Shema, S. J., and Kaplan, G. A. (1997) 'New burdens or more of the same? Comparing grandparent, spouse, and adult-child caregivers', *Gerontologist* 37, 505–510.

Strom, R. D. and Strom, S. K. (1994) 'Grandparent volunteers in the school: building a partnership', *Journal of Instructional Psychology* 21, 329–339.

Super, D. E. (1957) *The Psychology of Careers: An Introduction to Vocational Development*, New York: Harper & Row.

Suurnakki, T., Nygard, C. H., and Ilmarinen, J. (1991) 'Stress and strain of elderly employees in municipal occupations', *Scandinavian Journal of Work, Environment and Health* 17, 30–39.

Swan, G. E., Dame, A., and Carmelli, D. (1991) 'Involuntary retirement, Type A behaviour, and current functioning in elderly men: 27-year follow-up of the Western Collaborative Group Study', *Psychology and Ageing* 6, 384–391.

Swinnerton, K. A. and Wial, H. (1995) 'Is job stability declining in the United States Economy?' *Industrial and Labor Relations Review* 48, 293–304.

Szinovacz, M. (1992) 'Is housework good for retirees', *Family Relations* 41, 230–238.

Szinovacz, M. and Harpster, P. (1994) 'Couples' employment/retirement status and the division of household tasks', *Journals of Gerontology* 49, S125–S136.

Taiapa, J. (1994) *Ta Te Whanau Ohanga: The Economics of Whanau*, Department of Maori Studies, Massey University, New Zealand.

Tajfel, H. and Fraser, C. (1978) *Introducing Social Psychology*, Harmondsworth: Penguin.

Takahashi, K. and Hatano, G. (1994) 'Understanding of the banking business in Japan: is economic prosperity accompanied by economic literacy?', *British Journal of Developmental Psychology* 12, 585–590.

Taylor, M. (1996) 'Earnings, independence or unemployment: why become self-employed?', *Oxford Bulletin of Economics and Statistics* 58 (2).

Tepper, K. (1994) 'The role of labelling processes in elderly consumers' responses to age segmentation cues', *Journal of Consumer Research* 20, 503–519.

Thaler, R. H. (1980) 'Towards a positive theory of consumer choice', *Journal of Economic Behavior and Organization* 1, 39–60.

—— (1985) 'Mental accounting and consumer choice', *Marketing Science* 4, 199–214.

—— (1993) 'Mental accounting matters', paper presented at SPUDM 14, Aix-en-Provence, August.

Thomas, J. M. (1997) 'Public employment agencies and unemployment spells: reconciling the experimental and non-experimental evidence', *Industrial and Labor Relations Review* 50, 667–683.

Titmuss, R. M. (1970) *The Gift Relationship*, London: Allen & Unwin.

Toharia, L. (1994) 'Spain: modernisation of unemployment', in O. Benoit-Guilbot and D. Gallie (eds) *Long Term Unemployment* (pp. 111–120), London: Pinter.

Tomann, H. (1996) 'Private home-ownership finance for low-income households', *Urban Studies* 33, 1879–1889.

Toughill, E., Mason, D. J., Beck, T. L., and Christopher, M. A. (1993) 'Health, income, and post-retirement employment of older adults', *Public Health Nursing* 10, 100–107.

Tsuya, N. O. and Martin, L. G. (1992) 'Living arrangements of elderly Japanese and attitudes toward inheritance', *Journals of Gerontology* 47, S45–S54.

Tversky, A. and Kahneman, D. (1981) 'The framing of decisions and the psychology of choice' *Science* 211, 453–458.

—— (1991) 'Loss aversion in riskless choice: a reference-dependent model' *Quarterly Journal of Economics* 106, 1039–1161.

Tyszka, T. (1999) 'Transformation in Eastern Europe', in P. Earl and S. Kemp (eds) *The Elgar Companion to Consumer Research and Economic Psychology* (pp. 570–575), Cheltenham: Edward Elgar.

Tyszka, T. and Sokolowska, J. (1992) 'Perceptions and judgements of the economic system', *Journal of Economic Psychology* 13, 421–448.

Vanden Abeele, P. (1983) 'The index of consumer sentiment: predictability and predictive power in the EEC', *Journal of Economic Psychology* 3, 1–17.

van der Ploeg, S. (1994) 'Educational expansion and returns on credentials', *European Sociological Review* 10, 63–78.

van der Velde, M. E. G., Feij, J. A., and Taris, T. W. (1995) 'Stability and change of person characteristics among young adults: the effect of the transition from school to work', *Personality and Individual Differences* 18, 89–99.

van Raaij, W. F. (1991) 'Postmodern consumption', *Journal of Economic Psychology* 14, 541–563.

van Raaij W. F., and Gianotten, H. (1990) 'Consumer confidence, expenditure, saving and credit' *Journal of Economic Psychology* 11, 269–290.

van Raaij W. F. and van den Brink, P. (1987) 'Consumer confidence and the mortgage market', in F. Olander and K. G. Grunert (eds), *Understanding Economic Behaviour: Proceedings of the 13th Annual Colloquium of IAREP* (pp. 271–282).

van Raaij, W. F., van Veldhoven, G. M. and Wärneryd, K.-E. (1988) *Handbook of Economic Psychology*, Dordrecht: Kluwer.

van Veldhoven, G. M., and Keder, C. (1988) 'Economic news and consumers' sentiments', in P. Vanden Abeele (ed.) *Psychology in Micro and Macro Economics: Proceedings of the 13th Annual Colloquium of IAREP, Volume 3*.

Varlaam, A. and Shaw, A. (1984) 'Attitudes to school: a study of 5th year pupils', in D. H. Hargreaves (ed.) *Improving Secondary Schools: Research Studies* (pp. 1–42) London: Inner London Education Authority.

Veblen, T. (1899) *The Theory of the Leisure Class*, New York: Macmillan.

Vicenzi, G., Lea, S. E. G., and Rumiati, R. (eds) (1999) in *International Association for Research in Economic Psychology*, Proceedings of the XXIV Symposium 1, 315–327.

Vogler, C. and Pahl, J. (1994) 'Money, power and inequality within marriage', *Sociological Review* 42, 263–288.

Vuchelen, J. (1995) 'Political events and consumer confidence in Belgium', *Journal of Economic Psychology* 16, 563–579.

Vuchinich, R. E. and Simpson, C. A. (1998) 'Hyberbolic temporal discounting in social drinkers and problem drinkers', *Experimental and Clinical Psychopharmacology* 6, 292–305.

Wagner, J. and Hanna, S. (1983) 'The effectiveness of family life cycle variables in consumer expenditure research', *Journal of Consumer Research* 10, 281–291.

Wahlund, R. and Wärneryd, K.-E. (1988) 'Aggregate saving and the behaviour of saving groups in Sweden accompanying a tax reform', in S. Maital (ed.) *Applied Behavioural Economics*, Vol. 1, Hemel Hempstead: Harvester Wheatsheaf.

Walker C. M. (1996) 'Financial management, coping and debt in households under financial strain', *Journal of Economic Psychology* 17, 789–807.

—— (1997) 'The psychology of debt in the 1990s', Unpublished Ph.D. thesis, University of Exeter.

Wall, J., Covell, K., and MacIntyre, P. D. (1999) 'Implications of social supports for adolescents' education and career aspirations', *Canadian Journal of Behavioural Science* 31, 63–71.

Wallerstein, I. and Smith, J. (1991) 'Households as an institution of the world-economy', Chapter 9 in R. L. Blumberg (ed.) *Gender, Family and Economy: The Triple Overlap*, Newbury Park, California: Sage.

Ward, S., Wackman, D. B., and Wartella, E. (1977) *How Children Learn to Buy*, London: Sage.

Warnaar, M. F. and van Praag, B. (1997) 'How Dutch teenagers spend their money', *De Economist* 145, 367–397.

Wärneryd, K. E. (1983) 'The saving behaviour of households', paper presented at the conference, Saving in a Time of Economic Stagnation, Scheveningen.

—— (1988) 'Economic psychology as a field of study', in W. F. van Raaij, G. M. van Veldhoven and K. E. Wärneryd (eds) *Handbook of Economic Psychology*, (pp. 3–41), Dordrecht: Kluwer.

—— (1997) 'Demystifying rational expectations theory through an economic psychological model', in G. Antonides, W. F. van Raaij and S. Maital (eds) *Advances in Economic Psychology* (pp. 211–236), Chichester: Wiley.

—— (1999) *The Psychology of Saving. A Study on Economic Psychology*, Cheltenham: Edward Elgar.

Wärneryd, K. E. and Walerud, B. (1982) 'Taxes and economic behaviour: some interview data on tax evasion in Sweden', *Journal of Economic Psychology* 2, 187–211.

Warr, P. (1987) *Work, Unemployment and Mental Health*, Oxford: Clarendon Press.

Warr, P. and Pennington, J. (1994) 'Occupational age-grading – jobs for older and younger non-managerial employees', *Journal of Vocational Behavior* 45, 328–346.

Waterson, M. J. (1998) *Marketing Pocket Book*, London: The Advertising Association.

Watts, M. W. (1994) 'Was there anything left of the "socialist personality"? Values of Eastern and Western German youth at the beginning of unification', *Political Psychology* 15, 481–508.

Wawer, M. J., Podhisita, C., Kanungsukkasem, U., Pramualratana, A., and McNamara, R. (1996) 'Origins and working-conditions of female sex workers in urban Thailand consequences of social-context for HIV transmission', *Social Science and Medicine* 42, 453–462.

Webley, P. (1995) 'Accounts of accounts: en route to an economic psychology of personal finance', *Journal of Economic Psychology* 16, 469–475.

—— (1996) 'Playing the market: the autonomous economic world of children', in P. Lunt and A. Furnham (eds) *The Economic Beliefs and Behaviours of Young Children* (pp. 149–161), Cheltenham: Edward Elgar.

Webley, P. and Lea, S. E. G. (1992) 'Co moze nabidnout ekonomicka psychologie?' [Economic psychology in the market place], *Psychologie v Ekonomicke Praxi*, 2, 63–75.

—— (1993a) 'The partial unacceptability of money as repayment for neighbourly help', *Human Relations* 46, 65–76.

—— (1993b) 'Towards a more realistic psychology of economic socialization', *Journal of Economic Psychology* 14, 461–472.

Webley, P. and Nyhus, E. K. (1999) *A Dynamic Approach to Consumer Debt*, TMR Progress report no. 1, Tilburg: CentER for Economic Research.

—— (2000) 'Representations of saving and saving behaviour', in C. Roland-Levy, E. Kirchler and C. Gray (eds) *Lay Concepts of the Economy, Social Representations of Economic Phenomena.* (p. 85–102), Vienna: Weiner Universitäts Verlag.

Webley, P. and Plaisier, Z. (1998) 'The development of mental accounts', *Children's Social and Economic Education* 3, 55–64.

Webley, P. and Wilson, R. (1989) 'Social relationships and the unacceptability of money as a gift', *Journal of Social Psychology* 129, 85–91.

Webley, P., Lea, S. E. G., and Portalska, R. (1983) 'The unacceptability of money as a gift', *Journal of Economic Psychology* 4, 223–238.

Webley, P., Levine, R. M., and Lewis, A. (1993) 'A study in economic psychology: children's saving in a play economy', *Human Relations* 44, 127–146.

Weigel, R. H., Hessing D. J., and Elffers, H. (1999) 'Egoism: concept, measurement and implications for deviance', *Psychology, Crime and Law* 5, 349–378.

Weinstein, N. D. and Klein, W. M. (1996) 'Unrealistic optimism: present and future', *Journal of Social and Clinical Psychology* 15, 1–8.

Weisberg, J. (1995) 'Returns to education in Israel – 1974 and 1983', *Economics of Education Review* 14, 145–154.

Wellman, H. M. (1990) *The Child's Theory of Mind*, Cambridge, MA: MIT Press.

Wells, W. and Gubar, G. (1966) 'Life cycle concept in marketing research', *Journal of Marketing Research* 3, 355–363.

Westbrook, B. W. (1976) 'The relationship between career choice attitudes and career choice competencies of ninth-grade pupils', *Journal of Vocational Behavior* 9, 119–125.

Westbrook, B. W., Sanford, E. E., and Waters, S. (1999) 'Reliability and validity of a rating scale for assessing career choice appropriateness in adolescence', *Journal of Career Assessment* 7, 91–109.

White, B. B. (1977) 'Empirical tests of the life-cycle hypothesis', *American Economic Review* 68, 547–560.

Wilkes, R. E. (1995) 'Household life-cycle stages, transitions and product expenditures', *Journal of Consumer Research* 22, 27–42.

Williams, F. L. (1993) 'The family as an economic system: a conceptual model supported by empirical research', *Psychology and Marketing* 10 (2), 111–130.

Wilson, B. F. and Clarke, S. C. (1992) 'Remarriages: a demographic profile', *Journal of Family Issues* 13: 123–141.

Wilson, G. (1987) *Money in the Family: Financial Organisation and Women's Responsibility*, Aldershot: Avebury.

Wiman, A. R. (1983) 'Parental influence and children's responses to television advertising', *Journal of Advertising* 12 (1), 11–18.

Winefield, A. H. (1997) 'Introduction to the psychological effects of youth unemployment: international perspectives', *Journal of Adolescence* 20, 237–242.

Winefield, A. H. and Tiggemann, M. (1993) 'Psychological distress, work attitudes and intended year of leaving school', *Journal of Adolescence* 16, 57–74.

Winefield, A. H., Tiggeman, M., and Winefield, H. R. (1992) 'Unemployment distress, reasons for job loss, and attributions for unemployment in young people', *Journal of Occupational and Organisational Psychology* 65, 213–218.

Winnett, A. and Lewis, A. (1995) 'Household accounts, mental accounts and savings behaviour: some old economics rediscovered', *Journal of Economic Psychology* 16, 431–448.

Wren-Lewis, S. (1996) 'The truth about economic forecasts', paper presented to Exeter University business forum, 16th January.

Wright, J. P., Cullen, F. T., and Williams, N. (1997) 'Working while in school and delinquent involvement: implications for social policy', *Crime and Delinquency* 43, 203–221.

Wunderink, S. R. (1995) 'Is family planning an economic decision?', *Journal of Economic Psychology* 16, 377–392.

Yates, J.F. (ed.) (1992) *Risk Taking Behaviour*, Chichester: Wiley.

Young, B. M. (1986) 'New approaches to old problems: the growth of advertising literacy', in S. Ward and R. Brown (eds) *Commercial Television and European Children: An International Research Digest* (pp. 67–77, 82–83), Aldershot, Hants: Gower.

—— (1990) *Children and Television Advertising*, Oxford: Oxford University Press.

—— (1999) 'Differences and similarities between England and Sweden on their attitudes toward advertising to children', Report to the Advertising Association, London, UK.

Young, B. M. and Claessen, M. (1998) *Children's Categorisation of Foods*, London: The Food Advertising Unit, The Advertising Association.

Young, B. M., van der Valk, R., and Prat, V. (1997) 'The young child's understanding of advocatory communication', in I. Quintanilla and R. Luna (eds) *The Proceedings of the 22nd Annual Colloquium of IAREP: Volume II* (pp. 761–778), Valencia: Promolibro.

Zelizer, V. A. (1978) 'Human values and the market: the case of life insurance and death in 19th century America', *American Journal of Sociology* 84, 591–610.

—— (1994) *The Social Meaning of Money*, New York: Basic Books.

Zhao, Y. H. (1997) 'Labour migration and returns to rural education in China', *American Journal of Agricultural Economics* 79, 1278–1287.

Zullow, H. M. (1991) 'Pessimistic rumination in popular songs and news magazines predict economic recession via decreased consumer optimism and spending', *Journal of Economic Psychology* 12, 501–526.

Author Index

Subject Index